MADE F .. ꞮꞸꞸ🇩 Y

Barrie McDermott was born in Oldham in 1972. His career started with his hometown club before he moved to Wigan where he won a Championship winner's medal in 1994–95 and made his debut for Great Britain in 1994. He joined Leeds in 1995, becoming one of the top forwards in British rugby and a hero of Headingley's famous south stand.

Peter Smith lives in York and is a sports writer with the Leeds-based *Yorkshire Evening Post*, specializing in rugby league. This is his third book on the sport.

'I consider rugby league to be the most physically demanding sport possible. For Barrie McDermott to have represented Leeds, Ireland and Great Britain despite the physical disability of only having one eye is a totally remarkable achievement.'

Chris Brookes, Great Britain rugby league team doctor

Barrie McDermott

and Peter Smith

MADE FOR RUGBY

THE AUTOBIOGRAPHY

PAN BOOKS

First published 2004 by Sidgwick & Jackson

This edition published 2014 by Pan Books
an imprint of Pan Macmillan, a division of Macmillan Publishers Limited
Pan Macmillan, 20 New Wharf Road, London N1 9RR
Basingstoke and Oxford
Associated companies throughout the world
www.panmacmillan.com

ISBN-13: 978-1-4472-6981-6

A CIP catalogue record for this book is available from
the British Library.

Typeset by SetSystems Ltd, Saffron Walden, Essex

Acknowledgements

I have dedicated each chapter to groups and individuals who have helped, supported and inspired me throughout my career and my life.

For their help in the production of this book, I would like to thank Abe Kerr, Janet Harrison, Stuart Martel, Ray Fletcher, Bill Newton, David Howes and Roger Halstead; Ingrid Connell and Jacqui Butler and everyone at Macmillan Publishers; and Vicky Mathers, Steve Riding, Andrew Varley and Dave Williams for their pictures, plus the photographers of the *Yorkshire Evening Post* and *Oldham Evening Chronicle*. I am also grateful to my good friend Terry O'Connor for his foreword, and last but not least I would like to thank Peter Smith for helping me make sense of all the ups and downs.

Picture Acknowledgements

Pages 1 and 2: all photographs © Barrie McDermott.

Page 3: top © *Oldham Evening Chronicle*, middle and bottom courtesy of Barrie McDermott.

Page 4: top and middle © *Oldham Evening Chronicle*, bottom courtesy of Barrie McDermott.

Page 5: top and bottom © Dave Williams, middle © *Yorkshire Evening Post*.

Page 6: all photographs © Dave Williams.

Page 7: all photographs © *Yorkshire Evening Post*.

Page 8: top photograph courtesy of Barrie McDermott, middle © Dave Williams, bottom © *Yorkshire Evening Post*.

Page 9: top © *Yorkshire Evening Post*, middle and bottom © Andrew Varley.

Page 10: all photographs © Andrew Varley.

Page 11: top © Andrew Varley, bottom © Dave Williams.

Page 12: top © Andrew Varley, bottom © Dave Williams.

Page 13: all photographs © *Yorkshire Evening Post*.

Page 14: top © Andrew Varley, middle © Dave Williams, bottom © *Yorkshire Evening Post*.

Page 15: top and middle courtesy of Barrie McDermott, bottom © *Yorkshire Evening Post*.

Page 16: all photographs © *Yorkshire Evening Post*.

Contents

Foreword by Terry O'Connor *ix*

Introduction *xi*

1. THE ACCIDENT 1

2. EARLY DAYS 15

3. A YOUNG LION 28

4. TURNING PRO 42

5. BARRIE THE ROO 58

6. AMONG THE BEST 73

7. PROUD TO BE BRITISH 83

8. LEARNING HARD LESSONS 96

9. CROSSING THE GREAT DIVIDE 110

10. BAD BREAKS 125

11. 'ELLO, 'ELLO, 'ELLO 138

12. IN FROM THE COLD 153

13. TROUBLED TIMES 170

14. THE GREATEST GAME 181

15. INTERNATIONAL BREAKDOWN 193

16. THE NEARLY MEN 219

17. DREAMS AND NIGHTMARES 241

18. THE REAL ME 264

Postscript. ON TOP OF THE WORLD 277

Barrie's Record 293

Index 297

Foreword

All rugby players should be like Barrie McDermott: as tough as teak on the field and a lovely bloke off it; the sort who will knock your head off and then help you look for it. We have played with and against each other for more years than either of us cares to remember. In fact, I knew Barrie when he was a fleet-footed full-back, before he piled on the pounds and had to move up into the pack.

More often than not, Barrie and I have been on opposing sides. Even back in our teenage years he played the game hard as a really fierce competitor, something that has never changed. He played his youth rugby with two Pennine teams, Saddleworth and Waterhead, and you always knew you would be in for a battle against either of them if Barrie was in their line-up. I remember one year my amateur team from Widnes went to play away at Waterhead. We had only eleven players and no subs, but we beat them something like 60–0. Funnily enough, that is not in this book!

We both turned professional around the same time. I went to Salford and Barrie joined his home-town club Oldham, but we teamed up later on at Wigan and they were good days. I do not have many regrets about my playing career, but I do wish I could have played alongside Barrie at Wigan more often. He was not there very long, sadly, and we were only selected to start together once, in an away game at Castleford. Things obviously did not go according to plan, because the coach Graeme West never again paired the two of us in his front row after that. Unfortunately, things did not work out for Barrie at Wigan, but I think letting him go was one of the worst mistakes they ever made. He has gone on to prove them wrong, and not many players who leave Wigan do that.

As a front-row forward, Barrie has got everything it takes: skill-wise he can step off both feet, he has got great ability with the ball, he can tackle, and he is tough and aggressive. I have played with and against the top props in the world for a decade or so, as well as the best Super League has to offer, and in my opinion Barrie is better than any of them. He has not always had things easy off the pitch, and because of his reputation on it trouble has sometimes found him rather than the other way around, but he has come through some difficult times, risen above everything that has been thrown at him and emerged as a thoroughly decent bloke.

Barrie is as hard as they come on the field, but a soft teddy bear off it, and he dotes on his lovely wife and three beautiful kids. That is why I have never been scared of him when on the opposing team, because I have seen his other side! We spend a fair bit of time together socially and I always get a kick out of introducing Barrie to people who know him only by reputation. They expect to be meeting some kind of monster, but he is absolutely nothing like that when you get him away from the rugby arena and into civvies.

I am proud to call Barrie my mate, and it is an honour to write the foreword for what is a cracking autobiography.

Terry O'Connor
Widnes Vikings RLFC

Introduction

It is Valentine's Day, 1999, but love and romance are the last things on my mind. My team, Leeds Rhinos, are playing Wigan Warriors in the fourth round of the rugby league Challenge Cup, and it is one of the most important games of my life.

After a couple of years dogged by injury and suspension I am determined to put the record straight and prove I am still one of the best front-row forwards around. That is the plan, but unfortunately I am about to make a mistake, a big one. Twenty minutes have gone and we are leading, but Wigan are battling hard to get back into the game when one of their forwards, Simon Haughton, ball in hand, comes charging towards me. He tries to step past me, and I have a split second to decide how I am going to stop him. I get it completely wrong. Whack! I catch Haughton across the face, he goes down in a heap and the red card comes out. I am sent off. It is a disaster, and at that point I fear my career is over.

Fast forward two and a half months to another big Challenge Cup tie, but this time it is the final, at Wembley, Leeds versus London Broncos. We are red-hot favourites, but London are leading 16–12 and the game is well into the second half. Leeds need something special to turn the tide, and I am about to provide it. We get a penalty deep in London territory; our skipper Iestyn Harris taps the ball and turns it back to me about ten metres from the London line. I see a gap and go for it. The next thing I know I am over the whitewash, the ball is down and my team-mates are leaping all over me in utter joy. We go on to win the cup, easily, and I am back in business.

That is how it goes in professional sport. One minute you can be the villain, the next you are the hero – or vice versa. I have experienced it both ways, but in sport it is the bad times that make the good ones special.

'Notorious' is a word you will often see used when the media talk about Barrie McDermott. As far as the press, television and radio are concerned, I am the hard man who has had more punch-ups than hot dinners, appeared before rugby league's disciplinary committee over a dozen times, paid more than £5,000 in fines and missed at least forty matches through suspension. I have also been at the centre of a diplomatic incident between Great Britain and Australia, hit the headlines for a run-in with the police following a 'misunderstanding' outside a nightclub and got locked up for playing rugby in France when I should have been appearing in court in England.

As you will find out, all those stories – and more – are true, but they aren't the whole truth. There is a bit more to my life than that. This is the story of how a working-class lad from Oldham who had dreams of being a soldier or a professional boxer ended up earning more than a dozen caps for Great Britain in the hardest team sport of all, rugby league. You might call it a success story, but there have been plenty of ups and downs along the way. For every golden afternoon at Wembley there has been a miserable evening in the mud and the rain at Featherstone or Warrington.

Nobody's life is straightforward, and mine certainly has not turned out the way I expected it would. This book goes behind the headlines. I hope to reveal the true Barrie

McDermott, how I really am, not only as a rugby professional but also as a father, a husband and a friend. Some of it may make you laugh, some of it may make you cry. I hope, too, that some of what you are about to read will inspire you, but I am sure parts of it will leave you shaking your head in disbelief.

There is more to my life than just rugby league, but I have no doubt the sport has shaped me into the person I am now. Rugby league has been great to me, and as far as I am concerned it really is the Greatest Game. Rugby has taken me all over the world, from Ireland to South Africa and from France to Australia. I have made some lifelong friends and had experiences I could never have imagined growing up in the back streets of Lancashire. As much as this is my story, it is also a rugby league story, and I will always be grateful for the opportunities the game has given me.

There is an old saying, 'don't let the truth get in the way of a good story', but this account is as honest as memory and libel laws will allow. It has been a bumpy ride, I have made plenty of mistakes along the way and I would be lying if I said there were no regrets, but I am still happy with the way it has all turned out.

Hero or villain? Notorious or misunderstood? Make your own mind up.

1

THE ACCIDENT

To my mum, dad, sister and grandma.

I became a professional rugby league player by accident, or at least because of one. Until my final year at school I had my heart set on joining the army, but then something happened that changed my life for ever. When I was fifteen, I lost my right eye in an accident with an air rifle. It was just one of those stupid, freak things that happen, but it meant the army career went out of the window and all the plans I'd had were torn up.

It sounds a strange thing to say, but in some ways the accident was the best thing that could have happened to me. Obviously it was a terrible experience at the time, but in the long run it changed me as a person, and in many ways I think it did me a lot of good. If it hadn't been for the accident I would never have been paid to play rugby league, I would never have represented my country and I would not have the sort of lifestyle I enjoy now. When I was at school I thought the road I was going down was the right one, but things have certainly worked out well and, looking back, I'm sure that where I am in my life now is much rosier than where I would have been had things gone to the original plan.

As I get older, the accident itself seems less and less important. For a few years afterwards I could remember exactly how long it was since it happened and I used to talk about it to my mum and dad, but as time has gone on it has become less significant because of the direction I have taken with my life. Now, it's hardly ever mentioned. People have asked me about it in interviews, but this is the first time I have told the full story. Sometimes you hear people say that they can remember something that happened a long time in the past just as if it was yesterday. When it comes to my accident, that really is true. I can remember virtually everything about that day.

It was 5 December 1987. A friend and I had spent the morning wandering around Oldham's Tommyfield Market looking for a job, helping out on the stalls or whatever. We were trying to find something to earn ourselves a bit of pocket money to spend on the usual sorts of things teenagers spend money on. We didn't get anywhere, so we wandered back to our house. My mum was in at the time and I remember she made us some porridge for breakfast. I know it sounds daft, but I can still see all these things happening now. I suppose it just goes to show that things can happen to change your life when you least expect it.

After we had eaten the porridge we decided to wander over to where my mate lived, and on the way he said he had an air pistol and an air rifle at his house. Just like that we decided we would go shooting at a place called Medlock Valley. We weren't going to shoot at anyone or anything – not anything living anyway. We just wanted to have a bit of fun, like you do when you're teenagers. We knew we were too young to be using air guns, so I suppose that added to the excitement.

We began shooting things, stones and leaves and stuff like that, and then we found a plastic bottle, which looked like it would make a better target. I had the pistol and my mate had the rifle. I was watching how he was aiming it, and as I turned my head to glance at the plastic bottle, he fired. The pellet hit the bottle and rebounded into my face. It hit the corner of my nose and ricocheted at an angle across my eye, causing quite a lot of damage inside. Fluid began to leak out of the eye, which to be honest shocked my friend a lot more than it did me. I didn't really appreciate how serious it was, but he could see the fluid coming out of my eye and he panicked. I don't really blame him: it must have been a gruesome sight. He picked up the pistol and ran off, but I just kept blinking, thinking I had a bit of grit or something in my eye.

When I had done that a couple of times I realized something was definitely wrong, so I began walking to the nearest house, where an old couple lived. On the way there my friend, who was still panicking, came back and said maybe we should make up a story that I had been shot by a couple of lads. We knew we weren't old enough to be playing with air weapons and we were scared of what the police, and our parents, would say if they found out. The old couple phoned for an ambulance, which came quite quickly. All the way to the hospital my friend was still saying we had to make sure we stuck to the story. In the end, we saved Oldham police a few hours' overtime.

I was at the hospital, very frightened, when the police arrived. That was the first time I had ever met a policeman, although I have met plenty since! I think he sussed me out pretty quickly. He said, 'Look, son, tell us the truth. If you say it was two lads who shot you we will send as many policemen as we have got to go and look for them. But if you've done it with your mate and it was an accident, that's your business.' I replied, 'You're right. Me and my mate had an accident and we don't want to cause you any trouble.' And that's the last we saw of the police.

I never blamed my mate for what happened. It was just an accident, and I suppose it could just as easily have been him instead of me. We went our separate ways after the accident, although I don't think that was because of what had happened. I haven't seen him for quite a few years, but I would certainly speak to him if I saw him again. There are definitely no hard feelings, and I'm not bitter about it. My mate did go into the army, but I don't think that lasted long. He has been in and out of prison a few times, so perhaps what happened affected him more than I ever realized.

While I was in hospital just after the accident it seemed like a bit of an adventure. You know what it's like when you're a kid: I was thinking a black eye or a busted nose or whatever would be tremendous fun because I would get a lot of sympathy from all the girls. That has always been one of the better things about being injured throughout my rugby career. At the time I obviously did not know the full extent of the damage, and it never really occurred to me that what had happened was as serious as it turned out to be. I don't think I was in any pain, although I remember the shock of it all. I have been hurt a few times playing rugby, and it's strange, but you forget pain as soon as you start to recover. Your mind plays tricks with you and it disguises the fact that something hurts. I get battered just about every other day, either in training or in a game, but my mind blots out all the aching joints and the bumps and bruises. The same thing must have happened with my eye. I'm sure it did hurt, but I have no recollection of that at all.

The staff at the hospital gave me some drugs to calm me down and ease the shock, and it was only when they set in that I started being sick and began to realize I was pretty ill. Mum and Dad came to see me and they were obviously very upset. I remember being very dozy, maybe even asleep, on the bed in the hospital, and my dad was consoling my mum. She gave me a little kiss on the head and then they wheeled me off to the operating theatre. It's strange, but I can picture the scene as clearly as if I had been standing at Dad's side. I have no idea how, but I have got a very clear picture in my mind of lying there on the bed with Mum and Dad watching over me.

The surgeon operated on my eye for a couple of hours and did what he could, and when I got out of surgery I spent three or four days in hospital. All the kids from school came to see me, and they had clubbed together to buy me a cassette. It was *Now That's What I Call Music 10*, so that shows how long ago it was; we're on about number sixty now. My granddad Bryan, my mum's father, also came to see me, and I remember him complaining about the music on the tape, asking me, 'What's that rubbish?' People often say I am just like my granddad Bryan, very sarcastic and funny and everybody's friend. The song he was complaining about was 'Pump up the Volume', and the next tune on the tape was Nina Simone's 'My Baby Just Cares For Me'. On 20 December my granddad died in his sleep. He was a heavy smoker and he had suffered with angina for quite a while, but those songs always remind me of him. I can't help thinking that the stress of what happened contributed to the way he felt at the time, and it still saddens me that I never really got to know him.

Obviously that Christmas will not go down in McDermott family history as a very happy time, what with Granddad dying and me still being in a bit of a state after the accident. The doctors decided not to remove the eyeball straight away because they wanted to give it every chance to get better, but I had lost too much fluid. The eye was just a red ball with a black dot in the middle and it was easily noticeable by anyone who looked at me. I used to have to go to school in the middle of winter with dark glasses on, which was a bit of a joke in itself.

I still didn't realize the severity of it. Being a bit of a rough and ready sort of kid, I'd had plenty of black eyes and other bumps and bruises and they had always got better, and I suppose I thought my eye would too. But at the beginning of February 1988 I went with my mum to see a consultant at Oldham Royal Infirmary and he dashed all those hopes. He told me that what can happen in those circumstances is that the bad eye affects the good one, which then starts to deteriorate itself. I was never going to be able to see through my injured eye again and there was a real danger I could start to lose sight in the other one as well. He told me to go away and think about whether or not I wanted them to remove the damaged eyeball. We got the bus home and I told Mum, 'I'm not going to let them do it. I don't want anything artificial where my eye should be. I want to be normal.'

That bus ride was when it all began to hit home with a shattering thud. It was not an adventure any more, and it definitely wasn't funny. It was no longer about people coming to visit me in hospital and me being the centre of attention, it was about the frightening possibility of looking like a freak for the rest of my life. For at least two days I said no way, but Mum kept telling me I would lead a normal life and I wouldn't look any different to how I had been before. I thought my life would never be how I wanted it to be, but we talked about it long and hard, and eventually I decided to let them do the operation. I went into hospital in Manchester on Valentine's Day.

After your eye has been removed it takes about six weeks before you get a false one fitted; until then they give you a big plastic contact lens that slips under both your eyelids and stops them folding in. That is what I wear during games now. Originally it was just a clear, hollow shell, but when I started to make it into the big time and I began to see myself in the papers and on the TV I decided to customize it a bit. It's as crude as it comes, but I draw a black dot on the lens with a marker pen. It looks that bit more natural and it makes me feel a lot better. The first time I looked in the mirror and saw this thing in my eyeball was something I will never forget. It was a huge shock, but that sort of thing has helped make me mentally tougher, which is a big factor in a sport like rugby league. After everything I went through when I was fifteen, I know that nothing could ever happen in this game, no injury or disappointment, that could match that. I could have died, and I put my family through all kinds of pain and heartache. I'm used to it now, and the false eye is not something that bothers me much. I still don't like to look at myself in the mirror in certain situations, but I know if I hadn't been through all that I would not be the person I am now. I think I am someone who doesn't like to let other people down, someone who is determined to live his life to the full.

As I said, the accident ended my plans of going into the army, which was a huge blow at the time. I had been in the army cadet force since the age of twelve and I had already passed the entry tests, so I had really put all my eggs in one basket. I had never even thought about what I could do instead, and I was not exactly a star pupil at school. I never really paid much attention in lessons, but I had always enjoyed my sport, though I was a jack of all trades and master of none, mainly because I wasn't trying to achieve anything other than enjoying myself. Looking back at my school reports from my early teens, they all say things like 'Barrie is a capable athlete but will not apply himself because he has got no aspirations to become a sporting person'.

I played rugby league for the school and for a couple of local teams, Saddleworth and Waterhead, but that was just for fun. Before the accident I never thought about getting paid to play rugby. The sport I was really interested in was boxing, and I was planning on taking that seriously once I got into the army. I used to train as often as I could and I loved my boxing, but unfortunately I never got to fight (not in the ring, anyway). Obviously when I lost my eye the boxing went out of the window as well. I would have loved to give boxing a go, although I have gone further in rugby as a sport than I think I would ever have done in the ring. I used to love the training and the mental aspect of boxing. It's a gladiatorial thing: it's just you and your opponent, and there's nowhere to hide. You have to be tough all round to be a boxer, and that's something that has always appealed to me.

Another of the reasons I wanted to join the army was to do a bit of travelling and see the world. Missing that opportunity also seemed like a blow at the time, but there aren't many places I would like to visit that I haven't now seen as a result of playing rugby. I have played in Australia and New Zealand and been on pre-season training camps with Leeds Rhinos to the US and South Africa, so I have probably done more travelling than I ever would have in the army.

I don't think losing an eye has ever held me back, and I certainly don't consider myself to be disabled. I could go to the council and get one of those orange stickers for the car, but it might look a bit strange for me to park in a disabled space and then get out and go and play in Super League! Quite a few people have said to me, 'Imagine how good you could have been if you were playing with two eyes,' but I have often thought that if I did have two eyes I wouldn't be playing at all, and I definitely would not have the passion and burning desire I have deep within me to do what I do now. I know people accept that what I have achieved has not been easy, and probably a lot of other people would not have been able to do it, but I don't think I've been brave. I have just worked hard and had a bit of luck. Having only one eye has never been a point of reference for me. Other people say, 'Bloody hell, how do you do it?' And I say, 'I don't know, I just do.'

It was a reporter from the local paper, the *Oldham Evening Chronicle*, who first gave me the idea that maybe I could make it as a professional player. We had a rugby game at school just after I had undergone surgery to remove my eye, and I said I wanted to play. One of my teachers, Fred Laughton, who coached the team, said, 'Look, Barrie, you've just had a major operation, I can't let you play.' I told him I loved rugby and I was desperate to take part, but he insisted, 'I can't let you. I can't be responsible for you damaging your other eye.' That had never even entered my mind, so I kept on badgering him until he said I could play if I got a letter from my mum. I went home and pleaded with her, but she, too, said no way. It was the same message again: 'You're just a couple of days out of surgery, Barrie. Drop it, it's a non-starter.' But I didn't drop it, and I pestered her for a day or two until eventually I turned up to see Fred Laughton with a letter from Mum saying that I could play. She wrote that she didn't really want me to play, but she had seen how determined I was and she had decided not to stand in my way. Fred still wasn't keen, but he could see it was important to me and in the end he let me play.

I can still remember the game. I didn't play badly, although I didn't crack any pots, but a lot of people came up to me after the game and said well done. I hadn't gone into it thinking I wanted to do this to make people respect me; I just enjoyed it. Subconsciously, though, I think I was determined to prove everybody wrong and to earn their respect.

The *Oldham Evening Chronicle* got hold of the story and came and took a picture of me. Their reporter asked, 'Where do you see this going? Would you like to play professionally?' That was the first time it had ever been mentioned. I also remember a kid who was in the year above me at school coming up to me and saying, 'You'll never make a

professional.' I said, 'Why not?' and he replied, 'Because
you are nothing, and who would you play for? The blind
school?' I went home, thought about it and said to myself,
'I'm not having this idiot saying things like that and getting
the better of me.' That's when I really started thinking
about making a go of rugby league in a serious way. I
thought to myself, 'I'm good at this game. I'm not the best,
but I am good, and with a bit of luck, dedication and
application I can be even better. And I can be a lot better
than him.'

That all happened in the last six months of my school
days, and I started to develop a bit of a rebellious streak
from then on, which lasted for a long time. I was viewed as
a bit of a special case and, like any kid, I took advantage of
that. I wouldn't turn up for school until 9.30 or ten o'clock
some days because I knew I could get away with it. I went
through a spell when I didn't even bother wearing a tie.

Until then, I had never liked confrontation and I never
wanted to get into a fight or an argument with anybody; I
would rather have a laugh and a joke. Before the accident,
if I could use a joke to get out of a fight or a tricky situation
I would, but afterwards I became known as someone who
would stand his ground and would rather meet things
head on. I can't pinpoint exactly when that transformation
occurred, but it was during this six-month period at the
end of my time at school. Still, I like to think that I got on
with everyone at school and people enjoyed my company;
I certainly wasn't prepared for the stick I got when I started
work. When you are sixteen and you've got blokes of thirty
having a pop at you, you're not sure how to handle it. I
suffered a lot of abuse and mickey-taking about my eye,
and I took out my frustrations on my opponents on the
rugby field. I went from being a hooker who was quite
skilful but a passive tackler – that is, someone who will
tackle around the knees – to being a volcano who erupted

every time he got out on the pitch. I just wanted to smash everybody I came up against. I didn't just want to be the one who made the most tackles, I wanted to be the one who made the most big tackles. And I wanted to be the one who started the fight. Suddenly I wanted to be the one who knocked the other lad over so hard he couldn't get up. My sole focus had become to prove anybody and everybody wrong. I wanted to do whatever it took as an up-and-coming player to prove that I could make it.

I have had a bit of a reputation for as long as I have been playing the game, and most people involved in rugby league know about my eye, but it has only been mentioned on the field once, during the second Test in November 1994 at Old Trafford when I was playing for Great Britain against Australia. I came on as a substitute and got a great shot on Bradley Clyde, who I later played with at Leeds, and managed to jar the ball loose. About five of the Aussies took exception and started to smack me on the back of the head, and I ended up getting sent to the sin-bin. I had only been on a couple of minutes, and the whole incident was down to me being fired up from the moment I'd trotted onto the pitch because I heard one of the Australians, Ricky Stuart, saying, 'He's on, he's on. Let's get the one-eyed bastard.' I have to admit, that got to me. I thought, 'Right, I'm going to shut the lot of you up here. I'm going to hit one of you so hard you will all remember who I am.' At the time, Stuart was in what we call the bobbying position, which is a good ten to fifteen yards behind anyone else – and he needed to be. Had he been stood toe to toe with me he would not have said it.

Fans are a different matter. I suppose it's easier to make offensive comments about someone when you're standing with 5,000 other people than it is face to face, so as a player you are going to be on the receiving end of that sort of thing. I don't want to single out any one club, but I have

been at away grounds with thousands of so-called supporters all singing 'He's only got one eye' at me, and you would
have to have a heart of stone not to be affected by that.
I have always thought the best policy is to ignore it, and I
never, ever react. It's not that I can't hear what's being
said, I'm just not going to waste my time acknowledging
nobodies in the crowd. My attitude is always that they can
shout all they want but they will not upset my concentration
– and somebody in their team is going to get hit a little bit
harder in the next tackle as a result.

I have got used to the insults over the years and they
don't really bother me any more, but I will admit that is
the main reason why my family don't come to watch me in
away games. I don't want to have to explain to my kids
why grown men and women are being so hurtful. Whenever my dad went to away games, he was always getting
into rows with other fans who were giving me abuse.
Maybe I should take it as a compliment; perhaps if I was
no good they would just ignore me. But I do think it is very
small-minded. Fans pay their money and they have the
right to voice an opinion, but it's disappointing if they have
to resort to childish abuse. I suppose it's the same as racism:
no one should have to put up with that for any reason
either, even if they are playing for a different rugby team.
Of course I don't expect fans of other clubs to love me to
pieces, and I don't expect them just to let me get on with
my job, but I would like them to stop and think, 'Perhaps
that's a bit below the belt.' Unfortunately there are people
who watch the game who like to hurl abuse at players,
maybe so they can show off to their mates. But as I said, no
one has ever stood toe to toe with me and said anything to
my face. The fans who shout things at me from the terraces
wouldn't say anything if they met me in the street. They
know if they did challenge me they would have to deal

with the consequences, which would not be good for either of us.

I just want to get on with my job, which is playing the game. I have matured a lot now and I like to think I have left childish things, like hitting someone because they have called me a name, a long way behind me. I am a bigger person now, and I would like to think I can respond to people in better ways than that. But if a bloke stands in front of you and hurls an insult, it is a challenge, and you have got to react.

I don't think my so-called disability is an issue as far as my team-mates or opponents are concerned and it does not affect the way I play the game. All Super League teams do work on targeting weaknesses in the opposition, but I would be surprised if my vision was ever mentioned when they are working on ways to deal with me.

Because the position I play is in the middle of the field, there are naturally two or three other people alongside me, so it would be hard to isolate me in that respect. If I was playing out wide and I was involved in one on one situations more often I suppose it might be a problem, but my natural aggression has always carried me through.

Vision overlaps in the middle, it doesn't just stop at the side of your nose. Close one eye and you'll see what I mean. Although I have only got sight in one eye, my attitude is that I have lost 25 per cent of my vision rather than 50 per cent. Even though it is obviously restricted, I can still see left and right and am able to use my peripheral vision a bit more than most people. I can see things slightly out of my immediate focus.

I would like to think what I have achieved in rugby league is an example to other people who may have a diability. I hope the people I play with and against respect me for it and realize I have a bit of mental toughness.

There was another advantage, certainly when I started out in the professional game. I am fairly well known now, but people I played against in the early days have told me that I had quite a sinister appearance then and I was pretty scary to look at. A few of them have said they didn't fancy tangling with me just because of the way I looked, so that gave me a bit of an edge.

2

EARLY DAYS

*Thanks to everyone who helped me when I was
growing up: family, friends, teachers and coaches.*

My mum and dad always say they can't understand where
I get my size from. It's certainly not a trait in my immediate
family. Dad is just over five feet tall, and when he was a
youngster he was about eleven stone wet through. Mum is
even smaller, so I am the exception to the rule, though at
five feet ten inches and seventeen stone I am far from the
biggest rugby league player around. I do come from a big
family in another sense, though: my mum's mum was one
of thirteen, and Dad was one of five, so I have got aunts
and uncles and cousins all over the place.

Until I came along ours wasn't really a rugby-playing
family. There were a couple of rugby players in our
extended family – my grandmother's brother and my
granddad's brother-in-law both played for Rochdale – but
there was no strong rugby influence. Still, the family was
always a very sporting one, and I suppose I do come from
a typical working-class rugby league background. My
mum, Jacqueline, fell pregnant with me in her late teens.
When I was very young she did a lot of part-time jobs
because she wanted to spend most of her time at home
with me and my sister Alison, who was born three years
after me. When we were both out of nappies Mum worked

as a cleaner part-time while she went to college to get herself some qualifications. Now she has done really well for herself, as a senior doctor's receptionist. She has a single-minded attitude and she is very focused on what she wants to achieve for herself and her family, and I think that is probably something that has rubbed off on me.

My dad, Robert, was a worker at a local sheet metal firm. He worked very hard to make ends meet and he was always busy, but I used to spend as much time with him as I could. I loved to be around him because he was such a popular bloke. I used to go and watch him play football on a Saturday afternoon, and the other lads in the team often told me what a good player he was. From what I have been told, I think he could have made it as a footballer at a decent semi-professional level, but unfortunately he had a few injuries including a broken leg and I think that held him back. Although he was a talented player, Dad had a young family which did not give him much time to dedicate to his football, and he was not as single-minded as Mum was, but I know he has taken a lot of pride and pleasure from seeing me make it as a professional sportsman. He feels every game and every bump and bruise, and he always rings up to wish me good luck before a match. He rarely goes to away games, but he's always on the phone afterwards asking how I have got on, so he is very much involved in my career.

He's a real character, but he was a strict dad. I remember one time I got a good hiding for something I hadn't done. I used to share a bedroom with my sister and we were both upstairs playing. For some reason Alison had been chewing on a screw she had found somewhere and she had swallowed it. She was screaming her head off, and Dad came bounding up the stairs, picked me up, took his belt off and whacked me with it. I was saying, 'I haven't done anything!' and Alison was still screaming. Eventually it all calmed down and she told him what had really happened. I said to Dad, 'I told you I hadn't done anything,' but he just told me to get to bed. He still hasn't apologized for that. I have told him since, 'You know I didn't do anything.' He just says, 'Yes, well, you were always not doing anything.' But he was, and still is, a good father, and I try to model myself on him with my kids. Although he was strict, he was never unfair, and he was always funny. Even though he used to belt us at times, I know he didn't take any pleasure from it. Now, if I have to discipline my kids I sit them down and tell them why. I always say, 'You know why I must do this. I don't want to do it, but I have to because I love you.'

Mine was a great upbringing, and I couldn't have asked for any more. Looking back, though, I do remember being teased about the clothes I wore. There were a lot of girls in our family and I used to get their hand-me-downs. I got a lot of T-shirts, tracksuit tops and trainers off girls, and I got a lot of ribbing about that! Nowadays I have a bit of a fetish for trainers. I like to have nice trainers and to have a lot of them in the house, because I never had them as a kid. But Mum and Dad always did their best for me.

I think it was seeing my dad so involved in sport that got me interested. I was into all sorts of sports as a kid. As well as rugby I played soccer, cricket, softball, badminton and basketball, which I would have liked to take further. There was an opportunity for me because one of my teachers coached the local Oldham Celtics basketball team, but I was too short to get anywhere in that game. I played a lot of football, but Dad teases me about it. I seem to remember I was quite good, but he tells me I wasn't. He's always telling me I played football just how I play rugby. He says he always knew my future was in rugby, but he didn't want to push me. 'You know what it's like with kids,' he reasons. 'If you push them too hard in one direction, all they want to do is rebel and do something completely different.'

I was born in Oldham on 22 July 1972, and, apart from a spell in Australia playing rugby and six months in Leeds and Wigan when I had lost my driving licence, I have lived there all my life. As a town, Oldham is somewhere that has got a lot of bad press over the years, especially after the riots in the early 2000s. But for a kid it was a good place to grow up. There was a lot of open space near where I lived and we always used to entertain ourselves with a ball or on our bikes. I was a BMX kid, and I once won a competition when we were on holiday at Pontin's.

The place where I lived wasn't a council estate, but it was surrounded by them, and the kids I used to play with were very streetwise. Some of them were a bit wild, but I didn't get up to anything that could be called illegal, though I was mischievous. We used to live near a place called Park Cakes, a baker's. When Mark Owen left Take That and he was asked if he had any plans for the future, he said he was going to look for a job at Park Cakes. Everybody in Oldham got the joke, but no one else knew what he was talking about. We used to ride down there on our bikes and climb over the wall to pinch a few cakes off the back of the lorries, but that was just a bit of fun.

It's sad when I see what has happened to Oldham over the last few years. It has always been an area with a lot of different nationalities and that has never been an issue for me. I am upset about the way the kids are going now and what motivation they have got. No one seems to want to tolerate the other races any more, which is a real shame. We just got on with our own thing and race was never really a problem. My best mate, Alvin Carnekie, was a lad of mixed race so as I was growing up I was aware of the different cultures, but in our family we were taught to love everybody the same, no matter what colour they were or where they were from. It was always a case of, if they are a bad 'un don't bother with them, but it doesn't matter what colour they are.

I went to St Anne's primary school and St Alban's secondary, all in Oldham, and that's where I started my rugby, thanks to my mate's dad Dennis Maders. He'd had a spell as a professional with Oldham, but he was more of a character than a great player. He was always loads of fun to be around, and when I began senior school he really got me involved in the game. I had played it at St Anne's, but that was just mucking around really. We didn't have any set positions or anything like that, we just ran around with the ball, which isn't a bad way to start. Dennis saw me playing at school and asked me if I wanted to go to Saddleworth, which is an amateur club in the Oldham area. I was keen to go, but Mum and Dad didn't drive so Dennis said he would pick me up and take me. I remember the first time he collected me to take me to the rugby. He arrived in his Volvo estate and there were about nine kids crammed in the back. He used to pick me up every Sunday morning without fail. I had to go to nine o'clock mass at church and then run home to get back in time for Dennis to pick me up at 9.45.

Church was very important to our family and I didn't miss it, even for rugby. If we had an away game I used to go to mass on Saturday night, so I could be away a bit earlier the following morning. My parents thought going to church was an important part of my growing up. My grandma is a staunch churchgoer, and when I go now I sit at the back with her and all her pals. Very often I drop them off afterwards. They still insist on telling me where they live, even though I've been giving them lifts home from church for years.

I remember being a very quiet kid right up until my mid-teens, when I had the accident. I definitely was not a trouble causer. I have seen my headmistress and various teachers since and they have all said that when they see me on the TV playing the game they can't really believe it's the same lad, because I was so happy go lucky.

I wish I'd knuckled down and tried harder at school. I enjoyed my sports, but I wasn't really interested in the other lessons. I always blame the end of my schooldays on things that happened after the accident, and I probably use that as an excuse. I think the teachers, quite understandably, gave me a bit of a loose leash, but in the long run it didn't do me much good. It annoys me when I hear people say that rugby players aren't as intelligent as blokes who work in an office. Though I was lazy at school I am determined it will not be hard for me when my rugby career comes to an end and I am back in the workplace. I haven't got any qualifications yet, but that is something I am going to put right in the future. I fully intend to get a job that relies on brains rather than brawn. I was never top of the class, but I've got plenty of good ideas and I know I've got something to offer away from rugby league, though you do need qualifications to be taken seriously in this society.

When I was a kid, one of the most popular programmes on TV was *The Fall Guy*, starring Lee Majors as a Hollywood stuntman. If anyone asked me what I wanted to be when I grew up, I always said a stuntman or a professional sportsman. People were telling me I could have what it takes to succeed as the latter, but I needed a job as I worked my way up through the amateur and youth rugby league ranks. Unfortunately, there isn't much call for stuntmen in Oldham, so when I left school I served my time as a joiner's apprentice with a local firm. I began on a Youth Training Scheme earning £29.50 per week, which went up to £32 in my second year. I worked for three and a half years at the same place, so at least I learned a trade before I went out into the big wide world. I enjoyed the apprenticeship, but it wasn't always very successful. Monday mornings were a bit of a problem for a start. I was never much use on the first day of the working week, because I was either hung over or as stiff as a board after playing rugby all weekend.

In those days I used to play open-age rugby for a team called Chadderton on a Saturday. Chadderton was a pub team, a proper tough guys' side. It was run by Ernie Hall, the father of a girlfriend of mine. He was a really nice bloke and he looked after me, along with Eric Louther, the coach. I started with Chadderton when I was fifteen, playing open age in the Yorkshire League against some real bruisers. That definitely gave me the confidence for when I moved on to bigger and better things. I knew if I could handle myself in that sort of league, I could survive anywhere. We used to play with and against some real tough nuts, but they were great lads and good times. If we had an away match we used to travel in a little minibus. How it got us to and from Yorkshire every other week I will never know, but we would go over there, play the game and then chug back with a few drinks and a good sing-song on the way home. I was in my mid-teens and I'd be coming home with three cans of lager inside me, pissed as a rat.

Then I would be playing under-17s on Sunday mornings. I played for Saddleworth until I left school, then some of the lads at college, where I went once a week as part of my apprenticeship, got me playing for another amateur club in the area, Waterhead. Ken Wilson, who was the mentor at Waterhead, gave me the confidence I needed in the gym and on the track. I was fairly energetic and naturally quite strong at that age, but I didn't really excel at anything and I wasn't particularly fit. When I joined Waterhead I learned about the gym and how a bit of perseverance pays off, and to this day I still love being in a gym lifting weights.

With all this weekend rugby, plus a few drinks, getting into work on a Monday was, as I said, a struggle. I would try my hardest to get into work for eight, but I was nearly always late. I used to walk in with Dad, and we were supposed to set off at 7.30. Dad would be shouting at me from quarter to seven, and at about twenty-nine minutes past I would dive out of bed, go to the toilet, brush my teeth, jump into my jeans and boots and then dash out of the door with him.

When, in 1991, I got picked for a tour to New Zealand with BARLA – the British amateur side, and about as high up as you can go without turning professional – I told my boss at work that I needed five or six weeks away. He said he wasn't prepared to give me the time off. I had worked really hard to get called into the squad and it was a big opportunity for me. If I got a professional contract I knew that would be good for me and for the firm, but he wasn't interested. He told me he was sick of me. I remember him saying, 'You're a waste of space on a Monday and all you want to do on a Friday is finish at dinner time and get off. I'm not having it. You have got to make a choice now: it's either work or your amateur rugby career.' Not much of a choice really. I told him he could stick his job, and walked out. I remember walking home wondering if I had done the right thing, and what Mum and Dad would say.

One thing Dad had always drilled into me was to get work sorted out first before anything else. As a kid he had really hoped for a career in sport so he hadn't set his sights very high job-wise. He stuck with the same job for most of his life, and he didn't want me to put all my eggs in one basket like he had. He wanted me to have a good trade, one that meant I would never be looking around for a job or struggling for money like he sometimes was. So that evening when I got home I was pretty sure I was in for a telling-off. I was expecting Mum and Dad to tell me to get back there and beg for my job back, and to be honest I was thinking about doing just that. The last thing I wanted was to be skint and on the dole. But my parents surprised me: they said I had done the right thing and they wouldn't have stood there and taken it either, so that made me feel a lot better.

As it turned out, I wasn't unemployed for very long. Mick Slicker, who was the Waterhead first-team coach, knew the BARLA tour was a great opportunity for me and would also be a good thing for the club. He said he would look after me until I got a full-time job again, so I worked for him as a joiner for six weeks. That was great for me at the time, but by the end of it I think Mick was wondering what he had done. To say the least, I was a bit accident prone. By the end of my time with Mick I had managed to break almost everything I got my hands on. Mick is a good family friend and I still see him quite often. He always jokes about just what a disaster those six weeks were. We were fitting windows, and I must have cracked more glass through doing the glazing than anyone else in history. Mick never gets fed up of reminding me that I cost him more in breakages than I ever brought in.

When I got back from the BARLA tour I didn't have a job, but I was earning a bit of money because I had signed for Oldham just before I left. I signed amateur forms so I could go on the tour, before beginning my career as a professional player when we got back. But I was still trying to find work as a joiner. The building trade has picked up a bit recently, but in the early 1990s it was a poor industry to be in and I really struggled for employment. I was out in the big wide world for the first time, and that was an education in itself. On Monday mornings I never knew where I would be working for the rest of the week, because it was always a case of having to look around for jobs. A mate and I bought an old Morris van for £150 and we travelled around the Manchester area, looking for work. One day we got ourselves a job in Bury but the van conked out halfway there. It was actually in flames at one point. We couldn't afford anything more reliable, but fortunately we managed to keep it going most of the time, though it cost us a lot more money in repairs than we had paid for it in the first place.

I used to drive everywhere at the time, even though I didn't have a licence. I'd started driving when I was sixteen and I had various licences to operate fork lift trucks and other heavy equipment, but it wasn't until I joined Wigan in my early twenties that I actually passed my driving test. I always felt a bit stupid sitting in a Nissan Micra or a Mini Metro with a big L sign on, but that was a bit of vanity more than anything.

Part of my job-seeking problem was that I needed to work locally so that it would fit in with my rugby. Although my job was my living, my priority was always the rugby. I would never miss rugby for work. No matter where I was or what I was doing, I always had to be back at Oldham for training, either with the rest of the squad or working on weights on my own. Although I was a joiner by trade, I used to do other labouring jobs on sites just to ensure I could stay local. I worked for brickies and plasterers, doing odd jobs like sweeping up. I would get paid a day rate, which was a poor wage, but at least it meant I could stay in the Oldham area and I never had to miss training or games. If I am at training now and I hear players moaning about how long they have been there, I always tell them, 'There'll be a job going at the building site around the corner if you don't like it here.'

At the beginning of the 1993–94 season the work I had been doing in and around the Oldham area dried up, so I asked the Oldham chairman, Jim Quinn, if he could find me some employment. He gave me a couple of weeks' work at his firm in Oldham, which was tough graft for next to no money. But that work soon dried up as well, so after that I got a bit of work actually at the ground, helping to keep Watersheddings going for a bit longer. I was doing a bit of joinery and just generally tidying up. When that was finished, the guy who was looking after the ground put me on to painting the seats in one of the stands. He told me to charge my day rate and take as long over the job as I could, because when that was finished there was no more work. I spent the whole week painting the same seats over and over again, and everything would probably have been fine if there hadn't been a home game at the end of it. On the Monday I went into training and the club secretary shouted over to me and said she had taken some complaints from angry fans: about half a dozen of them had got red paint all over their suits and they wanted the club to pay their dry cleaning bills.

It was hard graft, but working in the building trade was a fantastic learning experience and I met some real characters. I wouldn't say I didn't enjoy it, but there were bad times as well as good ones. The good times were always connected with nice weather. It can be pretty miserable toiling on a building site in the freezing cold or waiting in a hut until the rain stops so you can get back to work, but in the summer and the hot weather it could be a good way to make a living. My spell working as a plasterer's labourer was probably the hardest job I've ever done. As well as mixing the plaster in a bath or a bucket, I had to get it to wherever the plasterer was working, which inevitably was up a ladder or on some scaffolding. There's no hod for plaster; it has to be carried in buckets. When the rugby season was over I would get really stuck into the labouring because I knew whatever happened I wouldn't put any weight on, and when it was time to report back for pre-season training I would be as fit as a flea.

You get to learn about real life working on a building site. When you don't know on Sunday night whether you will have any work to go to on Monday morning and you haven't got any money in your pocket, it puts things into perspective. That's something I have never forgotten in the job I have now. I am always aware that being a professional sportsman is a privileged lifestyle, but that it could change at any time and I might find myself back where I was when I was a teenager.

You were always working on a promise in those days. If you didn't do the work that was set out for you, you didn't get paid. If the bosses weren't happy with the work you had done, you didn't get paid. And if they didn't want to pay you, you didn't get paid. There was many a time I had done a week's work and then wasn't able to find the boss on Friday, which was pay day. When that happened it usually meant a return visit on the Saturday, to take apart whatever we had spent all week building. The building trade at the time was very cut-throat and people would rip you off without even thinking about it.

The last building job I worked on was for a subcontractor employed by a major firm to build a supermarket in Wigan. I had played for Oldham against Wigan when they won the championship in 1993, but the blokes I was working with hadn't heard of me and didn't believe me when I said I was playing in the first team.

I always used to take my tools home with me, but the weekend we played Wigan I left them at work for some reason and when I went back on the Monday they had been pinched. At the time I was close to signing a full-time professional contract with Wigan, and having my tools stolen was the final straw as far as the building trade was concerned. I just threw my bag in the bin, and that was the end of that. My rugby career had developed promisingly over the previous six years, and although I have never been arrogant or big-headed, I told the blokes I was working with, 'The next time you see my face, I will be on telly playing in the Big League.'

3

A YOUNG LION

*To all my friends at Waterhead, who taught me
how to enjoy sport. Thanks to everyone who went
with me to New Zealand with BARLA.*

Although I'd begun to play rugby with Saddleworth
Rangers, it was when I moved to Waterhead that I started
to make a name for myself – or, to be honest, several
names. Those were the days before clubs were called
Rhinos, Warriors and the like, but at Waterhead we could
have been known as the Brawlers, and of course that
reputation led to me having plenty of fun and upsetting
lots of people in the process.

Waterhead's ground was about a mile and a half from
my house, and a friend and I used to walk there every
Tuesday and Thursday for training, and on matchdays,
which was Sunday. I'd enjoyed my time at Saddleworth,
but it was further away from home and I got fed up with
the travelling. I didn't really want to leave, but the move
worked out really well and I'm glad I did. Waterhead were
always very good to me, and I've still got a lot of affection
for the club. I go back there as often as I can and there has
never been any jealousy or resentment because I have made
it in the pro game; they're just pleased to see one of their
old boys doing so well. I always feel completely at home
there and I enjoy a chat and a swift pint or two whenever

I pop in. I know I owe Waterhead a lot, and I have tried to pay some of that back by helping them out whenever possible, including three seasons there as coach, which I thoroughly enjoyed. I always try to chip in by donating some of my old playing shirts and other souvenirs whenever the players' fund gets a bit low.

The social side at Waterhead was excellent, and I loved the craic we had as mates and team-mates. When I was playing there we never had a great side and we didn't win a lot of games, but we didn't lose many fights. That has given me my philosophy on the game, something that has stayed with me throughout my career. You can lose games, but to come off the pitch having been beaten is far worse. I always try to give the best possible account of myself, and that is something I learned at Waterhead. The attitude there was always to keep going and never to lose your focus, even if the game might be a lost cause. I have had various bad patches throughout my career, both personally and team-wise, but the experience I gained at Waterhead has always helped me deal with that.

I am not one to hold back, and I was happy to put myself about a bit in the amateur game, which can be a bit rough at the best of times. I have never been afraid of physical confrontation and I always liked to go big lad against big lad, which led to some fiery encounters. That all came from my dad, who would tell me, 'Always pick on the big ones and the little one will leave you alone.' My tactic was to bluff my way through games by causing a fight with the biggest bloke in the opposition team, then hopefully the rest of them would keep their distance.

I had my fair share of dismissals and suspensions, but in those days I loved playing rugby simply for the enjoyment of it and I wasn't going to let the odd ban stop me. There were many times when Barrie McDermott was suspended but still turned out in disguise, under someone else's name. On one occasion a bloke I played with at Waterhead got picked for Lancashire and no one could understand why, because he wasn't the most talented of players. When he got to the trials no one knew who he was. The name the scouts had seen on the teamsheet when they had been watching Waterhead was not the player who turned up. I had been banned at the time, so I had played under his name for a few weeks, had three or four good games and got picked for the county, all under someone else's name.

I spent around three seasons as a teenage player at Waterhead, but the height of our ambition was just to go out and enjoy every game and not worry too much about whether we won or lost.

Like any young lad, I would have played every day of the week if I had been allowed. At one stage, I was playing open age for my pub side Chadderton on a Saturday, for Waterhead on a Sunday and with Oldham's under-19 district team in midweek. The district team played in the British Coal National Youth League, which was a pro-am competition, though we were unique because we had no professional players in our side. We had a good run in the competition in the 1990–91 season and qualified for the last four with a 48–42 extra-time win over Leigh at Watershed-dings. I got over for a hat-trick of tries, though I remember that game for more painful reasons.

One of the Leigh players was Jason Donohue, who later had spells as a professional for Leigh, Leeds and Bradford. I got a really good shot on him, a legal tackle which just about knocked him out of his socks. He went down like a sack of spuds, and as he was lying on the ground I stood over him and said, 'How do you like that, Donohue, you soft git?' Unfortunately, as he got up he punched me, hard, between the legs. I thought my balls were going to come out the top of my head. This time it was me rolling around on the ground in absolute agony as Jason stood over me and said, 'How do you like that, McDermott, you soft git?'

I scored two more tries in a big win at East Hull in the semi, and we were through to the championship decider, which was the first big final I ever played in. Our opponents, York, had five players who were playing in the Second Division that season and they beat us 36–20 at Watersheddings, but I had the consolation of scoring one of our tries.

Because most of the teams included professionals, the National Youth League got plenty of attention in the press and I began to get some good write-ups. After the Leigh game the *Oldham Evening Chronicle* described me as 'big, strong, rough and fast' and said Wigan, St Helens and Leeds were already watching me, which was a big boost to my confidence and a tribute to the work various coaches were doing with me, principally Mick Slicker, who went on to coach at Halifax and one or two other sides in the professional game. He was the first one to notice my offload game. He convinced me that I had some ability with the ball and that I wasn't just a big, tough lad. A lot of the things he taught me have stayed with me throughout my career.

I played for the district side for a couple of seasons, and at one stage Brian Gartland, the coach, decided to leave out me and a mate of mine, Roy Jewitt, to try some new blood. It was Roy's birthday on the day of the next game, so we decided to finish work early, go for a couple of drinks to celebrate his birthday and then go and watch the game and support the lads. We finished work just after lunchtime, had half a dozen beers and were pretty merry by the time we got to the ground to watch the game. Brian saw us arrive, and the first thing he said to us was, 'Have you brought your boots?'

'I have, Brian,' Roy replied, 'but I have had a beer this afternoon.'

Brian told him he was short of players, so he would have to play, then he turned to me. I hadn't got my boots with me, so I thought I was off the hook. But Brian said, 'We are desperate. You're going to have to play.' I ended up borrowing some boots and playing without a gum-shield, and after twenty minutes, with all that beer sloshing around inside me, I was about ready to die. It's strange how things work out, but I stayed on, somehow managed to have a good game and scored a couple of tries. St Helens had a scout at the game and they were interested in signing me on the strength of it, but I didn't really take them seriously and nothing came of it. At that stage I still couldn't imagine a top club wanting to take me on.

The social side of amateur rugby was always as import-ant as what happened on the field in those days, and we had some good times at Waterhead. One year we went to Blackpool for a night out. The coach driver gave us a strict departure time of midnight for the trip back to Oldham, but that proved to be wildly optimistic. We went to the Pleasure Beach and the front, visited a few pubs and clubs and had a thoroughly good evening, and by the time we'd finally finished carousing it was well past two a.m. We went back to the park thinking the bus would be waiting for us, but it was long gone and we were stranded in Blackpool with no money and no way to get home. There were only three coaches left in the park, but luckily one of them was from Oldham, so we thought we'd sneak on board, keep our heads down and stow away for the trip home. Unfortunately, its passengers turned out to be a hen party, so there wasn't much chance of us keeping a low profile. They let us on, but the girls savaged us all the way home. I have since played against some pretty fierce opponents and I have been involved in a few hair-raising antics on and off the field, but coming back from Blackpool on a coach full of pissed-up women was easily one of the most frightening experiences of my life.

From my mid-teens I regularly played outside my age group, but playing open age on Saturdays and youth rugby on Sundays was a bit of a mixed blessing. My coaches at Waterhead thought I was picking up bad habits turning out for the roughnecks at Chadderton, but playing against big blokes and bashing them around a bit gave me plenty of confidence, and when I came up against people my own age I knew I could handle anything they threw at me.

My disciplinary record probably held me back a bit, but I did begin to get noticed, and in 1988 I got called into the under-17 Lancashire squad to face Cumbria, though I wasn't selected for the actual side, which included lads like Tony Barrow junior, Shaun Casey, Bobbie Goulding and Chris Joynt, who all went on to have good professional careers. I was disappointed not to make the team because it would have been my first taste of representative rugby. I hadn't really expected to get in, but once I'd had that taste of being involved in a representative squad I realized it was something I was more than capable of doing and I began to set my sights quite high.

I was always an enthusiastic trainer, but my experience with the under-17s gave me a bit more incentive to have a strong pre-season and to play some good rugby, and that paid off a couple of years later when I was called into the county under-19s squad. That was the first time I properly met Terry O'Connor, who played for the Widnes Tigers amateur club and was one of the stars of the county team. We had fought a few battles, literally, and been sin-binned together a few times so we were aware of each other, but we hadn't really spent much time together. It was a bit of a stand-off at first because we were both quite wary, but when we eventually became friends it would last for ever, even though more often than not we have been playing for opposing teams. Though neither of us would ever back down in a confrontation, I know if I was going into battle I would want Terry in the trenches with me, and that's something that is very important in this game. It's very much a macho game, and a game of trust: you have to have faith in the people you are playing with.

My first representative rugby, then, was in the back row for Lancashire under-19s at St Helens in 1990 opposite Darren Fleary, who I later played with in the front row at Leeds. He got man of the match because he dropped a goal to win the game for Yorkshire. I also played in the second game of the series, against Cumbria, and that led in January 1991 to selection for the Great Britain under-19s side away to France, which was the first time I ever played for my country.

The feeling the first time I pulled on the Great Britain jersey was one of sheer elation. I got a bit carried away with the whole thing and went out before the match and had a British lion tattooed on my arm. I regret that a bit now because it is permanent, but it seemed like a good idea at the time as I was so delighted to have been chosen to represent my country. People laugh now and ask what I was thinking, but I really thought that was as good as it was going to get and I wanted to mark the event. No one believed that someone with less than twenty-twenty vision could play at such a high level. It took me a long time to realize I could go as high as I wanted to in this game, but getting picked for that Test against France was the start of that self-belief. From then on I knew that if I got the right breaks and had a bit of luck, and if I worked hard, I could go a long way. The harder you work, the harder you train and the more experience you get, the more you realize that, touch wood, you are going to be all right.

There were a few tears when I lined up with Great

Britain for the first time. It was very emotional, and I still feel the same way now. I always feel I am representing myself, my family and anyone who has ever had anything to do with my career, and that's a big responsibility. I am a very proud person, and I play with pride whichever team I'm playing for, but you can't do any better than representing your country. The full internationals at the time, people like Kelvin Skerrett and Andy Platt, were big heroes of mine and I wanted to emulate them. I never thought I would, but I always wanted to.

We won the first game, in Bordeaux, 24–6, with Terry O'Connor picking up the man of the match award, and completed the double against them with a 20–2 win in Whitehaven two months later. That game is famous in our family for my dad's first meeting with the Great Britain coach Malcolm Reilly. Malcolm later coached me in the full Great Britain side and was assistant coach at Leeds, but that night at Whitehaven he was sitting in the stand watching the game a few seats away from Mum and Dad. My dad is a bigger kid than me, and he has always been a bit star struck. Mum could sense Dad staring at Mal Reilly and she kept telling him to pack it in, so she was pretty horrified when Mal got up at half-time to go to the toilet and Dad got up and followed him. Dad stood next to Mal at the urinals, totally star struck, and all he could think of to say was, 'All right, Mal?' Mal said hello back and that was the full conversation, but Dad remembered that experience for a long time. A lot of water has passed under the bridge since then, if you will pardon the pun, but when Mal coached me later in my career Dad used to say, 'Ask him if he remembers having a pee next to me at Whitehaven.'

Those games against France were important because Great Britain under-19s were gearing up for a major tour to New Zealand at the end of that 1990–91 season, in June and July, and everybody knew that if they played well they would have a great chance of being on the plane. I must have impressed because I got selected for the tour, which at the time was by far the biggest honour I had ever received.

Before the tour party was named, Mike Morrisey, who was chairman of the BARLA youth committee, had told me that he'd watched me play and had liked what he'd seen. He also said that I needed to curb my temper and think about my game a bit more, and if I did that I had a chance of being picked for the Young Lions. I have always been a bit of a goal-setter so I kept telling myself, 'I'm going to New Zealand.' I used to write B McD 4 GB & NZ. I was at college at the time on a block release during my apprenticeship as a joiner, and it was a bit of a standing joke, because no one thought I had a cat in hell's chance.

The morning I got the letter to say I was selected to tour New Zealand I was thrilled to bits, and Mum and Dad were equally pleased. We went out together as a family to celebrate and there was quite a big article about it in the local paper, which said it could be 'the start of a great career'.

Players on amateur tours have to raise the money to pay for the trip themselves, and Waterhead did a great job collecting enough cash to make sure I could take up my place. I had a benefit at Waterhead and at a local working men's club, and the Oldham amateur rugby league organized a do with footballer Mike Summerbee as the guest speaker. In the end I managed to raise quite a lot more than the £1,200 I needed, so I could fit myself out with some new trainers, new boots, some smart kit and have a bit of spending money as well.

We went out to New Zealand that summer with a twenty-six-man squad, most of whom have gone on to play in the professional game. Terry O'Connor was picked along with Daz Fleary and Paul Anderson, who I have had a few battles with in his time at Bradford Bulls, and there were people like Simon Knox, Leigh Deakin, David Bradbury, Jeremy Dyson, Gary Burns, Gary Christie and Stephen Holgate in the party as well. We also had a really good backroom team, coach Brian Chambers, Robin Divorty, Geoff Owen, Jackie Reid and Gerry McDonald all doing a great job keeping us in some sort of order. Our kit for the tour was sponsored by British Coal, who backed the full GB side, and that made me feel even more proud, to be wearing the same jersey as all my heroes. It felt like I had taken another step closer to my dream.

When we arrived in New Zealand we were staying in a moorai, which is like a hostel, with everybody sleeping on mattresses on the floor in one big, long room. It was a bit like a scene out of the TV series *Auf Wiedersehen, Pet*. That was an experience in itself. For the first couple of days we were just trying to get over jet lag, but you couldn't get a good night's sleep even if you wanted to, because the bloke next to you would have been out for a few beers and he would come staggering in during the early hours tripping over bodies and waking everyone up. But it was a great laugh and it just added to the experience.

New Zealand was a bit of a culture shock, especially as we had to rub noses with the people who greeted us at the airport. That's not something you do very often in Oldham. The queen of the Maoris turned up to welcome us to New Zealand, and everyone we met was really friendly, but it was a completely different matter once we got out on to the pitch. I have never met a small Kiwi, and some of the so-called under-19s we came up against were massive, which made for some fun and games in the heat of battle.

The first game was against Waikato in Hamilton. Our coach, Brian Chambers, who was also in charge of Lancashire, came up to me before the game and said, 'They've got a big number eight. I want you to intimidate him, get stuck into him and make your presence known.' I have always been a bit confused about instructions like that. I didn't know if Brian wanted me to big-hit him, run at him or just plain hit him on the chin. In those circumstances I always went for the third option, because it was the easiest.

We got out on to the pitch and of course I was looking around for the big number eight, but he was nowhere to be seen. We were ready for the kick-off, but there was a delay and we were all asking each other what we were waiting for, until we noticed they only had twelve players on the field. Eventually the thirteenth man came trotting out and he was absolutely huge. The shirt he was wearing had been sliced up the side and was stuck together with tape because the jersey that had been provided wasn't big enough. I don't know how old he was, but he must have been in his mid-twenties. Of course, when he turned round I could see the number eight on his back. I thought, 'Brian Chambers has really stitched me up here.'

The first twenty minutes were fairly quiet, but then Dave Bradbury went in for a big shot on the number eight and managed to dislodge the ball, which led to a bit of pushing and shoving. I was a few metres away, but their big fella turned to me and started to head in my direction, so I thought, 'Here we go, this is my chance.' I brought a punch up from my feet and whacked him right on the end of his chin.

I'm not sure how fast my fist was travelling by the time it got all the way up there, but it connected with a huge wallop. As I swung round with my right hand, I saw the other front rower coming for me, so I threw a left hand at him. I wouldn't normally do that, because it's my weaker hand, but I managed to slot him on the chin as well. Two punches, and when I looked down both Waikato props were lying flat out on the ground at my feet. Unfortunately, they didn't stay that way for very long. They both leapt up very quickly looking for revenge, and it was all on in a huge brawl. We didn't video the game, but I really wish we had because all the people we were staying with said it was one of the best punch-ups they had ever seen. The thing I will always remember about it is our winger Darren Williams being chased all round the pitch by one of their lads. I later learned it was Martin Moana, who played in England for Halifax, Wakefield and Huddersfield among others.

As it turned out, that was a big turning point in the tour. We won the game 56–4 and it really brought us together as a team. I escaped being sent off, but I was sin-binned, and to avoid any more bother I went straight into the changing room. I was sitting there thinking, 'I've done it again. I've come all this way and I have let myself down.' Then Brian Chambers came in with a face like thunder and I thought I was in for a real rollicking. I was sure he was going to tear strips off me, but he broke into a big grin and said, 'Barrie, what a cracking punch that was!' As everybody came in at half-time they were all patting me on the back and saying what a good job I had done, which made me feel a lot better. I went back on for the second half, and fortunately for me the big number eight, who had also been sin-binned, only lasted a couple of minutes before going off with a leg injury, which meant he couldn't get his own back.

The second game was against Auckland. Their side included Willie Poching, who I later played with at Leeds, but I remember the encounter fondly because it finished nine against eleven. Paul Anderson had a huge fight with Jason Temu, who played in England for a while with Hull and Oldham, and they both got sent off early in the game. That set the tone for the rest of the match, and there were brawls breaking out every four or five minutes, with people being sin-binned or sent off all over the place. The match, which we lost 32–13, even made the news, the presenters saying, 'How did Great Britain let such a bunch of thugs get on the plane and come over here?' What they failed to point out was that the New Zealand players gave as good as they got, and in most cases started the fighting. We were so tight as a unit we were prepared to stand up for each other: if one of their blokes had a go at one of ours, we would all pile in to sort it out.

We played two Tests on the tour and I was named man of the match in the first one, which we lost 34–16. I had a skirmish with one of their players after about ten minutes, but oddly enough that made me really popular with the New Zealand fans. They enjoyed the physical side of the game and they really took me to their hearts. Wherever I went I got a great reaction from the locals, especially if I was able to have a chat and a beer with them after the game. I have always enjoyed the bad guy image on the pitch, but I have never tried to continue it off the field. That's far too much like hard work; it's much easier to be the nice guy after the match is over.

The first Test was in Greymouth, which was a real one-horse town. There were two pubs, and only one of them was any good. It was a hard-fought game and we were looking forward to a few beers and a night on the town to relax afterwards, but we ended up in the same pub as the Kiwis. It was a bit tense at first, but after we all had a few drinks everyone began to lighten up. The replay of the game came on the TV, we all sat down, had a good laugh at the fights and the big hits, and had a thoroughly good time.

The second Test was the final match of the tour, and three nights before the game Brian Chambers decided to impose a curfew of midnight, which was probably a good idea but didn't seem that way to a lad in his late teens on his first big trip away from home. Me, Colin Hodgkinson,

Richard Chamberlain, Leigh Deakin and Simon Holgate all went well over the curfew, and instead of getting back at midnight we found ourselves sneaking into the hotel at 2.30 a.m. Brian caught us in the act and he dropped us for the Test, which was a big disappointment.

In fact, we were gutted. The rest of the squad got together, and for a while it looked as though they would refuse to play if we weren't reinstated. In the end the game went ahead and Great Britain lost heavily, but I still think the result could have been different if we had played. That was a disappointing end to what had been a great experience.

4

TURNING PRO

To everyone at Oldham RLFC,
who opened the door to my career.

When I started to make a name for myself in the amateur game, scouts from professional clubs began to turn up at our matches. I must have impressed them because Wigan, Wakefield Trinity and Sheffield Eagles were all keen to sign me. Any of those would have been a good option for an up-and-coming eighteen-year-old, and originally I began talks with Wigan through an old scout, Derek Standish, who had asked me to go for a trial. I was a bit low on self-worth at the time and I was unsure whether I should go, but I got the phone call after an under-19s game for Waterhead, and after a few pints some of the lads persuaded me to go for it. I had got a bit of Dutch courage inside me, so I decided I would play in the trial, which was a reserve team game against Leeds at Central Park. It's strange how things turn out. I suppose if I had played in that game and done well the whole course of my career could have been different, but after all the agonizing about whether or not to go, the match was called off at late notice.

There was no Wigan A team game for a few weeks after that, and before the next one came along I met Peter Tunks, who was the Oldham coach. Peter is a great salesman, and he managed to talk me out of going to Wigan and into signing for Oldham. Peter came round to our house and had a chat with Mum and Dad, and he certainly won them over. My mum is a pretty good judge of character, and when Peter left she said, 'I like him. I think he is true to his word and he will look after you.'

So that was more or less that as far as deciding who I would sign for went. I had always wanted to play for Oldham, but as I'd got older I had set my sights a bit higher and I'd been hoping to sign for one of the really big clubs. But sometimes you have to take a step sideways to go forward. Wigan were the best team in England at the time and I knew my first-team chances there would be limited, for a while at least. Oldham had just been relegated that year, and I thought if I could get a few senior games under my belt I should be able to put myself in the shop window and hopefully attract one of the really big clubs. Either that or really get myself established at Oldham and become one of the mainstays there, which was in fact very much my favoured option.

I shook hands with Peter Tunks and he arranged for me to go up to the old Watersheddings ground to actually put pen to paper. I signed amateur forms in 1991 before the BARLA tour to New Zealand and officially joined up with Oldham as a professional player when we got back, along with Abraham Phillip, Gary Christie, Gary Burns and David Bradbury, who had all been in the Young Lions squad with me. I had my picture taken for the newspaper wearing an Oldham shirt, shaking hands with the coach. That was obviously a big day for me and my family.

I signed in the afternoon, and that evening I played for Waterhead in what turned out to be a dramatic Oldham Cup final against Salem Hornets. We were trailing 12–10 with four minutes to go, but a storming finish saw us win 22–12. I came off the bench just after half-time and scored a couple of tries, which was enough to earn me the man of the match honour, despite not playing the full game. The fact that it was Peter Tunks who was doing the choosing was just a coincidence, but I got plenty of stick from the lads afterwards. They were all joking and saying it was a fix.

At that time, Oldham had two changing rooms for training, one for the first-team squad and the other for the rest of the lads. When I started I got a spot in the first-team changing room, on the number four peg, right next to Charlie McAllister, who was a hero of mine. That gave me a clue that I might be in the running for a first-team place at the start of the 1991–92 season, but I was determined not to take anything for granted and I made sure I worked really hard at pre-season training all through the summer. I ensured I was always up there with the fast ones at training, which sometimes did not go down too well with the older heads in the squad. It didn't occur to me at the time, but now that I'm getting towards the end of my career I have learned that it's not nice when a young kid comes along with a lot of enthusiasm and determination and leaves you standing in training.

I made my debut in that summer of 1991 in a friendly against Dewsbury at Mount Pleasant and got over for a try in a narrow win. Peter Tunks must have been quite impressed because he picked me for the club's pre-season tour to the south of France, which became famous for one of the biggest brawls ever seen on a rugby pitch.

I was delighted to get on the tour because they only took twenty-one players, and a couple of lads who had signed at the same time as me were not selected. The first game was against Pia, but I had picked up a bit of an injury in the Dewsbury match and I wasn't chosen to play. I did, however, make the side for the second game, which became known as the Battle of Carcassonne, for reasons that will become obvious. The rugby league writer from the *Oldham*

Evening Chronicle, Roger Halstead, went with us on the tour so the game got huge coverage back at home, and of course I was right in the thick of it.

The game was reasonably quiet until midway through the first half when I took the ball up and one of their back rowers stiff-armed me right across the nose. As he moved his arm away I did something I hadn't done before and have never done since: I bit him. He responded by pushing me and then throwing a punch. I looked around to see if anyone else was getting involved, but the ball had gone and the referee had waved play on, so I thought, 'I'm not letting him get away with that.' And I whacked him back. We exchanged about half a dozen punches and the next time I turned around everyone else was fighting in lumps all over the field. It was like a barn dance – grab your partner, but in this case hit him as hard and as often as you can.

When we watched the tape later, it was absolute chaos. All the subs were on the pitch, Peter Tunks was chasing a bloke who had kicked one of our players, Richard Russell, and there were fists flying all over the place. Every time it looked like things were calming down another fight would break out. In the end, three local gendarmes came onto the pitch and managed to restore order. Believe it or not, the referee, Maurice Fabre, had actually allowed play to go on until Daniel Divet scored a try for Carcassonne. We had already had experience of local French referees in the first game, when Pia scored two tries while they had fourteen players on the field. The Carcassonne game was eventually lost 30–12.

Things got even more heated during the speeches after the game when one of the Carcassonne committee men said it was a pity the English did not understand the meaning of a friendly match. But the French had given as good as they got, and none of our lads had been prepared to take a

backwards step. Our director, John Chadwick, said afterwards that a lot of our team had gone into the game as
boys and come out as men, which was right.

That night we went out for a few beers in one of the
local towns and I didn't have to pay for a drink all evening.
All the older lads were saying what a great craic they'd
had. It was years since they'd had a brawl like that.

I stayed in the side for the third and final game, which
was a much more peaceful affair against Villeneuve, and
I was happy with the way I played, even though we lost
the match. Tunks must have been pleased with me as well,
because I was named in the side to face Sheffield Eagles at
Don Valley Stadium in our opening Second Division game,
my professional debut on 1 September 1991. I was on the
bench, and more or less my whole family travelled to South
Yorkshire to watch the game. I did reasonably well, made
a few nice runs and slipped out a few good passes, but it
almost turned into a disaster in the final minutes.

We were leading by four points, but Sheffield were
attacking near to our tryline. Hugh Waddell, who had been
a big star for Oldham and had played for Great Britain in
the famous Test win over Australia in 1988, was the next
man in their attacking line, and like any budding enforcer
I shot out of defence determined to get a good hit on him.
Unfortunately for me, Mick Cook, who had the ball, threw
a beautiful dummy for the first and only time in his career
and shot through a huge gap, where I should have been
standing, to score by the posts. It was my fault, and it
looked like I might have started and finished my career on
the same afternoon, because if we had lost it would have
taken me a long time to get back in the side. Mark Aston
lined up the conversion attempt, and not for the only time
in my career I said a quick Hail Mary and a 'please look
after me'. Thankfully, he missed the goal kick and we got
away with a point. Funnily enough, Mick Cook later turned

up as assistant coach at Leeds during my time there, but I don't think he realized how close he came to ruining my debut.

Until I joined Oldham I had managed to stay reasonably injury-free, despite all the usual bumps and bruises you get playing rugby at any level, but that all changed right at the start of my professional career, and for a while it looked as though injuries would force me to hang up my boots.

Playing in an A team game against Wigan I badly dislocated my right elbow, and that was a problem that haunted me for years. The injury forced me to start wearing an elbow pad, which has become a bit of a Barrie McDermott trademark. At first I used pads bought from sports shops, but they weren't exactly what I wanted so I began to customize them to suit me, and eventually I started designing my own range in partnership with the manufacturer Kooga, which has proved a nice sideline.

I spent about seven weeks on the sidelines, which was five less than the medical staff expected but was still very frustrating at that early stage of my career. Throughout the time I was injured I just wanted to get back onto the field and show what I could do. I eventually came back at least a month too early, making my return in an A team game at, of all places, Hemel Hempstead. I got through the first twenty minutes or so all right, but then the elbow went again and I found myself in a Hertfordshire hospital facing another three months out of the game. The lads had a few more drinks after the game than they would normally have and stopped off at the hospital on the way home to pick me up, so at least I wasn't stranded down there, which sometimes happens if a player ends up in hospital after a game in the south.

I got through the rest of the season without too much trouble, but about four months into the 1992–93 campaign I went to put a big shot on Rochdale's back rower Cavill

Heugh and yet again my elbow went the wrong way and dislocated. This time I went to Highfield Hospital in Rochdale to see their resident specialist. By now I was getting a bit disillusioned and was starting to wonder whether playing rugby was worth all the bother. I was insured, but that didn't amount to much, and it certainly couldn't cover the money I was losing by having to take time off work whenever the arm went. As a joiner you are using your arms all the time, hammering, sawing and things like that, so obviously that's impossible if one of your arms is in a sling. Each time I did it, for the first month or so I had no money coming in.

The specialist told me I had badly damaged the ligaments and tendons. He said, 'They aren't pieces of elastic, eventually they stop going back. Once they get stretched it takes them a long time to go back into place. If you do it again, you will seriously have to consider giving up rugby, or you could end up permanently damaged.' That was a frightening prospect. The doctors talked about plastic joints and screws and bolts and plates, none of which appealed to me much. I went home and talked to my parents about it. Mum said, 'You have started down this road now. If you walk away you will have to deal with that for the rest of your life.' I knew Dad didn't want me to pack it in either. He hadn't been able to play sport at a professional level, but he was getting a lot of pleasure from seeing me do it and I didn't want to let him down. For my parents' sake, I decided to give it another bash. Fortunately, there weren't many games left that season. I got through them all right, had a good off-season, and so far the elbow hasn't really bothered me since.

During that off-season in 1993 I got the chance to play in Australia, but, as I will explain in the next chapter, that landed me in bother with Oldham when I got back. I stayed in Australia a bit longer than first planned and the Oldham management weren't very happy about that, especially as I returned home with a hamstring injury which put me out of action for the first three weeks of the English season. I had to start the 1993–94 campaign in the A team, but luckily for me and unfortunately for him, our front rower Tiny Solomona had broken an arm. I got recalled pretty quickly, and once I got my first-team place back that year was probably the best I had with Oldham. A lot of that was down to the hard work I had put in and the experience I had gained from training and playing in Australia.

In February 1994 Peter Tunks was on his way and Bob Lindner took over as Oldham coach. He was a big fan of mine, and one of the first things he did was take me to one side for a pep talk. 'You are one of the best front-row prospects I have seen in this country,' he said. 'You will get all the help I can give you.' I am always desperate to play the game, and in those days I spent a lot of time worrying about whether I would be in the first team. If I was in the reserves, I was always bitterly disappointed. Bob assured me I would be one of the first names on his team-sheet, so having that pressure taken off did me a lot of good.

Andy Goodway was second-in-command at Oldham at the time, and he was someone else who took me under his wing, tutoring me on various technical aspects of the game, which I had never properly been taught before. Until then I had got by on a combination of brute strength and heart, and my style was simply to try to run at the opposition a bit quicker and a bit harder than they ran at me. I always had an offload and a good passing game, but I had never really used it because I didn't know how to. Bob and Andy taught me a lot in that respect, and that stood me in good stead later in my career.

I spent three seasons at Oldham, and over that time my reputation as a bit of a firebrand grew. I got into more than my fair share of punch-ups on the field, and various people told me if I didn't acquire some self-control I could destroy my career. Fairly early on Eric Fitzsimmons, who was assistant coach during Tunks's time at the helm, took me to one side and told me I wasn't doing myself any favours by getting into fights and giving away penalties. 'You've got to learn to be an aggressive player with a disciplined outlook,' he said. My attitude was that I wanted to be The Man. I wanted to be the bloke other teams were worrying about two weeks before we played them.

At the start of my career, gaining such a reputation was a big motivation for me. I wanted to grab the respect of people I was playing with and against. I had idolized a lot of the lads in the Oldham team when I was a kid and I wanted them to be proud to be playing with me, but sometimes I overstepped the mark.

Cumbrians always seem to be tough players, and one I had a memorable run-in with was Gary Tees, who played for Warrington and was at the time coming back from injury or suspension in an A team game against Oldham at Watersheddings. He came through as a dummy runner, and my attitude in those situations has always been to take him whether he has got the ball or not. I body-checked Gary, but he didn't like it and took a step back with his fists up, as though he was getting ready to unload a few punches. I decided to get my retaliation in first, so I walloped him with two massive punches right on the chin. I stepped away, thinking he would be down on the deck, but when I took another look he was still standing right in front of me as if nothing had happened. Gary was a big, thick-set lad and I hadn't even parted his hair. He grabbed hold of me and we ended up wrestling in the mud, with me making a mental note to avoid picking unnecessary fights with Gary Tees in future.

A few weeks after that incident Warrington played Hull on Sky TV. Gary took the ball in full bore against Mark

Jones, who was a big, tall ex-Welsh rugby union forward. He wasn't particularly known as a hard man, but he was definitely someone who could take very good care of himself. Gary ran into Jones and for some reason the Welshman took exception and laid him flat out with one punch – so that was someone else I decided not to upset in a hurry.

The first time I got a red card set a new Oldham record. It was April 1993, and we were playing Huddersfield in a Monday night game at Watersheddings. I went on as a substitute after twenty-nine minutes, and a mere four minutes later I was sitting in the bath after being sent off for a high tackle on Gary Coulter. It was believed to be the quickest red card in the club's history. I had been a professional for nearly two years by then and that was my first dismissal, but I still picked up a two-match ban after the RFL disciplinary committee decided not to believe my pleas of innocence, or insanity!

I came up against some real hard types while I was playing for Oldham, but one of my toughest opponents was Gary Price's mum. Gary was a forward with Featherstone Rovers, who play at Post Office Road, one of the most intimidating grounds in rugby league. Featherstone is a real rugby league area and the crowd there are always quick to let visiting teams know exactly what they think of them. It's a tight little stadium, with the crowd right on top of you, and there's a big slope down from the changing room end to the opposite terrace.

That particular afternoon, 7 November 1993, Craig Richards was in the front row alongside me, and for the first twenty minutes we gave Rovers a real good going over. Their props, Steve Molloy and Leo Casey, were both Oldham lads, and of course up against those two I was determined to make my presence felt. I spent the first quarter of the game just looking for a chance to get a good shot off on someone. Eventually, Gary Price came through with the ball with Leo Casey as dummy runner. I had been lining up to hit Leo, but when Gary came through with the ball I had a split second to change direction and I got it completely wrong. I caught Gary very high with an awful shot – though it wasn't intentional – and he stayed down, obviously in a lot of discomfort. He hadn't seen me coming and he was a bit off guard, which made an already bad tackle that bit worse. Any boxer will tell you the one you aren't looking for is the one that will knock you out.

Inevitably I got my marching orders, so I had to walk from the halfway line, where the tackle happened, up the hill to the changing rooms, which you reach by going up an alleyway between the main stand and a terrace in front of the clubhouse. As I walked past the Featherstone fans they were spitting at me and throwing coins and cans. I kept my head down, thinking, 'I have let myself down again. I hope that lad isn't badly hurt.' Just before I got to the changing rooms I felt someone bash me on the shoulder, and I turned round to see a very angry woman chasing after me, walloping me with an umbrella. I had no idea who this woman was, but she chased me into the changing rooms, and as I was sitting inside I could hear her carrying on at me, calling me a dirty so-and-so and creating a big commotion. Ken, our kit man, came in and told me it was Gary's mother, so I couldn't really blame her for being so upset. I have played against Gary plenty of times since and I still see him around. Fortunately there are no hard feelings, though I'm not sure if his mum ever forgave me.

Oldham were not the best team I have ever played with, but a lot of the lads just breaking into the side in those days have gone on to bigger and better things, and I often think it's a shame the club couldn't keep them all together, because they would have been a match for anybody. Oldham has always been a breeding ground for good rugby players, but most of them inevitably drift off to the wealthier clubs, which is what happened to me. For a while during my time at Leeds I shared a car from Oldham to training with two other Great Britain internationals, Iestyn Harris and Kevin Sinfield, which shows just the sort of talent coming out of the town. St Helens' Paul Sculthorpe, who was Man of Steel in 2001 and 2002, was from Waterhead, and many of the British game's really successful sides have had an Oldham lad or two playing for them.

While I was with Oldham, Chris Joynt played in the back row and Tommy Martyn, who later went on to win every available honour alongside Chris at St Helens, was a class act in the back division. Richard Russell, who later had a spell as hooker at Castleford, was in the team in those days too, and we also had Ian Bates and Richard Pachniuk, who used to travel over from Dewsbury together, competing for the hooking spot. Richard Pachniuk was a quality player; later, when he was playing for Hunslet, there was even some talk of St Helens swapping Keiron Cunningham, who's the best hooker around, for him. I don't suppose that was ever a serious possibility, but it shows how highly he was thought of. I think he could have gone to the very top if he had made a few better career decisions.

Ian Bates, or Blaster as everyone called him, was supposedly a scrum-half, but he was so tough that Peter liked to put him in between the big lads in the pack to do the tidying up for them. He would get through thirty or forty tackles every game. He wasn't a big lad, but he wasn't a passive tackler either. He would put his full weight into every shot. I remember one A team game against Halifax, who had, for some reason, included a lot of their first-team players. One of those was the giant prop Brendan Hill, who should have been called Brendan Mountain he was that big. Anyway, the inevitable fight kicked off, and somehow Blaster found himself tussling with Brendan, who must have outweighed him by about nine stone. I was in the thick of it myself, but when it all broke up I looked around and Brendan was lying poleaxed on the floor with Blaster standing over him.

Over more than ten years as a professional I have come up against some very good and very tough props. One of the most intimidating was Tim Street, who was my front-row partner when I was just starting out at Oldham. He was a good bloke to have at your side, and whenever trouble erupted, no matter what he said to the referee, he was always the instigator. Not surprisingly, he has a similar disciplinary record to mine.

There were some really good people involved at Oldham off the field as well as on it, like the A team coach John Prince, physio Nick Hodgson, John Watkins, who was a sort of general helper, and three stalwarts of the club: Tom Patterson, Mike Winterburn and John Chadwick. One of the real characters at Oldham was Alex Givons. He was at the club for about sixty years as a player, coach and eventually kitman. He was a Welshman who Oldham signed from Huddersfield, and he was a real cranky old so-and-so, but he had a heart of gold and he was a legend in rugby circles in the town.

The first time I met him was on our ill-fated French tour. The physio, who was sharing with Alex, had told me to come to his room at 7.30 a.m. for a massage on a leg injury. I arrived at about 7.15, knocked on the door and asked if the physio was in, and a Welsh voice from inside the room said, 'No he bloody well isn't, now piss off.' That was the first time I ever spoke to Alex, but he became a good friend of mine. He was one of the old-style rugby men, and as long as you treated him right and showed him a bit of respect he would treat you right in return. I think it was Alex who made sure I got a spot in the first-team changing room when I joined the club. Alex lived in the next street along from Watersheddings and he was never the same after the old ground got knocked down to make way for housing. One of the new streets was named after him, which shows how highly he was respected.

With the quality of players we had on board at Oldham, we were a bit too good for the Second Division. The first season I was there, 1991–92, we finished third, missing out on promotion by one place. The following season we went one better, finishing as runners-up to Featherstone and gaining a place in the Stones Bitter Championship for what turned out to be my last year at the club.

Missing out on promotion in my first season was disappointing, but we did go on to reach the Second Division Premiership final, which was played at Old Trafford. The Premiership was an end-of-season play-off competition, and in the final we faced Sheffield Eagles, who had finished top of the table. Unfortunately, I broke a bone in my hand a few weeks before the end of the season and when it came to the big day I wasn't selected. I was heartbroken because I thought I deserved a place, and the fact that I was part of the squad and got involved only by running on with water during the game didn't make me feel much better. (Sadly, I was to experience a case of déjà vu later in my career.) As it turned out, we lost 34–20, and Daryl Powell, who I later played with and was coached by at Leeds, got the man of the match award after scoring three tries.

I had some great times at Oldham, and I felt proud to play at the ground where I had spent so much time idolizing my heroes, even to run out alongside a few of them. Oldham have fallen on hard times recently and it makes me sad to see what has happened to them. I'm sure they would get back to the glory days if they had local lads from the town playing for them instead of elsewhere.

As I have said, playing for your hometown club is something special, but it can be a problem at times as well. One of the things I enjoy now about playing for Leeds and living in Oldham is the fact that I can leave work behind sometimes and I'm not being mithered all the time about what's going on and why someone's being picked when someone else isn't. When I'm in Oldham people tend to know who I am, but generally they will leave me alone. I have never minded signing autographs and talking about rugby, but sometimes it's good to have a bit of time off.

Playing for Oldham was certainly something you did for the love of the game rather than the money. I signed on for two years for £2,000. That's £1,000 per year. That wasn't a lot even in those days, but I suppose I was a bit of a gamble. I didn't have the best of disciplinary records and I was visually impaired as well, so I wasn't the safest bet as someone who was going to make it in the professional game. Wages in those days were £150 if you won and £50 for a loss; later on, in the Super League days, it would be everything for a win and nothing after a defeat. Nowadays a lot depends on where you finish in the league, the pot being divided up among the squad depending on how many games you play in and how many you win.

I certainly didn't get rich playing for Oldham, but we had a few laughs, not least on the annual end-of-season trip. After my final season at Oldham, before I joined Wigan, a big group of us went to Tenerife on a holiday that was booked by Charlie McAllister. He'd obviously forgotten to tell the travel agent we were a rugby team on an end-of-season piss-up, because we found ourselves staying in a family hotel. We had a lot of rules to make sure there weren't too many sober moments. As a result we were pissed for the majority of the week, and I'm sure the rest of the holidaymakers weren't exactly thrilled to have us there.

I was all set to join Wigan at that stage, in the summer

of 1994, and Andy Goodway, who was on the trip, pulled me over about halfway through the week and warned me to ease back a bit and to make sure I wasn't getting legless every evening with the rest of them. It was good advice, but I didn't take much notice of it, even though I wanted to. The following night we went out as usual and I didn't get back to the hotel until nine a.m. On my way back I stopped off to buy myself a paper and a bottle of milk, and just as I walked into reception Goodway was getting back from a jog on the beach. He thought I had just got up, and he was delighted I had taken his advice about not getting drunk and staying out all night.

5

BARRIE THE ROO

To everyone at Wyong, especially Bob Holloway and Rip Taylor, and David Stephenson.

Australia is a fantastic place: sun, sea, sand, surf and, fortunately for me, rugby league. After a winter playing at Watersheddings, which was one of the coldest places on Earth, I always fancied getting a bit of sun on my back, so in 1993 I took the plunge and began looking for a club to play for Down Under.

I was still fairly new to professional rugby at the time and the idea was to go out to Australia and spend a winter – which is, of course, our summer – over there learning my trade, and also to have some fun and see a bit of the world. Oldham knew I would come back a better player, especially after missing so much of the 1992–93 English season after dislocating my elbow for the third time, so they were all for it and they helped me find a club out there.

While I was making my comeback from injury in the A team I met Peter Walsh, an Australian who was coaching Workington. He was keen to take me up to Cumbria on loan, along with my team-mate David Stephenson, but I didn't see that as a step forward. I wanted to battle my way back at my hometown club, so I said no. With about six games of our season to go I told Peter Tunks I fancied going to Australia to gain a bit of experience and he said that Spider, as Peter Walsh was known, could sort me out with a club. I thought he might not be too keen to help after I had knocked him back at Workington, but he came up with the goods and fixed it for me and David Stephenson to join a club called Wyong, based on New South Wales's central coast, about an hour's drive outside Sydney. Ironically, considering future developments, Wyong played in the same green and gold kit as Australia's national side and were known as the Kangaroos.

I managed to find a sponsor to pay my air fare and off we went. The whole thing seemed to have been organized on a wing and a prayer, with notes about where we were going and who to meet written on the back of matchboxes and beer mats. Spider is a really easy-going bloke, and to pin him down to any firm arrangements was just about impossible. All I really had was the date I was going and a description of two blokes who were going to meet me at the airport. Spider said, 'One of them's a typical Aussie, with grey hair and glasses, and the other is the captain-coach, who is a scrum-half but looks like a prop.' I spotted them straight away. The typical Aussie was a bloke called Bob Holloway, who owned the local second-hand car dealership in Wyong. He turned out to be a great bloke, and a decade on I still keep in touch with him and send him pictures of my family. The captain-coach was Robert Taylor, who everyone called Rip. He had the biggest forearms I had ever seen. He was only about five feet tall, but he was also five feet wide, a massive bloke.

Wyong had fixed up a flat for us, which wasn't quite ready when we first got there, and a car from Bob Holloway's yard, an orange four-gear Datsun. It was a bit of a banger, but we ran it into the ground. On the first night we thought we had better get involved in some Aussie culture, so that meant a trip to the Wyong Leagues Club. Leagues clubs are a bit like social clubs over here, but with the emphasis very much on gambling. It is the leagues club that generates most of the income for the rugby team. The Wyong one was a massive operation, open day and night, with something like a hundred poker machines. If you went on the wrong one, some local woman would come up and whack you around the head with her handbag because you were on her machine.

We introduced ourselves to our new team-mates at a training session in the afternoon and then Stevo and I went home to get changed for our first night out in Australia. I was a pretty fashionable lad in those days and I wanted to look good, so I put on my dark jeans, white T-shirt and black leather jacket. I had long Elvis-style hair at the time, so that was all greased back, and out we went. To say we were overdressed was an understatement: the rest of the lads were there in shorts, T-shirts and flip-flops. They fell about laughing and then told us to go home and get changed into something a bit more casual.

Anyone going out to Australia knows the Aussies have a reputation for liking a drink or two, and as proud Englishmen Stevo and I were determined not to let the side down. The local haunt was a nightclub called Oz's Bar, which everyone called Sillies, because that was the state most people got into by the end of a night there. Stevo was feeling the effects of jet lag quite early in the evening so he was having trouble staying awake, but I was more concerned about getting used to schooners, little half-pint glasses. Two gulps and they were empty. I was in a really good groove, knocking the schooners back, while Dave was sitting next to me dozing off. Rip kept hiding his beers, because he couldn't keep up. He had never seen anyone empty a schooner so fast. I had flown 12,000 miles to one of the beer capitals of the world and I was with a mate who wouldn't drink because of jet lag and a coach who couldn't drink. It looked like the whole social side of the trip might be a bit of a washout, but I soon discovered the Aussies really can knock them back when they are in the mood.

The club had also arranged for me to get a concreting job, working for a bloke called Ralph Poppie. He was an ex-player who was heavily involved with the Wyong club and he used to employ a lot of the lads in the team. I'd get picked up from the leagues club early in the morning in time for start of work at around six a.m. We would have a bottle break – a litre bottle of Toohey's beer – at nine o'clock, a sandwich for lunch, and then we would be back in the leagues club for a few more bevvies by mid-afternoon. We all got paid $100 a day, which was decent money, around £40 or £50. That was enough to keep the two of us English lads in the essentials of life – videos and McDonald's. I really enjoyed the craic with all the lads, and though the weather wasn't exactly cracking the flags, it was a lot warmer than an Oldham winter.

Two Englishmen coming to Wyong to play for the local team was quite a big event locally and we attracted a lot of attention in the media when we arrived, especially the British lion I have tattooed on my arm. The day after we got there we had our photos taken in the gym with our training vests on, and the local *Wyong Shire* paper made a big thing of the tattoo. The story predicted we would not have a problem settling in as the Australian winter would be a virtual heatwave in Lancashire and we were already used to Aussie beer because Castlemaine sponsored Oldham.

For the first week we were there we lodged with one of the women who was involved in the running of the club, until the flat was ready and we could move in. It was brick built, and as they don't have central heating over there and we arrived in the middle of the Australian winter, it got pretty cold. The solution was to buy an electric heater, with a fan on it. One afternoon we were sitting in the changing room before training when a bloke came down the stairs from the leagues club looking for the two Poms. We stuck our hands up, and he said, 'Can you hear those fire engines outside?' We said yes, and he told us, 'Well, they're all going to your house. It's on fire.'

We lived about a hundred yards away from the leagues club, so we dashed up the street and there were three fire engines parked outside, with ladders and hoses strewn about all over the place. We had left the fan heater on to make sure the flat was warm when we got back and somehow it had fallen over and set fire to the carpet. We came running up, asking the firemen what was happening, and as Wyong didn't have many English residents they recognized us straight away from the paper. I had to show the firemen my British lion tattoo before they would go in and put the blaze out.

What with the tattoo and the fire, we quickly became fairly well known in Wyong and, fortunately, we managed to be quite successful on the field as well. We lost our first game, which was against a club called The Entrance, but I got a try and that began a scoring streak I haven't been able to equal since. We got off the mark in our second game, a 6–2 victory over Umina, and though I have never been noted as a try-scorer, I managed to get over the whitewash something like eight times in my first five games.

At that time the fashion in Australia was for big tacklers, going for a quick play-the-ball and not worrying about yardage or offloads. I have got a bit of footwork and I like to offload, so my own way of playing the game served me really well. I have scored only two hat-tricks in my entire career. One of them was for Leeds against Dewsbury in a Challenge Cup tie, and the other was in one of my early games for Wyong, against a side called Munmorah. Not only that, but I did it as a speedy winger. Well, a winger, at least. I played the first half of that game, which we won 68–2, in the front row as usual, but we got a few injuries so I found myself in the back row, then in the centres. I had scored two by then and I was taken off for a breather, but I was keen to get back on and complete the hat-trick, so they shoved me on the left wing and I duly got over for a third try, which was something I dined out on for quite a while.

Although we were in Australia mainly for the rugby, we were keen to see a bit of the country, and after we had been there a few weeks we arranged to go into the outback on a hunting trip. One of the blokes on the club committee had a friend who owned a couple of thousand acres in Queensland, in the north of Australia. Every so often he used to go up there to do a bit of pest control with his rifle. Kangaroos are considered to be vermin because they eat the crops and damage fences and so on, so they have to be controlled. The idea was for us to go up there and spend a week living off the land, which sounded like a good idea at the time.

I have always fancied myself as a bit of an outdoors type, but Stevo was not keen at all. In the end he agreed to come, but only under protest. It took us a good six hours to get there, even driving flat out on the dead-straight roads, and once we arrived we set up camp in a little shack in the middle of nowhere. The scenery out there was absolutely stunning and we spent a whole day driving around on quad bikes just getting a taste of the outback before our first hunting expedition, on the second night. I had eaten rabbit stew before and I was quite keen to taste kangaroo, which is supposed to be a bit of a delicacy. But there's a difference between eating meat you buy from a supermarket and catching and killing it yourself.

After watching the guys we were with skinning a few rabbits and kangaroos, I began to feel a bit green around the gills. The plan was to make rabbit stew in a big pan with some vegetables, but I was rapidly going off my food. By the end of the evening, if I had never seen a piece of meat again it would have been too soon. Stevo, who hadn't wanted to come in the first place, was completely the opposite: he absolutely loved it. He was riding around like a maniac shooting everything that moved, and at one stage he was wearing the insides of a kangaroo around his shoulders like a necklace. I practically became a vegetarian there and then.

We were there a whole week, and I couldn't wait to get back to Wyong. I felt sick the entire time. I have always been a big animal lover and I have owned quite a few dogs. I felt like I had betrayed every one of them. The rest of them were gorging themselves on rabbit stew and kangaroo meat, but I just couldn't touch it. Mind you, once we got back to civilization it wasn't long before I was back on steaks and Big Macs.

That sort of experience was a big culture shock, but it was what I went to Australia for, to broaden my horizons and experience different ways of life. I had never been away from home for any great length of time before and I was really dependent on my family. When I went away I didn't really have a clue; I didn't know how to use a washing machine, and just about all I could cook was beans on toast. But in Australia I got into cooking (which I still love), I learned how to wash and iron, and basically I grew up a bit. Before then I didn't realize that clothes didn't iron themselves; I had no idea there were a couple of stages in between throwing clothes into the wash basket and getting them out of the wardrobe. Roughing it in Australia for six months really taught me how to live on my own initiative and it improved me as a person, as well as a player.

Living in a flat with Stevo and other occasional lodgers was an experience as well. He worked at the leagues club, and if he couldn't get any employment there he would stay at home and look after the flat. I had no trouble getting work in the building trade, and I always found it really strange how Australians construct their houses from the inside out. The first thing they put together is the inside walls; the brickwork and the roof are done last. In Oldham, you get your brickwork up first and the roof on second, because you want to be dry when you're working.

I did a bit of joinery, and then I worked doing a spot of hod carrying for a couple of bricklayers. The guy I worked for there was the bloke whose position in the team I had taken, so we didn't really see eye to eye. But he needed a labourer and I needed work, so we put our differences to one side. The concreting job was the one I enjoyed the most. After playing on Sundays we would all go back to the Poms' house for a party and I always struggled to get up on Monday mornings. Nearly every time, the blokes I worked with had to call round to wake me up, and they would be stepping over sleeping bodies and the wreckage of the previous night.

For a while we had a French lad, Pierre, living with us. He was a cracking lad, a couple of years younger than us, but all we did was abuse him. His family had a bit of money so he didn't need to work; he had just come out to play rugby and see a bit of the world. He wasn't much good, but he managed to get the occasional game in third grade. Pierre used to call us 'stupid rosbif' – the French slang for an Englishman, from 'roast beef' – and he was always 'the lazy French bastard'. One of the reasons he was in Australia was to broaden his cultural horizons, but living with Stevo and me there wasn't much chance of that.

Pierre didn't drink, and he would get really annoyed with us whenever we brought the lads, and some girls, back after a game. He didn't mind the parties so much, but he hated the fact that he was always the one who had to clean up afterwards. One weekend he managed to get a game for the third grade, and afterwards he was drinking Tequila Sunrises in the leagues club. He had no idea what he was supping and within an hour of his first drink he was completely off his trolley, throwing up everywhere. The bar steward made us take him home, so we popped him on the roof of the Datsun, drove the short distance back to the flat and threw him into bed. Stevo, being the demon that he is, couldn't resist shaving off one of Pierre's eyebrows. I have never been in favour of that sort of prank, because there are always serious repercussions. In the morning all we heard was 'You Pommie rosbif bastard!' Pierre had to spend the next few weeks with a plaster over his eye, until the eyebrow grew back.

Off the field, everyone looked after us really well, but of course Poms were a big target during matches and as usual I got myself into a fair bit of trouble. There was plenty of sledging going on, which wasn't really a problem, but I think I was treated pretty harshly by some of the referees. Rip got pretty fed up about that, complaining to the league that I was being harassed and discriminated against. The local paper did a big story about it, and Rip told them, 'With Barrie's English background I suppose it's only natural that he gets some sledging from opposing players, but it shouldn't come from referees.'

Of course, Sod's Law struck the week that article was printed when I was sent off during a game against a team called Erina. And this time I couldn't have any complaints. It was a big game for both clubs, because Wyong had beaten Erina in five successive games, including the previous season's Grand Final. I was down getting treatment on an ankle injury when the Erina winger, Brett Jackson, made a break straight towards me. He thought he was clean through and obviously he was confident he wouldn't have a problem beating me for speed, but I jumped up, ran across the pitch and, just as Jackson handed off our full-back, I came in and lamped him. I knocked his head right back and he went down in a heap, spark out. I knew straight away I was going to get sent off, and I did feel quite bad about it. Of all the times I have got the red card, about 50 per cent of the time I have meant to do it; this was one of those occasions when I hadn't. I had meant to stop him, and to hurt him when I was stopping him, but I hadn't aimed to catch him as high as I did. I wasn't too popular with the Erina supporters. There were no barriers to keep the crowd away from the players, and as I walked off towards the changing room I got spat at and manhandled. To make things worse, we lost 16–14. I bumped into the guy I had hit a few weeks later and apologized to him. He just told me to forget it and we had a drink together.

That red card meant a trip to disciplinary the following week. It might have been a different country, but I felt right at home there. I took Rip and Bob Holloway with me to help plead my case and basically I just lied my way through the hearing. I told them I had been captain of all the teams I had played with, I had never been sent off or been in any kind of trouble, I was really, really sorry, and I would never do it again. Of course the committee didn't believe a word I said and I ended up with a four-game ban.

Funnily enough, years later at Leeds I played alongside Dave Barnhill, a tough Aussie who came over for a spell in Super League. We both played for Ireland in the 2000 World Cup and I was introduced to his dad, who is also called Dave, in a bar in Dublin. When I said hello, he said, 'You don't remember me, do you? I was on the disciplinary committee when you got sent off playing for Wyong. I must say you put forward a really, really good case and you sounded like a very rounded individual. But when you left the room we all burst out laughing because we all knew what a pack of lies it was.'

Wyong were one of the best teams in the Carlton Central

Coast Division competition, and the year I was there we finished top of the table, as minor premiers, and got through to the Grand Final, which decides who wins the title. I came back from my ban in time for our major semi-final in the championship play-offs, when we beat Woy Woy 17–12, but I tore my hamstring in that game which meant I was in doubt for the Grand Final. I had treatment all week in the lead-up to the final, even going to see an acupuncturist because I was absolutely desperate to play. In fact I was so desperate I landed myself in serious trouble with Oldham and Peter Tunks.

Wyong's Grand Final was at the same time as the start of the 1993–94 league season back in England, and in between me getting sent off and the team reaching the Grand Final I had received a phone call from Peter saying Oldham wanted me back. They had signed Craig Richards, but he had got an injury and another forward, Tiny Solomona, was out for the season, so they needed me back in the side as soon as possible.

That was a really big disappointment. I had been playing well and I was training really hard, starting at five o'clock in the morning five or six times a week before I went to work. A bloke I met in Wyong took me on forty-five-minute bush runs every morning – that is, literally running on nature trails through the bush on the outskirts of the town. At that time in the morning everything's moving and there are all kinds of things shooting out of the undergrowth at you – snakes, spiders and other creatures I couldn't identify. As you're running along, it's quite damp and misty, the bushes are moving and there are things skittering and sliding all over the place. That obviously added a few yards to my speed while I was out there.

So when Tunksy phoned me up and told me to come home, it was a big blow. Basically, I told him to shove it. I had come out to Australia to play in a Grand Final, I had worked hard for it, and I wasn't going to miss out now I had got the chance. That didn't go down too well at Oldham, but Peter and co. were 12,000 miles away so there wasn't an awful lot they could do about it. We had a big argument, but in the end Peter said I could stay for the final but I would have to fly home the following Wednesday. That suited me down to the ground, because it meant I could play in the big game and enjoy the social side of things afterwards.

The Grand Final was played at Grahame Park in Gosford, a picturesque little ground surrounded by palm trees with a harbour at one end behind the goal posts in which yachts bobbed up and down. It was about as far removed from Watersheddings as it is possible to get. Our opposition were The Entrance, who had already beaten us twice that season.

All week leading up to the game the town was decorated with banners supporting the Roos and there was a really good atmosphere around the place. It was my first experience of a big final so I was really looking forward to it, and I kept quiet about just how bad the hamstring injury was. I started in the front row; Stevo, who played in every game while we were out there, was on the bench.

The Entrance had a big front rower, a policeman from Manly called Dave Steptoe. He was massive, six feet five inches tall and nineteen stone. All week the media were building up the clash between the Aussie policeman and the Pom. I have never been frightened of anybody in my life and I like to rise to a challenge like that, so it was inevitable there was going to be fireworks.

Throughout my career people have said I am easily goaded and I get wound up during games. That is true, but when it happens, whoever is doing the goading has to cope with the consequences, because I enjoy a fight.

Twenty minutes into the Grand Final I was pulled off for a bit of a breather, and just as I left the field the big policeman went on. As soon as I sat down I spotted him, so I asked Rip to put me straight back on. Rip took off our other front rower, Doug Edwards, and I was back in the action. The first time I took the ball up I ran straight at Steptoe and he caught me with a really high shot. The ref blew for the penalty, but as soon as I heard the whistle I dropped the ball and we were off, fists flying. We each threw a good dozen punches, which is a lot in anybody's book, and ended up wrestling on the floor. When I watched the video afterwards, the commentators were falling about laughing. They said the game was too close to call and they couldn't predict who was going to win, but a huge fight between us two was an absolute certainty. One of them said it was a better punch-up than Larry Holmes's world heavyweight title fight against Evander Holyfield.

Sadly, though, that was the highlight of the final from Wyong's point of view. We had been dominant all year, but we were well beaten in the big game, when it really mattered. The first half was pretty close, though. They went ahead early on, but we pulled it back to 6–6 and things were looking quite encouraging until they got their second try just before half-time. We couldn't get back on terms after the break and the final score was a bitterly disappointing 23–12 to The Entrance.

I was quite happy with the way I played. I drove the ball in strongly, got some good offloads away and even did a bit of general kicking. The commentators picked me out as Wyong's best player, though I was secretly relieved not to win the man of the match award because the prize was a king-size bed and I would have had trouble stowing that in my hand luggage on the flight home. It was nice to hear people afterwards saying what a big impact I had made that season, but that was no real consolation because I had set my heart on jetting back to England with a medal.

Fortunately, in Australia, when it comes to Grand Final

day, the game is only half the fun. We spent the Sunday night getting legless in the leagues club, in what we called the Dungeon. That was a little snooker room under the main bar where all the poker machines were. The wives and girlfriends were banished until the following day and no one was allowed to go home. We stayed there the whole night drinking, playing games, including a spot of naked touch rugby, and messing about. The following day was what is called Mad Monday, which is an Aussie end-of-season tradition that is beginning to catch on over here. At nine a.m. they unlocked the doors and allowed us to go home, freshen up a bit and get changed, but we all had to be back at ten for more drinking. In between me going home and getting changed, they stripped Rip completely naked, egged him and floured him, and he had to stay like that for the rest of the day. At lunchtime we had a barbecue and Rip was given something to eat, but he wasn't allowed to get dressed. All the wives, young kids and just about everybody else in Wyong came along to look at the first-team head coach, bollock naked and covered in flour and eggs.

Wyong has its own small racecourse, a bit like Pontefract or Thirsk, and on the Tuesday we went to the races, still all completely legless. Wednesday was the day we were due to fly home, so Stevo and I went to the bar to say goodbye to the lads, and they told us, 'We're coming to the airport to see you off.' Everyone had been drinking for three days solid by this stage and quite a few of them were in a filthy state. The two of us had been home to pack and sober up a bit, but the rest of them were absolutely steaming.

We had only been on a three-month visa and we had been in Australia for almost twice that long, so we were trying hard to act sensibly to convince the officials at the airport how sorry we were about staying two months longer than we should have done. Somehow we got away with it, but the sight of all the other herberts from Wyong singing, shouting and generally causing chaos in the bar outside didn't go down too well.

Stevo's appearance didn't help either. They say an elephant never forgets, but neither do French rugby players. Pierre had been waiting two months for his revenge, and he got it the night before we left Australia, when Stevo passed out in the bar. That's why he flew 12,000 miles home with no eyebrows.

6

AMONG THE BEST

To all those players at Wigan who stuck by me
when things went wrong.

About halfway through the 1993–94 season I was contacted by an agent, Derek Parker, who was based in Todmorden near where I lived. He was aware of the interest in me and the speculation surrounding my future and he offered his services to help make a possible move go more smoothly if I did decide to leave Oldham.

To be honest, I didn't particularly want to move, but I thought having an agent wouldn't cost me anything if I stayed where I was, and if I did move on he would be able to help me get a good deal. At the time I was getting quite a decent reputation as an up-and-coming youngster, and Derek did a good job putting my name around as someone who might be looking for a change, so a few clubs began to show an interest. That was flattering, but in my heart of hearts what I really wanted to do was stay at Oldham. Ever since turning professional I had imagined myself as a one-club man, and I wanted to do it with my hometown side.

Loyalty is very important to me, and I had strong feelings and a lot of passion for Oldham. Unfortunately, the board at Oldham didn't seem to feel the same way about me in return, at least not until they thought they could make a few quid out of me. The Oldham chairman, Jim

Quinn, knew exactly how I felt about the club, and in my opinion he used that to his advantage. I was the sort of bloke who would play for nothing, and the club's attitude obviously was, if he enjoys his rugby that much, why pay him for it? I was on a pay-as-you-play contract at Oldham for three years which earned me almost nothing, and much as I enjoyed it there that began to bug me when I saw what some of the other players were on. Wally Gibson, who was Oldham's import at the time, was on something like £20,000, and I was aware what Ian Sherratt, my front-row partner, was earning, so I knew what I was worth.

I had a meeting with Jim Quinn. I told him I'd had other offers but that I wasn't looking to leave. I made it clear I would like to stay for another year under Andy Goodway because I thought I could learn a lot off him and I was keen to play under a coach I really respected. Warrington, Widnes, Leeds, Wigan and St Helens had all offered me terms and some of the deals were as high as £14,000 per year. If Oldham had been willing to pay me half that I would have stayed, but Jim offered me £4,000 for the year. My reply was simple: 'Thanks, Jim, that concludes our business for the day. I will be moving to another club.' Jim tried to change my mind, but as far as I was concerned he was disrespecting me and he had made it clear I wasn't valued as highly as his other players.

Moving on was a huge wrench, but I spoke to the clubs who were interested and right from the start Wigan was always the most attractive choice, though they had actually offered me the least money. I had a meeting with the chairman Jack Robinson and John Martin, who was one of the directors. They took me into the boardroom, which overlooked the Central Park pitch, and showed me around the ground, the changing rooms and all the facilities. After Oldham and Watersheddings, it seemed like another world.

Kelvin Skerrett, who was one of the Great Britain props

at the time, was a Wigan player, but he was getting towards the veteran stage of his career, and Andy Platt, another world-class front rower, had just left the club, so there was an opportunity for me to break straight into the first team. Terry O'Connor had just signed for Wigan as well, which was another huge lure. I knew we would both be chasing the same spot in the team, but I thought having a mate there would make the move a bit easier, so I went home, thought about it and decided to do the deal.

Coming from Oldham, I had always been brought up to be very jealous of Wigan's success, so it was quite something actually to be signing for them, especially at a time when they were the best club side not just in England but in the world. One of the first people I saw when I was leaving the ground after agreeing to join Wigan was Shaun Edwards, who was one of their biggest stars. Shaun was known as Giz, after Gizmo in the film *Gremlins*, mainly due to the fact that he wasn't exactly an oil painting. He was a player I had always admired and I knew he was a great professional, but as a person he was someone I never really expected to like. As it turned out, I was wrong. I soon found out that Shaun is a thoroughly nice bloke, and we got on very well. The last game I played for Oldham was against Wigan. I had enjoyed myself and played well, but because of that game I still had it in my head that Shaun was the enemy. Whenever I played against him I had wanted to really hurt him, so when he came over to me, shook my hand and congratulated me on joining Wigan, that was a bit of a shock.

It was also an important lesson learned, and something I kept with me for the rest of my career. In sport, you should never take it for granted that your enemies are going to be your enemies for ever. You never know when you're going to be playing with or against someone in the future. I am always going to make enemies on the pitch

because of the way I play and the way I am, but when the
whistle has blown my attitude is that it's over and done
with. After having a good ding-dong with anyone I'm
always the first to go over, shake his hand and congratulate
him.

Moving from the part-time environment at Oldham to a
full-time one at Wigan was a major shock to the system,
and I was a bit worried about how I would cope with the
new training regime. The best advice came from Giz, who
told me it was just like starting work later and finishing
earlier. He told me just to make sure I was always on time
and I was always prepared right mentally.

The fact that Giz made me so welcome took a lot of the
pressure off. Oldham was a small pond, but on moving to
Wigan I was suddenly rubbing shoulders with some of the
brightest stars in the game and I wasn't sure how they
would accept me, especially as I had tried to bash a few of
them around when I had played against them in the past.
Slowly but surely, everyone came over and introduced
themselves, which is something I have carried on with new
players at Leeds. There are very few egos in rugby league,
and the first thing you should do when a new player comes
into the club is introduce yourself, ask him if he needs any
help and generally try to encourage him to settle in, because
you never know when you're going to be in that position.

It's a strange thing, but as soon as word got out that I
had decided to join Wigan, Oldham's valuation of me went
through the roof. Those were the days of transfer fees even
for players who were out of contract, so despite the fact
that Oldham hadn't made any serious attempt to keep
me, they weren't going to let me leave for nothing. Jim
Quinn reckoned that because Wigan had recently paid
£250,000 for the New Zealand rugby union centre Va'aiga
Tuigamala, who had not played league before, I was worth
£750,000, even though he had only offered me £4,000 a

season. That was in all the newspapers, which was very embarrassing. Once I had actually signed a contract with Wigan, Jim found out and sent me a contract offer worth £25,000 a year for two years. He knew that when it went to a transfer tribunal, the panel would base the fee Wigan would have to pay for me on what I had been offered by Oldham.

The tribunal was an experience in itself, and I had to take my hat off to Jim for the way he handled it. He had produced a fantastic tape of some of my best moments for Oldham, a sort of Barrie McDermott's greatest hits. It was an eight-minute video, and watching it in the hearing I was quite impressed myself. Jim also had references about my ability from Bob Lindner and Andy Goodway. Wigan had offered a down payment of £15,000, going up to £40,000 if I played Test rugby. In the end, the panel – which was made up of Sir John Wood, former Castleford chairman David Poulter and ex-Saints chairman Joe Seddon – decided I was worth £40,000 straight away, rising to £100,000 depending on appearances and whether I played for Great Britain, which I think both clubs were fairly happy with. Wigan would have to pay an extra £20,000 after thirty first-team appearances, another £20,000 after sixty and an additional £20,000 if I got a full cap, which at the time did not seem very likely, not in the near future anyway.

In 1994, that made me a big-money signing, but I never felt under any pressure because of the transfer fee and none of the players at Wigan ever gave me any grief about it. I was made welcome straight away, and I relished being around the enthusiasm of people like Denis Betts, Phil Clarke, Jason Robinson and Andy Farrell, who was just starting out and went on to become Great Britain captain and one of Wigan's finest ever servants. Having Tez there was an advantage too, and I enjoyed learning off everyone at Wigan. I can't say the front rowers were particularly forthcoming or keen to offer me advice, but the other players did everything they could to help me.

Kelvin Skerrett was probably one of the last people to talk to me, though over the course of the season he turned out to be a lovely lad and he did his best to get on with me. Although he was always a very tough player and a real enforcer on the pitch, off it he was quite quiet and shy. He was someone I liked and respected. When I signed, people at the club had said that the way I played reminded them of Kelvin, so I think he had it at the back of his mind that I was there to replace him. At the time I thought he was being a bit stand-offish, but later on in my career I could understand exactly how he felt.

When I had played in my final game for Oldham against Wigan I had enjoyed a good tussle with Kelvin and I had given as good as I got. I probably slightly outplayed him that day, though the fact that he was due to play at Wembley in the Challenge Cup final the following week maybe had something to do with it. But I marked that down as one in the win column, and I kept thinking that perhaps that was the reason why he wouldn't talk to me. It seemed like he was holding a bit of a grudge, though later on I found out that was not the case. It was simply due to shyness; there was no malice there at all.

Tez and I probably did not help ourselves when Kelvin came over in the gym one day to invite us to his wedding. The whole squad were going, though it can't have been easy for Kelvin to invite the two new front-row prospects. Unfortunately we had both already got something arranged for that day and we turned him down flat, which didn't go down too well. That was something he never forgot, and he still takes the mickey about it now when I see him.

At the time I joined Wigan, they were known as the Invincibles. Wigan have always been one of British rugby league's top clubs, but they had gone into decline in the late 1970s and eventually got relegated for the only time in their history in 1980. They got promoted the following year and struggled a bit until the mid-1980s when Graham Lowe took over as coach. He and chairman Maurice Lindsay turned the club around, mainly by buying the best players in the world.

I had a good pre-season with Wigan, playing well in a couple of trial games and getting some positive write-ups in the press. My first appearance was in a friendly at Leigh, when Tez also made his debut. We actually lost 30–29, but I was pleased with how I played and the local paper said afterwards that of the two of us, I looked more ready. The game after that was a Locker Cup match against Warrington, and I scored a couple of tries, one in each half, which was very unusual for me. I obviously made a good impression on head coach Graeme West and the rest of his backroom staff because when they named the team for our first competitive game on 21 August 1994, against Featherstone Rovers at Post Office Road, I was in it. I remember sitting on the toilet reading the programme – which is my traditional pre-match ritual – and seeing my name alongside people like Tuigamala, Skerrett, Betts, Clarke, Offiah, Botica and the rest. My name looked out of place.

The game was live on Sky TV, and when I got home my dad wanted to know what Shaun Edwards had said to me. At one point I had tried to play the ball, but one of the Rovers players had knocked it out of my hands. They got the benefit of the doubt and the referee awarded a knock-on against me. On the tape, you could see Shaun Edwards throw his hands in the air and start shouting and bawling. I had my back to him, so I didn't realize what had gone on until I watched the game again at home. People might have thought it was the experienced player having a dig at the new boy, but it wasn't. If you make mistakes, you have to accept the consequences. Shaun was just trying to gee the whole team up. It wasn't personal and I never took anything like that to heart.

I made a decent start at Wigan and I got on a bit of a roll as a try-scorer. Martin Offiah, Shaun Edwards and I got seven tries between us in my second game, against Sheffield Eagles: they both got hat-tricks and I got one. I also scored in a big home win over Leeds, and in the following match, when we hammered Widnes 46–12. Jason Robinson and Denis Betts both got hat-tricks that afternoon, which just goes to show what strike power Wigan had at the time. I was pleased with the try against Widnes because I had to show a bit of pace, running forty metres to the line after their full-back, Stuart Spruce, had chipped a clearing kick straight at me.

I was delighted with a return of three tries before the end of September, but the next one I scored was in the Regal Trophy final four months later, and that proved to be my last for Wigan.

My good early-season form, however, earned me a place in the Great Britain side for the Tests against Australia, and therefore cost Wigan an extra £20,000, which they had to pay Oldham under the terms of my transfer. Unfortunately, I picked up a groin injury during the second game of the series and had to have a painkilling injection before the decider a couple of weeks later, which turned out to be a bad move in the long run. Your body gives you pain when it doesn't want you to use a particular muscle; pain is a signal to your brain to shut that muscle down and let it heal. By masking the pain you can usually play on, but you only end up doing more damage, and that inevitably results in a longer spell out injured. That is what happened to me. I don't regret it, because playing for your country is something every player aspires to, and if the chance arises you can't turn it down, but it did have a big effect on my season at Wigan. I played in the back row in the two club games immediately after the third Test, but I wasn't fully fit, I played poorly and I ended up losing my place.

The first game after the Elland Road Test in November 1994 was against Featherstone, and that led to a major row in the changing rooms between me and Martin Offiah, who was one of the game's biggest stars in those days. Kelvin Skerrett scored a try against Featherstone, and afterwards Martin began ribbing him about it, asking him, 'What are you doing scoring tries? That's my job.' I got involved, a bit tongue-in-cheek, and told Martin, 'What are you saying that for? We don't say things like that when you make a tackle.' Martin took that the wrong way and really laid into me, saying things like, 'Who the hell do you think you are? How many games have you played?' I took it all quite personally. I was a part of the squad and I thought I was beginning to make headway in the team, so there was no need for one of the senior players to be trying to put me down. Martin was a nice bloke and I hadn't had any problems with him before then, but that incident made me realize what a tough job I was going to have getting accepted into the environment they had at Wigan, where virtually everybody was a big star. I definitely was not looking for special treatment, but I thought I deserved to be classed as an equal.

I was at Central Park from July 1994 to September the following year, starting eight games with another five appearances off the bench, but I never really settled or felt like I fully belonged. The players there were colleagues rather than friends, and I found that very hard to come to terms with after the environment at Oldham where we had been like a family. It was a very auspicious environment to go into, probably one of the most successful British teams of all time in any sport, and virtually everybody else in the changing rooms had a pile of winners' medals, inter-national caps and big games behind them. They had all been handpicked to do a specific job and they were very good at what they did. I came in, kicked the door down and said, 'I'm going to make a name for myself here,' but when I kept getting injuries that made it really difficult. You can train as hard as you like, but there's a saying about certain rugby players that they train like Tarzan and play like Jane. What that means is unless you can back things up on the field, people won't take you seriously. The culture at Wigan was such that no one ever accepted second best and, other than the odd game, I wasn't able to show them what I was really capable of. At Wigan, when you were in the first team you were made welcome and really looked after, but if you were outside that elite no one could care less.

The fact that I was very naive when I signed for them did not help me, and it was one of the reasons why I got into bother a few times off the field. I had been used to driving the vans around at work, even though I had never taken a driving test, and the Wigan board were a bit shocked when they asked for my licence so they could arrange a sponsored car for me and I told them I didn't have one, but that I had coped fine without one. They knew there and then that they were going to have to teach me a few things. I had my photo taken with my sponsored car and then it had to go back and sit in the showroom until I passed my test. I took a block course of lessons and passed first time, on a Friday morning. I got a lift to Wigan to pick up my sponsored car, which had my name written all over it, and I was driving along the motorway back to Oldham less than two hours after the test.

But it was the injury I sustained playing for Great Britain that meant I didn't get back into the Wigan side for a long time, and I never really felt part of things after that.

Having a ball.
Here I am, aged two,
ready for a game of
football with my dad.

The McDermott
family. Aged five,
I'm all spruced up
for a family wedding,
along with little sister
Alison and my
Mum and Dad.

Little cherub.
This fresh-faced
youngster is me,
aged six.

My first big game. St Albans under-14s line-up, before a cup-final clash with Saddleworth. I am second from the right in the front row. Seven from this team went on to play professionally.

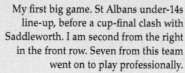

In action for Chadderton 'Brawlers'.

Cheers. Celebrating the end of the BARLA tour to New Zealand. Left to right: Ian McRae, Darren Carter, Gary Christie, Sean Casey, Gary Burns, Richard Chamberlain and me.

A big day. Shaking hands with coach
Peter Tunks after signing my first
professional contract for Oldham.

Ready for battle. Tim Street and I
prepare for action during Oldham's
ill-fated French tour, which featured
the notorious Battle of Carcassonne.

Wild men. It's supper the hard way
for Dave Stephenson and me during
our hunting expedition deep into
the Australian bush.

Touchdown. Scoring for Oldham against Leigh on my home debut in 1991.

Driving in. For Oldham against Featherstone at Post Office Road, scene of one of my most spectacular sendings-off.

The dynamic duo. Terry O'Connor and I pose for the cameras on the pitch at Central Park, for the first time, just after joining Wigan.

Crunch. The tackle that sparked a diplomatic incident. Aussie hardman Paul Sironen gets in the way of a McDermott elbow during the 1994 tour game at Central Park. It earned me a two-match ban and my first GB call-up.

A dream come true. Coach Ellery Hanley and I pose for the cameras after I was named in the squad for my Great Britain debut against Australia in 1994.

Always an honour. Lining up for Great Britain ahead of the second Ashes Test at Old Trafford in 1994.

The greatest
team ever?
Celebrating
with Wigan
after our 1994
Regal Trophy
triumph,
in a season
that saw
us win every
available
honour.

Getting the
ball away
against
Warrington
Wolves
in Leeds'
first-ever
Super
League
game, at
Headingley
in 1996.

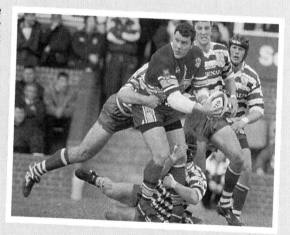

Tanks a lot. Posing with my Rhinos teammates Anthony Farrell, Jamie Field, Terry Newton and Adrian Morley on a pre-season Army training camp in Wiltshire.

My favourite try. I am about to score against Warrington, after fooling the defence by dummying to kick a drop goal.

On the mend. Recovering at home in Oldham with Jenny, Billy and our dog Tyson after breaking my leg in 1997.

My wedding day.
Dressed up for Jenny's
and my big day
with (left to right)
my brother-in-law
Michael Unsworth,
Ian Sherratt,
Terry O'Connor,
Darrel Rogers
and my dad, Bob.

Outcast. Batley Bulldogs
are the opposition as I drive
the ball up during my loan
spell with humble Bramley.

Off. Simon Haughton goes
down in a heap and the red
card comes out. At the time
I feared this incident in a
1999 Challenge Cup tie might
mean the end of my career.

7

PROUD TO BE BRITISH

*To all my antipodean friends – with or against you,
it was always great fun.*

Australians. Love them or hate them, in rugby league you can't ignore them. Over my career I have played with and against loads of Aussies, and the majority of them have been great blokes. But that hasn't stopped me trying to knock seven bells out of as many of them as possible, and vice versa, and some of my most memorable and enjoyable moments have been in games against Australia.

The rivalry between Great Britain and Australia is fierce in any sport, and particularly in rugby league, where they have had the upper hand for more than thirty years. The last time Great Britain won the rugby league Ashes was way back in 1970, and that's something generations of British players have been trying to put right ever since. Things were fairly even in the early 1970s, but then the Aussies began to pull away from us, and between 1978 and 1988 we couldn't get anywhere near them. Australia won fifteen successive Tests against Great Britain in that ten-year period, but we began to get back on to more of an even keel in the late 1980s and early 1990s, and by the time I had my first crack at them in the autumn of 1994 we felt we had a real chance of a series win.

The 1994 Australian touring side was as strong as any

they have sent over in the past, with great players like Bradley Clyde, Mal Meninga, Wendell Sailor, Laurie Daley, Steve Walters, Paul Harragon, Ian Roberts, Brad Fittler and Paul Sironen all in the party. In those days touring teams played a game against every club side in the First Division, as it then was, as well as the three Test matches. At the time, Wigan players made up the majority of the Great Britain squad so our showdown against Australia at Central Park was billed as the unofficial fourth Test.

I had set myself a goal at the outset of the season to be in the squad for the clash with the Aussies. I played in most of Wigan's games leading up to the tour match, starting a couple of them, and was going reasonably well and managing to enhance my reputation a bit. That October, Great Britain's leading prop Kelvin Skerrett was looking like missing the Test series after fracturing his cheekbone playing for Wigan against Leeds. John Martin, the Wigan director who had played a big role in taking me to Central Park, was quoted in the press saying that if the selectors were looking for a front rower to take over Kelvin's mantle, Barrie McDermott was the one. That was the first time I had ever been mentioned in the same breath as Great Britain, and I was chuffed to bits. I even went to see John afterwards to thank him for what he had said.

Still, I didn't think I was seriously in with a chance of making the Test squad, but I was named on the bench for Wigan against Australia on 8 October, which was one of the standout games of my career. I was not to know it beforehand, but that match would land me in the middle of a major diplomatic incident.

In those days my tackling technique still needed a bit of working on, and my natural aggression when I played meant I would sometimes make mistakes. I liked to shoulder charge, but if I felt I was going to miss, rather than adjusting my feet I used to change the position of my arm. Nine times out of ten I would get it right, but on the other occasion I inevitably missed and caught the ball carrier around the head with my elbow, which is what had happened the week before against Sheffield Eagles' Paul Broadbent. Graeme West, the Wigan coach, called me into the office a few days after that game and said he had received a letter from an old lady saying it was the worst foul she had ever seen. He added, 'Frankly, Barrie, I agree with her. It's not a good thing to do and you wouldn't like it done to you, so cut it out.'

All of which was fair enough; it wasn't something I had meant to do. But before the Australia game, when we were relaxing a couple of hours ahead of kick-off, Mick Cassidy asked me what had happened and I showed him on one of the punch bags in the gym. So when I was sitting on the bench waiting to get into the action, the seed had been sown and there it was, lurking in my subconscious.

After about half an hour I got thrown on for my first crack at Australia. Ex-policeman Paul Sironen, the Balmain back rower, was one of their hard men on that tour, a big, tough forward with hands like shovels and a reputation as someone you didn't mess with. We were losing quite heavily and I just wanted to get on and make an impact, even if it was only by causing a bit of a scuffle. Whenever I have gone on as a substitute I have tried to lift everybody, because that's what you want from your bench men. So on I went, and one of the first things I did was play the ball and push Sironen out of the way. He didn't like that, shoved me back, and punches were thrown.

Minutes before half-time we restarted after an Australia try and Sironen was on the back line to receive the ball. I didn't mean to do what happened next, but it is in my nature to get stuck into the biggest bloke on the pitch. Sironen caught the ball and I raced up at a hundred miles an hour to make the tackle, with Mick Cassidy moving up alongside me. Mick is predominantly a legs tackler, but because of the size of Sironen, Mick tackled him ball and all, around the chest. In those circumstances you have microseconds to make your mind up as to what you are going to do in terms of adjusting your feet, arms and body position to make the tackle. I had to make a split-second decision, and because Mick had gone high I thought I had better go higher in an attempt to get a good contact.

My timing was completely off, and I caught Sironen right on the chin with the corner of my elbow. It happened in a flash and virtually nobody – the referee David Campbell, players or fans – saw what had happened. Sironen went down like one of Fred Dibnah's chimneys being felled, play was stopped, and he got lifted up and carried off. I remember the Aussie physio had to leave him on the side of the pitch for a second to pick something up, and when he turned around Sironen was staggering about wandering back onto the field. He hadn't a clue where he was or what was happening.

Half-time came and went, and I didn't think much about it. The game went on and we lost, but I had played reasonably well, and more than anything I had got stuck in. I was quite pleased with how things had gone, but I didn't realize the consequences of what had happened in that tackle. When I got home and watched the video they were replaying the incident time after time, people were commenting on it at half-time and full-time, and the Aussies were threatening to cite me to try to get me banned.

All the hoo-ha was a bit of a shock. I had spent most of my time playing out of the limelight with Oldham and I wasn't used to such scrutiny. I had done similar things before in my career and no one had taken much notice, other than the player on the receiving end. I can recall one tackle on Sheffield's Nic Grimoldby that was much worse. I had never really imagined I would get called up for the

Test series, and now I reckoned the Sironen incident would leave any talk of it dead in the water. I felt like I had blown my big chance just through being that bit overzealous. But after reading the papers and hearing what other people in the game were saying, things began to look a bit different. Nobody was saying they were happy at what I had done, but they did like the fact that I had taken on the biggest guy in the Aussie squad, knocked him out and had him carried off the pitch. There was a definite fifty-fifty split, with half the people wanting me banned for life and the rest saying I should be picked for Great Britain.

Inevitably I got cited, which meant yet another trip to see the disciplinary committee, though this time it was an international panel rather than the usual Rugby Football League one. The tribunal that day was made up of Jack Robinson, the Wigan chairman, former League chairman Bob Ashby and RFL director Harry Jepson. John Martin, the Wigan director, was representing me, and we travelled over to Leeds for the hearing in the same car as Jack Robinson. During the journey, Jack and John were talking about what punishment I was going to get, with me listening in. A couple of years earlier the Great Britain prop Ian Lucas, who played his club rugby for Wigan, had had his career ended by a bad tackle from Australia's Paul Harragon in a Test match in Sydney, and I think Jack thought what I had done was payback. I went into the disciplinary and got fined an international record £1,000, which was a lot of money, more or less what I had been paid for the entire previous season at Oldham. I was also banned for two games, which meant I would be available for the first Test at Wembley.

I still wasn't expecting to get picked, but later that week I was named in the initial squad and asked to go along to Great Britain training. At that stage I had played only five games for Wigan, but all the lads came over to shake my hand and congratulate me when the news broke, which was a nice moment. It was another step on the ladder, and quite a daunting experience, as well as a brilliant opportunity for someone who had been working on building sites a few months before.

Ellery Hanley was the Great Britain coach. I had played against him when he was at Leeds and I had managed to get one over their big prop Harvey Howard, which I think made quite an impression on Ellery. After training he pulled me to one side and said, 'I'm going to put you on the bench for the first Test. When you get on, just go mental and get stuck into them.'

I will never forget that day at Wembley. Even years later it is still a fresh memory and one of the highlights of my career. It might sound like a bit of a cliché, but it really was the stuff of dreams. My mum and dad were sitting in the stands, and Mum was in tears. I had a highlights tape of the 1992 Lions tour to Australia and New Zealand which I used to watch to psyche myself up before games, and the background music was the hymn 'Jerusalem'. So when we walked out at Wembley and that was playing, it was a very emotional moment.

Before the game we stayed in a hotel in London, and I shared a room with one of my ex-Oldham team-mates, Chris Joynt. I was taking everything in, and I had to stop myself shaking my head because six months before I had been playing in the reserves after coming back from a ban, and a year earlier I had been in Australia playing for a country side and I couldn't get my spot back at Oldham. I couldn't believe this was really happening.

When we got to the ground there were huge crowds of people waiting to cheer us off the coach, but the first thing I saw was Steve Whitmore and a few other lads from my amateur club, Waterhead, carrying a loaf of bread between them, which was a bit surreal. I found out later that loads of lads in the team had signed the loaf of bread and they were taking it to every game as their lucky charm. Seeing a few friendly faces settled me down a bit, but the nerves started again when we got into the changing rooms and I began thinking about all the great sportsmen, not just rugby players, who had been through those doors in the past. The whole experience was overwhelming and very humbling, and to be in the company of great players like Jonathan Davies, Alan Hunte, Karl Harrison, Lee Jackson, Chris Joynt, Bobbie Goulding, Allan Bateman and Daryl Powell, as well as all my Wigan team-mates, raised my standards to a new level.

Most of the lads had a walk round the pitch for a feel of the turf, and by the time they came back in I had strapped myself up, rubbed myself down, got my kit on and was jogging on the spot shouting 'come on!' to myself, all with a good ninety minutes to go until the warm-up, never mind the actual game. Blood was pumping around me and the adrenalin was flowing. I wasn't punching lockers, but that's only because there weren't any. Phil Clarke turned to Denis Betts and said, 'Have a word with Barrie and calm him down or he's going to blow a gasket.' Denis pulled me to one side and told me to sit down and read the programme to occupy myself and relax a bit, otherwise I would be knackered by kick-off.

Just walking out onto the pitch was an incredible experience, and I sang the national anthem as loudly as I could. I had sung the anthem at home with my dad and in the stands watching Test matches, but to be out there myself was making all the hairs on the back of my neck stand up.

I got on after about twenty minutes in place of Daryl Powell, who had to go off with a dead leg. Australia had been penalized and Karl Harrison, who was the other prop, needed a bit of a breather, so it was my job to take the ball up from the penalty, straight into a reception party of Paul

Harragon, Glen Lazarus and my old mate Paul Sironen. I remember thinking that I was either going to be hiding from these lads all game or I was going to run at them and let them know I wasn't scared. So I ran the ball in as hard as I could at Sironen. He shot out of the line to bash me, but I bumped him away and made five or six yards upfield, which was much better than anyone could have hoped for in the circumstances and put paid to all my nerves in the space of six seconds.

I went on to have a good game in what turned out to be one of Great Britain's best ever wins against Australia. We were the underdogs anyway, but when Shaun Edwards got sent off twenty-five minutes into the first half it had looked like mission impossible. Bradley Clyde had made a bit of a break and Shaun came out of nowhere and whacked him really high, around the nose. Clydey was unconscious before he hit the ground. Talking to him years later when he played at Leeds, he said that was the best shot he had ever taken. He never saw it coming and it just cleaned him out. The ref, Graham Annesley, stopped play, got out his red card and waved Shaun off. I had to stop myself walking off with him out of force of habit.

It would have been easy to think 'That's it, the game's gone', but there was no way I was going to give up. We all got together, and the senior players were saying, 'This isn't an excuse. There's no way we are losing this game. We can still win it if we dig in.' It was a really close, low-scoring game, but Jonathan Davies kicked us in front with a penalty goal and then dummied to pass to Gary Connolly and shot past Brett Mullins to touch down at the corner for a brilliant try. The second half was very tense, but our defence held out until eight minutes from time when Steve Renouf scored. Then, with a couple of minutes to go, Harragon was penalized for holding me down in a tackle, Bobbie Goulding kicked the goal and that was it, we had won 8–4.

Afterwards I was exhausted, but I was so pumped up I felt I could have played for ever. One of my great memories of that afternoon was during our celebrations at the end, when Ellery Hanley came over, shook my hand and said, 'I told you. All you had to do was be yourself.'

The public reaction to our win was tremendous and we got a lot of very positive coverage in the media, which made a nice change. Jonathan Davies, or Jiffy as everyone called him, got a lot of the attention because of his try, but unfortunately he picked up a painful injury late in the game. Or, to be a bit more accurate, I injured him. It was a tight game all the way through and being a man short meant we were under intense pressure every time Australia had the ball. As things got really tense midway through the second half we had a spell defending for our lives near our own line. It seemed as if eventually we would cave in, but like the rest of the boys I was defending my nuts off and I remember thinking, 'I'm going to keep the Aussies out if it kills me.' Somehow we managed to dislodge the ball, and Jiffy, who was the nearest British player, dived on it, which relieved the pressure on our defence. I was standing quite close to Jiffy and, being young and enthusiastic, as he dropped on the ball I clamped it to make sure he wasn't going to knock on and then landed right on top of him, with all my weight. Jiffy took a long time getting up, which the Aussies and people in the crowd probably thought was time-wasting, and had to be substituted straight away; Allan Bateman, another convert to league from Welsh rugby union, came on in his place for the final twenty-two minutes. At the time I didn't realize what had happened, but Jiffy told me later that my weight had basically squashed him so much I had dislocated his shoulder. I was there, rubbing him on his head and saying 'Well done, mate', and he was in absolute agony. To make things worse, he didn't play in either the second or the third Tests.

The second Test, which was played in November at Old Trafford, was a big contrast to the one at Wembley. We went into it thinking we had a genuine chance of reclaiming the Ashes, but finished up on the end of a 38–8 hiding. It has been a similar scenario every time I have played for Great Britain. I have always felt there was a great chance of a series win and then been bitterly disappointed when it didn't happen.

I was on the bench again, but this time the Australians were ready for me. Years later I met up with Steve Walters, their hooker, in a bar in New Zealand, and I asked him about it. He told me that Australia's coach, Bob Fulton, had said to them, 'If McDermott starts messing about, all of you get stuck into him.' I came on after about an hour, having been prowling the touchline since the twenty-minute mark, waiting for my chance. I had been getting more and more agitated, and when I got on I was ready to rumble. My first action was a good shot on one of their forwards. I did a bit of chasing, took the ball in once, and then landed what I thought was a good ball-and-all tackle on Bradley Clyde. I hit him with a decent amount of force, knocked his head back and landed on top of him, with him facing the other way. That was the cue for all the other Aussies to come piling in and start hitting me on the head. I stood up, threw a few back and got sin-binned after less than five minutes on the pitch, so suddenly I was sitting back down again thinking, 'That didn't go too well.'

I did better in my second spell, but obviously Ellery had looked at it and thought that having me getting worked up on the sidelines was not the best policy, so he decided to give me my first start for Great Britain in the third Test at Elland Road later that month, which was the series decider. That was up there as one of the best atmospheres I have ever played in. It was a full house, with around 40,000 packed in, and again we thought we had a good chance of winning the game and taking the series, even though we had been a very poor second at Old Trafford.

The plan was for me to come off after twenty minutes for a rest. In those days, once you had been substituted you couldn't go back on again, but we had come up with a bit of skulduggery that would allow me to return to the action in the second half and give Karl Harrison a breather. The idea was to give Karl a bit of a nick with a razor around his ear during half-time so that he could go into the blood-bin, which would have allowed me to go back on in his place for a fifteen-to-twenty-minute all-out stint before he took over again for the final quarter. The blood was gushing out of Karl's ear in the changing room, but as soon as he went out for the start of the second half and began to run around, the bleeding stopped. No matter how much he pulled at his ear, he couldn't get it to start again, so I didn't get back on.

We had been well in the game at the break, just 7–2 down, and we pounded their line for the third quarter, but we couldn't get over and they pulled away near the end to win 23–4 and retain the Ashes yet again.

Once the Test series was over, hostilities ceased and we had a chance to get to know a few of the Aussies socially. They were staying in a hotel in Leeds, and Shaun Edwards, who knew several of them, was invited down for a few drinks. It was a good opportunity to swap stories and show off a few battle scars. He asked me to go with him, along with Gary Connolly and a few others, and we had a good night, especially as Ian Roberts, their big front rower, had a free tab running, along with all the other Aussie lads.

It was the first time I had really met Ian off the pitch and I was a bit dubious because, as everybody in the game was aware, he is gay. I knew exactly how to treat him on a rugby field, which was to batter him as hard as I could, just like any other opponent, but I wasn't too sure how to act around him socially. Ian told me and Shaun about his free tab and said any time we wanted a drink just to give him a shout and he would get the round in. I kept giving Ian a wave and he kept getting the drinks in. As the night wore on I began to get a bit paranoid, and I started thinking, 'I hope no one thinks there's anything going on between me and Ian Roberts just because he's buying me drinks.'

Later, a big group of us were sitting around having a chat and Ian was enjoying a bit of a dance, and for the first time that evening he looked less than totally macho, if you get my drift. To this day I am still deeply embarrassed about what happened, but at the top of my voice, and without thinking about it, I announced to the entire room, 'Hey, Roberts, I hope you don't think just because you've bought me a few drinks you're going to shag me. I bat for the home side.' I remember the room falling silent and everyone else shaking their heads and thinking, 'What a complete tool.' Ian, though, must have been used to that sort of remark because he just said, 'Don't worry, Barrie, you're not my type.' Everyone had a laugh at that, but a few minutes later paranoia set in again and I piped up, 'What do you mean? What's wrong with me?' I had gone from being offended that he might fancy me to being equally offended that he didn't and upset at the fact that he thought I was a big, fat, ugly git.

Ian was a great bloke and one of the hardest forwards in the game. It must have taken some guts to come out and announce he was gay when he played an intimidating game like rugby league, so that shows how tough he was. There was one incident during a club game in Australia when one of the opposing players called him a poof and Ian beat ten bells out of him. From that day on, no one took liberties.

Overall, losing that 1994 Test series was a huge disappointment, but at least I had the memory of the first Test to look back on and I thought I had gone some way towards establishing myself as an international prop. I didn't realize then that it would be five long years before I would get to pull on a Great Britain jersey again.

8

LEARNING HARD LESSONS

To all my doubters. I say we all make mistakes,
but the real man gets back up, picks up the
ball and runs in again.

I wish I had done better at Wigan, but I have no regrets about the time I spent there, and at least I came away with a taste of the big time. The Regal Trophy against Warrington on 28 January 1995 was the only final I played in with Wigan, and it was my first real experience of a major occasion at club level in England, but Wigan won every trophy available in 1994–95 – the Championship, the Challenge Cup and the Premiership, as well as the Regal Trophy – and I am honoured to have been a little part of rugby league history.

The Regal Trophy was scrapped in 1996 when Super League came along, but in its day it was quite a prestigious competition with the big matches broadcast live on the BBC. It was a mid-season tournament, and I missed the early rounds because I was struggling with my groin injury.

The game before the final had been at Doncaster, and that was the first time I came across Vila Matautia, who went on to have a glittering career with St Helens. He was playing as a centre for Doncaster and he hit Scott Quinnell, who was in the Wigan front row alongside me, as hard as I have ever seen anyone hit on a rugby field. Scott ran on to a ball and Vila absolutely smashed him, shattering his nose. Scott didn't know where he was, and he got up and played the ball facing his own line, to one of the Doncaster players. His number went straight up and he got hauled off. It was one of his first games after switching codes, and he told me afterwards, 'I never had anything like that playing union!'

That ended any hope Scott might have had of playing in the Regal Trophy final, so it came down to me or Terry O'Connor. The squad was named on the Wednesday before the game and Tez was included instead of me, but he had a slight hamstring strain so I was told to keep myself ready. I didn't get my hopes up because I knew Tez would want to play in such a big game, but on the morning of the final he rang me up and said, 'I'm no good, I can't play.' Graeme West, the coach, had told him, 'If you aren't right, don't play. If you say you are fit and then you break down and you have to come off, it will be a long time before I pick you again.' It wasn't an ideal way to get into the team, particularly at the expense of such a good mate, but I had a smile a year later when Wigan got to the Regal Trophy final again and Tez had a real stormer. I think he was playing two games in one that day.

But beggars can't be choosers, so I was determined to make the best of it. Because I knew I was playing only a few hours before kick-off I went in nice and relaxed and I had a fair game. We won easily, 40–10, which was a record score for a Regal Trophy final and made up for the previous year when Wigan had been thrashed by Castleford. All the damage was done in the first half as we built up a 28–4 lead, Va'aiga Tuigamala getting a couple of tries and Frano Botica and Gary Connolly also touching down. I came on for Neil Cowie at half-time and got over for a try with a few minutes left, which made my day. Apart from my early burst that season I have never been much of a try-scorer. I'm very much a hard-yards man, but I always enjoy getting over the whitewash, and the occasion made that one of my most memorable tries. Martin Offiah scored our final touchdown and Phil Clarke got the man of the match award, even though Frano had one of his best games for Wigan, kicking eight goals from nine attempts to go with his try.

Frano Botica was one of the best goal kickers rugby league has ever seen, and that day was a real master class. Funnily enough, he hadn't been able to practise properly because of bad weather during the run-up to the game, so he had spent some time sitting in his car in a traffic jam just visualizing how the kicks would go over, which is exactly the sort of professionalism that made Wigan so successful.

There were a few times at Wigan when I really felt part of things, and the Regal Trophy final was one of them. The lap of honour probably meant more to me than the rest of the lads, because I had never experienced it before. That was the first rugby game ever played at the McAlpine Stadium in Huddersfield and it had nearly been called off because of blizzards a few days earlier. There was snow piled up around the edges of the pitch, and as I was wandering round afterwards, waving to the crowd, someone threw a snowball at me, which hit me full in the face. I had been enjoying myself so much I hadn't noticed we'd gone past all the Wigan fans and were walking in front of the Warrington supporters. All the rest of the lads had speeded up and left me behind, so I obviously made a tempting target. My first reaction was to go and sort the snowball thrower out, but as I started to move towards the stand I realized there were about 5,000 people all looking at me and daring me to have a go. In such circumstances discretion is the better form of valour, so I changed my mind and had to be content with pointing out that I had a winners' medal and they hadn't. Unfortunately, I haven't got it any more as it was stolen from my car a few weeks later.

I should also have got a First Division Championship medal that year, but I never bothered to pick it up. You had to play in thirteen games to qualify, so I just scraped in. The medals were not presented, they were just delivered to the club, and you went up to the office to pick yours up. At the time I didn't really feel I had contributed to winning the title, so I never bothered, and presumably someone else got mine. I haven't won many medals in my career, but the ones I do have I have earned. I wouldn't want to get one by default, so it's not something I regret.

Wigan was a hard school, but it taught me a lot of valuable lessons that have stayed with me ever since and have definitely made me a better player and a better person. From 1995 I became more focused and determined not to make a mess of my career.

In my early days at Central Park I was rarely on time for matches or training, I never had my kit sorted out and I was always having to ask to borrow someone else's boots. When I was at Oldham I only had one pair of boots, I used to train and play in the same T-shirt every session, and my training gear was something I never thought about. A few of the senior players at Wigan had to have a word with me, to tell me to get myself sorted out and to start acting like a professional. Being professional is as much a state of mind as anything else. I was being well paid, but in plenty of other respects I was still a rank amateur.

When I left Wigan I thought I was putting my time there behind me and making a clean break, but in fact it has had a huge influence on my career ever since. I made a lot of mistakes, and when I see lads at Leeds doing exactly the same I can sit down with them and tell them I know just what they are going through and how to put it right.

One of the big differences between an amateur or semi-professional environment and a full-time one is the amount of time you have on your hands. When I was at Oldham it was a case of working, training and sleeping; there was never any time for getting into trouble. But at Wigan I had so much spare time I didn't know what to do with it, and that led me into bother. Some of the things I did when I was a Wigan player were funny at the time but make me cringe now when I think about them. One of the most embarrassing took place on the day of the 1995 Challenge Cup final against Leeds at Wembley.

Wigan were the undisputed cup kings, and that year saw their eighth successive Wembley victory, which is a staggering record and one I don't think will ever be matched. When summer rugby started the Challenge Cup became an early-season competition for a while, but in those pre-Super League days the final was played at the end of the campaign and it was always the highlight of the year.

Any hopes I might have had of playing at Wembley effectively ended during a game against Castleford when I dislocated my shoulder. I went to tackle Lee Crooks, got it wrong and the shoulder popped out. Very painful. By the time Wembley came along I was making my comeback in the A team and I wasn't expecting to get picked for the final, but I had joined Wigan to play in the big games and I was still pretty upset when I wasn't included in the squad.

All the Wigan players travelled down to London a few days before the final, and on the day of the game those of us who weren't playing got to Wembley really early, with plenty of time for a look around. We did the usual things – had a walk up and down Wembley Way and chatted with the fans – then we decided to go to the pub for a few drinks to take our minds off the fact that we weren't in the team. I was with a few of the A team lads, Craig Murdock, Andy Craig and Matt Knowles, and we all had tickets for the final. Because I had played in the first team my ticket was one of the most expensive ones, in with all the directors and players' wives, while the others had cheaper tickets, but still decent seats. On the way to the pub we saw a few touts hanging around buying and selling tickets, so on the spur of the moment I sold one of them our tickets. We got about £50 for them, which we then spent in the pub.

At the celebration do that evening Scott Quinnell told me it hadn't taken the other players long to rumble what I had done. 'I knew you had sold the tickets,' he said, 'because I was sitting there in the posh seats with all the other lads and the wives and this big, bald-headed Leeds fan came and sat next to me. I told him he couldn't sit there, but he said, "Yes I can, I've got a ticket." As soon as I saw the ticket I thought, I bet I know where Barrie is.' Fortunately the Wigan directors didn't find out, but after that I had to put up with all the lads asking me if I had a spare ticket every time we played a big game.

The coach trip back from Wembley that year is famous among the players of the time for the antics of Martin Offiah. I couldn't count Martin as a friend, but he's a decent bloke and he is straight down the middle with anyone he meets, which made what happened even funnier for the rest of us.

A couple of weeks before the final we had been having a meal after training when Phil Clarke threw a banana at Martin Hall. He saw it coming and ducked, and the fruit hit Martin Offiah smack on the back of the head. Offiah turned round, saw Martin Hall laughing and completely snapped, which was very much out of character. I don't know if he was reading something into the incident that wasn't there, but he was furious. Martin Hall denied having anything to do with it and Offiah later found out that the real culprit was Phil Clarke, which was something he must have been stewing over for weeks.

On the way home after Wembley all the players were sitting at the back of the bus, having a few cans of lager and the odd short, when someone produced a bottle of rum. No one wanted to touch it, but Martin Offiah, who didn't drink at all, shocked everyone by saying he liked rum. Then he proved it by knocking most of the bottle back. I had never seen Martin drunk before, but it wasn't long before he was totally inebriated, and he went through all the classic stages very quickly. First he went into the love stage, during which he staggered up and down the bus going up to everyone and telling them what good players they were. Then, minutes later, he went into the nasty stage and started shouting at people. There was a partition in the middle of the bus, separating the directors and coaching staff at the front from the players at the back, and Graeme West heard all the commotion and came through to see what was happening. In no uncertain terms, Martin told him to get lost. Westy must have been as surprised as everyone else, but he eventually went back to his seat after Martin had threatened him a few times, though of course nobody took what he was saying seriously.

Martin then went into the tired stage and fell asleep, but that was quickly followed by the throwing-up stage, all over himself, the table, his seat and a couple of players who were sitting near him. This brought Westy back to our end of the bus, and he obviously decided Martin needed removing from the action, so he threw him over his shoulder and carried him off to the front of the coach. As he was being carried away, Neil Cowie slapped Martin on the back of the head, very hard. That had no effect on Martin, who was asleep again. But when he woke up he obviously felt it because a few minutes later he came storming back, demanding to know who had hit him. I think Martin must have remembered the fruit-throwing incident, because he charged to the back of the coach and swung a punch at Phil Clarke, missed completely, spun right round into a seat and immediately fell fast asleep again.

It may sound like the players at Wigan did not get on, but that wasn't the case, even though a lot of us didn't have much in common outside rugby. One player I did struggle with at Wigan was Neil Cowie. He was a fringe player before I signed and I think he expected to move straight in when Andy Platt left the club, so Tez O'Connor and me coming on the scene made him very uncomfortable. He would never give me the time of day or an inch of respect, which always grated with me. Later, whenever I played against him he always seemed to have a secret smile on his face. I think he thought he had won the battle because I had left Wigan and he was still there.

But as I said, what made Wigan so successful was the teamwork ethic and the winning attitude, which went right through the club. They had deliberately gone out and signed the best players in the world and put them in an environment that was totally geared towards success. In players like Dean Bell, Andy Platt, Frano Botica, Gary Connolly and Va'aiga Tuigamala they had people who were at the very top of their profession and who were great role models for all the younger players trying to make their own mark. A lot of them probably would not have got on in other walks of life, but put them together on a rugby field and they just clicked. Just about everybody got on, although we weren't all close mates. Everyone was winning and earning good pay, and when that's the case you are prepared to put up with people you might not otherwise want to spend time with.

The success Wigan had did more than anything else to raise standards in the British game in the 1980s and 1990s, when they were so far ahead of everyone else the other clubs had to find ways of closing the gap. People say it isn't healthy for one club to be so dominant, but it certainly gave the others something to aspire to. In any British sport, if you are doing well you are up there to be shot at, and

Wigan were no different. There was a lot of jealousy and animosity towards Wigan, and fans of other clubs hated us with a passion, because we were so good. That was something that was very evident to the players, and it was a shock to me when I first arrived. A lot of people seemed to think Wigan must be cheating because they won everything and because we were bigger, fitter and stronger than everyone else. The reason for that was we trained harder than anyone else. There was nothing underhand about it at all.

We were the only full-time professional players at the time, though Leeds also went fully pro in the early 1990s, and that gave us a huge advantage over the rest. We had one day off during the week, usually a Wednesday, but the rest of the time we were training every day, and training hard. In that environment rugby was the only thing that mattered, so when we came up against players who trained a couple of nights a week and worked the rest of the time, they couldn't compete.

Tuigamala, who everyone called Inga, was someone I very much admired, though he hadn't been playing rugby league long after switching codes from rugby union. Physically he is a very imposing bloke and he's as tough as they come on the field, but off it he is one of the nicest men you will meet and a very committed born-again Christian. His attitude towards life rubbed off on quite a few of the boys at Wigan, including me. When he saw me going through some bad times he tried to tell me to take comfort in the Lord rather than in a pint of lager, which I thought was the better option at the time.

Inga had a greater influence on Jason Robinson and was at least partly responsible for helping him become one of the biggest names in world rugby, in both league and union. Jason was a bit of a lad in his early days at Wigan and we spent quite a lot of time together because we were both single and, like me, Jason enjoyed a night out and a drink. Jason was even worse than me at turning up late for training, and at the start of his Wigan career he was pulled into the office and told that his attitude had to improve. He was always a talented player, but there was a danger of that being wasted until Inga took him under his wing. That obviously did the trick, because Jason is now one of the cleanest-living blokes you will ever meet and his attitude is spot on. As a player he has got freakish ability, and physically he is ideally built for rugby. Even in the days when he wasn't bothering to train he was a complete Adonis when he took his shirt off, which pissed everybody else off no end.

I did a lot of specific training with Inga because we were similar body types, but after I dislocated my shoulder I got moved into another training group, with the waifs and strays. I found it difficult to adjust to being on the outside, and that was probably the first time I began to realize things were going wrong for me. Still, after the traumas of 1994–95 I was determined to make a real go of it at Wigan in 1995–96, which was rugby league's final winter campaign. I spent the 1995 pre-season working with Graeme West, who had decided he was going to keep a very close eye on me. I put in a lot of time training with some of the younger guys, and particularly Inga, who, as a big man, liked to train all year round rather than take a total rest and then have to get his basic fitness back. As I said, Inga is a lovely bloke and he had lots of tolerance – far more, as it turned out, than the Wigan board were prepared to show me.

Throughout my career, just like Inga, I have tried to make sure I never have more than a couple of weeks off at any one time, because if I do that just makes it harder to get back. Even if I'm having a break I don't stay away from fitness work completely; I will go to the gym or play a bit of squash just to keep myself moving. As a bigger bloke you have got to keep your body ticking over as much as you can.

I got to know Westy quite well that summer and I thought I made some headway in terms of trying to right some of the wrongs of the previous twelve months. It looked to me like Wigan were prepared to give me another chance, but that went down the pan – quite literally – the week before we were due to play Leeds in the season-opening Charity Shield in Dublin.

I had moved into a house on my own in Wigan and had started doing my own cooking and looking after myself, which wasn't the best idea as it turned out. Though I enjoy cooking, I'm not the world's best chef, and I managed to give myself food poisoning just as pre-season training was coming to its peak. For the next three or four weeks I was in a terrible state. As soon as I ate anything spicy or had a beer, it was coming out of both ends. In the week leading up to the Charity Shield I couldn't train, but I still thought I would be involved somehow, even if it was just as a member of the squad.

Wigan decided to take some twenty players over for the game and I wasn't selected, which really upset me because I had worked hard and built up a good relationship with Westy. I thought I deserved to be going, and I made my mind up then that if Wigan didn't want me I would find a club that did. That's a decision I have regretted ever since, not because I didn't want to leave or because the time wasn't right, but because I walked away. It's the only time in my career I have ever thrown the towel in, and I'm not proud of it.

Things came to a head the week after the Charity Shield, on 17 August, when I played in an A team game against Hull at the Boulevard. Hull moved to a new stadium in 2003, and I can't say I was sorry. For some reason the Boulevard was a ground where I always seemed to have real battles, and the atmosphere there was very intimidating. On this particular occasion, the scene was set for fireworks. I went into the game with a bee in my bonnet about being left out of the Charity Shield side and I was determined to have a good game and prove a point. Right from the start, things went wrong. After twenty minutes we were losing and I was having a bit of a nightmare. A young kid called Steve Craven, who had just joined Hull from York, was giving me a really hard time, hitting me with some good shots and dislodging the ball once or twice. I was getting angrier and angrier, and it all exploded after one challenge when the ball came loose. I stood up, butted him, threw a few punches and got sent straight off. I got a load of abuse off the Hull fans as I went to the changing rooms and I knew then that that would be the last time I would ever wear a Wigan shirt. After that, there was no way they would give me another chance.

I can't really blame them, because along with eye gouging, butting is one of the worst things you can do on a rugby field. It's a cardinal sin, and fortunately it's something you don't see very often any more. But that was one of those occasions when the red mist came down and I totally lost it. Craven had done a number on me, and I will always remember him laughing at me as I walked off. I have played against him quite a few times since for Leeds, and though he had a good, long career at a high level, I'm surprised he didn't go on to even bigger and better things.

The sending-off meant yet another trip to the disciplinary committee in Leeds. I pleaded my case, said what had happened, described what frame of mind I was in and outlined all the things that had happened to me over the past few months. As usual, they took absolutely no notice and gave me a five-match ban.

Because that was rugby league's shortened centenary

season there were two games most weeks, so I wasn't going to be out of the game for a long period of time. Soon after I picked up my ban I got a message from Jack Robinson, the Wigan chairman, saying he wanted to see me at his business premises in the town. When I arrived, Jack asked me how I was and what I was doing with my time while I was getting over the suspension. I told him I felt fine, I was getting stronger, my shoulder was OK and I was enjoying training, though I had been disappointed to miss the Charity Shield.

Then Jack told me that he had spoken to Hugh McGahan, who was the assistant to Leeds coach Dean Bell, and they were interested in taking me over to Headingley. Jack wanted to know what I thought, but my first reaction was that I had started something at Wigan and given the right amount of time I could get my place back and rebuild my reputation. But I think Wigan had already decided I didn't have a future there. Jack told me I was behind Kelvin Skerrett, Neil Cowie and Tez O'Connor, who were first-choice props, and that Scott Quinnell was ahead of me in the pecking order as well, so if I was going to stay I would be fifth choice for the front row. My opportunities for first-team rugby with Wigan were obviously very limited, so Jack asked me to go home and think about what I wanted to do, because the chance to join Leeds would not be there for ever.

Around the same time I got a phone call from an agent, David McKnight, who said he was a friend of Dean Bell and that he could get me on board at Headingley, though St Helens were interested in me as well.

Well, if you're going to leave Wigan, there are only a few clubs that aren't a major step down. Leeds is one of them, so once I heard they were interested I didn't need a great deal of persuading. Leeds was my preference because I could see an opening there for me to go straight in as one of their first-choice props and I knew they were a club that could match my ambitions.

Dean was out of the country promoting his autobiography, but I had a chat with Hugh McGahan and everything was agreed quite quickly. When Dean got back he told me that Denis Betts, who had played with Dean at Wigan and Auckland, had recommended me and said I would be a good bet if he was looking to shake his side up a bit. Dean had inherited a team from Leeds' previous coach Doug Laughton and was looking to stamp his authority on the place, with me being the first step. Leeds inserted a clause in my contract that allowed them to fine me £500 every time I got sent off and a similar amount per match if I picked up a ban, but even so, Dean wanted me, as he put it, to add a bit of 'mongrel' to the Leeds pack.

9

CROSSING THE GREAT DIVIDE

*For everyone at Headingley. You opened your hearts
and minds. I hope you have enjoyed my company
as much as I have enjoyed yours.*

When I signed for Leeds in September 1995, it was a dream
come true. I'm an Oldham lad and I'm proud of my
Lancashire roots, but I always followed Leeds as a youngster and ever since I moved to Headingley I have considered myself an honorary Yorkshireman. There's a lot of
rivalry between the west and east of the Pennines, but I
have always been made very welcome in Yorkshire and
whenever I have played for Leeds I have always had real
pride in my shirt.

I knew the first time I walked into Headingley that I
would be right at home there. As far as I'm concerned,
Leeds is the biggest club in the game with a rich history
and a great tradition, and ever since I signed for them I
have been determined to be part of that. Right from my
very first day I set out to be talked of alongside the Leeds
greats as one of the best front rowers the club had ever
had, which was a big task considering I was following in
the footsteps of people like Joe Thompson, Dai Prosser,
Mick Clark, Steve Pitchford and Lee Crooks.

My arrival at Headingley came as a huge shock to most
of the national media. Leeds called a press conference to

announce a major signing, but didn't tell anyone who it was. The pressmen thought it was going to be Frano Botica, the former All Black goal kicker who had been such a big hit at Wigan. He had close links with Dean Bell, having played with him for Wigan and New Zealand, so the press put two and two together and got five. Quite a few of the papers that morning announced that Leeds had signed Frano Botica.

Stuart Duffy, the Leeds media manager, got in on the joke. He kept me out of sight at the start of the press conference and then told the reporters, 'Ladies and gentlemen, meet our new signing – Frano Botica.' And then I walked into the room.

People were a bit shocked that I had jumped from the best club at the time to the next best, but I saw it as a real step forward and I thought Leeds were in a position then to halt Wigan's dominance. As it turned out, I was joining Leeds at one of the lowest points in their history, though that did not become clear for a few months.

I saw out the rest of my suspension and made my debut against Bradford on 22 September 1995 in front of a big crowd at Headingley, but it wasn't an auspicious start. I'd had a top game for the A team a couple of days before and twisted my left knee, which has been a bit of a problem throughout my career. I shouldn't have played the following weekend, but obviously I was determined to get my debut out of the way, so I declared myself fit.

That was a mistake, as the Bradford game was the last one before a break for the Centenary World Cup, when I was likely to be playing for England. Looking back, I should have sat the Bradford game out and given my knee a chance to recover, but I was desperate to make a big impression.

I only lasted twenty minutes. I did some quality things early on, but then slipped and twisted my knee again and

had to come off. As I limped out of the action I could hear
the Bradford fans – at least I like to think it was the
Bradford fans – singing 'what a waste of money', which
was most upsetting. The injury kept me out of the World
Cup, which was a shame, but not a huge disappointment
because my main concern was getting myself fit to play for
Leeds.

The first game after the World Cup was, ironically
enough, against Wigan, again at Headingley on 3 November. I'd had two pressure games one after the other, and I
remember thinking what a contrast that was to my Oldham
days, when everything we got was a bonus whether we
played well and lost or by a strange twist of fate or a big
slice of luck we managed to win.

My first tackle against Wigan was a big shot down the
side of the South Stand. That prompted a huge roar from
the crowd, and I thought at the time, 'I like this. I'm going
to enjoy it here.'

We won both my first two games and went on to finish
second in the championship to Wigan, which was a fair
achievement; we thought it would set us up nicely for
the 1996 Super League season, marking the British game's
switch from winter to summer rugby league. Unfortunately,
my first couple of seasons at Headingley were a real transi-
tional phase for the club. The team I joined in 1995 was made
up of the old guard, people like Garry Schofield, George
Mann, Alan Tait, Richie Eyres and Esene Faimalo, plus some
up-and-coming youngsters including Nick Fozzard, Adrian
Morley, Mick Shaw, Francis Cummins and Graham Holroyd.

I was mates with Jim Fallon, a winger Leeds had signed
from Bath Rugby Union Club. I had no transport at the
time because of a drink-driving ban so I moved over to
Leeds and I lived quite close to Jim, near a pub called the
Chain Bull where the players used to go after a game on a

Sunday afternoon. The full-time professional era had just started, but the social side was still very important at Leeds and if you didn't go to the pub after a game it was frowned upon. At the time, as they do now, Leeds had a lot of travellers, players they had signed from other clubs who still lived outside the city. After a night out everyone tended to crash out at Neil Harmon's house in Leeds. Neil's place was known as the Palace and we all used to spend a lot of time there. Terry Newton, Phil Hassan, Adrian Morley and I would hang around together because we were all travellers and were a bit younger than most of the lads at Leeds, who were well into their thirties and were very much into their own company.

That final winter season ended in January 1996, but before the Super League began a couple of months later the early rounds of the Challenge Cup were played. We were drawn away to Swinton, a Second Division side, and only just managed to scrape through thanks to a couple of late tries after Swinton had been in front for most of the game. Dean Bell was heavily criticized for that performance, and he responded by dropping me for the next round, which was away to Warrington. I think Dean felt he had to make changes after such a poor team display, and as I was one of his signings he felt well within his rights to leave me out. Harvey Howard came in for the Warrington match and had a great game. He kept his place for the cup semi-final against Bradford at Huddersfield, which marked the start of Leeds' problems and Bradford's rise.

Because Harvey and Neil were ahead of me in the pecking order at the start of Super League, I ended up with the squad number 15. I'm a bit superstitious about shirt numbers: I won't wear 8, 12, 14 or 16. In the days before squad numbers, if I was in the front row I liked to wear 10, 11 if I was playing back row, or 15 if I was on the bench.

When I didn't get the number 10 shirt I opted for 15 because that had been lucky for me for Great Britain and in a couple of other games.

Dean began a clear-out: Garry Schofield left to join Huddersfield, Jimmy Lowes and Paul Cook went to Bradford and Craig Innes joined Manly in Australia. Innes is up there among the best centres I have played with. He was a New Zealand All Black who was one of Doug Laughton's star signings for Leeds. When I joined Leeds he was one of the few players there with any real ambition. It took him a while to get to grips with league, but once he got it he was sensational and it was a real shame he wasn't at Leeds longer. Losing players of that quality left us up against it, and right from our first Super League game, at home to Warrington on 31 March 1996, it was obvious we were going to struggle. A young kid called Iestyn Harris tore us apart in that opening game and we lost our first five matches before we finally got a win, at home to Sheffield. In the end we won only six matches that year, and for a long time it looked as though we might get relegated.

As implied by his clear-out, Dean had been determined to give some of the club's young players a chance and that meant that kids like the Gibbons twins David and Anthony, Gavin Brown, Marvin Golden, Lee Maher, Leroy Rivett and Adam Hughes all got thrown in at the deep end. Things got so desperate at one point that Dean himself came out of retirement for a game, a bottom-of-the-table clash with Paris at Headingley. We won that one, Dean scoring a try, and we finished the season tenth out of twelve, with only Paris and Workington below us. We took some real beatings in the process too, conceding more than sixty points a couple of times and getting fifty put past us by Bradford home and away, which must have been hard for the Leeds fans to take.

I was an ever-present that season – the only time I have

ever gone through a whole league campaign without missing a match – and I felt I played pretty well in a struggling team, but it wasn't enough to earn me an international recall. At the end of Super League I, in the autumn of 1996, Great Britain went on tour to New Zealand, but I was left at home. I deserved to go, but the coach Phil Larder thought otherwise and I wasn't selected. Rowland Phillips and Neil Harmon, who was without a club after walking out on Leeds midway through the season, got the front-row spots instead.

As far as I'm concerned, Larder made a mistake by not picking me. It was heartbreaking to miss out, but it proved to be a blessing in disguise because the tour was a total fiasco, a shambles from start to finish. The second-string players were all sent home before the end of the trip as a cost-saving measure, and Great Britain got whitewashed 3–0 in the Test series. To say the organizers didn't know what they were doing is an understatement. Around a month after the tour finished I checked my bank account and found that I had been paid a big chunk of money by the Rugby Football League, which I hadn't been expecting.

It was just coming up to Christmas, so I did what comes naturally and spent it. About a week later I got a call from one of the girls at Red Hall, the RFL headquarters, saying I had been paid Brian McDermott's tour fees and could I please send Brian a cheque for the amount as soon as possible. By that time I no longer had the money, so in the end they had to send Brian, the Bradford Bulls front rower, another cheque and I paid the RFL back a little later. At least the unexpected loan kept me going over Christmas.

In one way I was glad not to have been picked for the tour. My girlfriend Jenny, who is now my wife, gave birth to my son Billy that autumn and I would have missed it if I'd been chosen to go to New Zealand. Rugby league is my job and it's something I care passionately about, but you have to get your priorities right. As far as I'm concerned, my family comes first. If I had missed the birth I would always have regretted it, so on that front Larder did me a favour.

While Great Britain were being beaten in New Zealand, there was plenty going on at Leeds with the club facing a bigger crisis off the field than we had just gone through on it. The club had built up a huge debt over the previous few years and it had got to the stage where there was a real danger of them either going bankrupt or having to leave Headingley to share Elland Road with Leeds United. That was something nobody wanted, but I wouldn't have been surprised to see it happen. That sort of thing has followed me through my life. My first infant school is now a tennis court, my secondary school is a housing estate, there are houses on Watersheddings in Oldham, and Wigan's old Central Park ground is a Tesco. If Headingley had been demolished and turned into a supermarket, people would probably have blamed me.

I've been lucky because I've never been at a club where the players have been frightened they were not going to get paid, but that was becoming a real possibility at Leeds towards the end of 1996. It was a really hard time, and I just couldn't see where Leeds were going, so when Bradford Bulls showed an interest in signing me I listened to what they had to say. This has never been made public before, but I actually signed for Bradford at the end of Super League I. At a hotel just off the M62 motorway in Brighouse I met their coach Matthew Elliott and put pen to paper on a contract. I was under contract at Headingley for another year, but I agreed personal terms with Bradford and all they had to do was sort out a fee with the management at Leeds, which considering their financial difficulties would not have been much of a stumbling block. One of the things I have always enjoyed about being with Leeds is playing at Headingley, and when I thought the ground would be sold I just couldn't see much keeping me at the club. Fortunately, while I was speaking to Bradford, Gary Hetherington and Paul Caddick got on their white horses and rode in to save Leeds from going bust. They took over the club in the autumn of 1996 and immediately announced that they would be staying at Headingley. Which presented me with a bit of a dilemma.

I heard the news on the radio in the car on the way home from training, and with Gary and Paul at the helm at Leeds I knew I didn't want to leave. Gary began by having meetings with all the players, and luckily I was one of his priorities. I knew him from when he had tried to sign me for Sheffield – he founded and coached the club before he came to Leeds – and from when he had been assistant coach with Great Britain, so I was aware he liked me and rated me as a player. Bradford had contacted him to ask if he would be willing to let me go, but I told him I was keen to stay at Leeds if he wanted to keep me. Gary said he would match the deal the Bulls had offered me, which wasn't a huge increase in money but meant an extra twelve months on my contract. You have to look after yourself and your family, but money has never been the most important factor in my career. It has always been more important to me to know I am wanted and that I will be part of a club's plans. Once Gary said he saw me as an integral part of the Leeds pack over the next few years, the Bradford deal went out of the window.

I know what you're thinking: does he regret that now? The answer is no, I don't regret staying at Leeds, but I would be a liar if I didn't admit that I have sometimes thought 'What if?' Since 1996 Bradford have won the Challenge Cup, the minor premiership, the Super League and the World Club Challenge, and of course it would have been nice to be part of that. But I don't wish I had moved to Bradford; rather, I wish Leeds had enjoyed the success the Bulls have had.

The takeover at Leeds was the start of a couple of encouraging seasons at Headingley. Dean Bell stayed on as coach, but there was a bit more money to strengthen the team and Gary brought in some players who went on to give really good service to the club. Anthony Farrell, Ryan Sheridan and Dean Lawford all came from Sheffield, Paul Sterling was signed from Hunslet, Richie Blackmore joined from Auckland Warriors, and Wayne Collins, Damian Gibson, Martin Masella and Jamie Mathiou were the overseas recruits. The last two were both props, which gave me a bit of competition but also took some of the burden off after I had been the most experienced forward at the club in my early twenties. I thought Martin was a really good player, but, as I will explain later, I had a few run-ins with Jamie Mathiou over the years and our relationship was always pretty icy.

Wayne Collins was a good bloke, and he was responsible for giving me one of my nicknames, which wasn't too flattering. I have always been famous for having a bit of a fat arse, and Snoopy, as Wayne was known, started calling me Barrie Bikerack. He said every time I lay on my front he wanted to park his cycle in the crack in my backside. I much preferred being called Barrie Benchpress.

We got to the Challenge Cup semi-final again in 1997, and for the second successive year we lost to Bradford at Huddersfield, though this time we went down fighting. It was a really bruising encounter, and their prop Brian McDermott (who is no relation) got sent off late on after a punch-up. Brian was an ex-Royal Marine who had been a heavyweight boxer in his younger days and was a really tough bloke on the pitch but a gent and a joker off it.

We had quite a few tussles over the years, but he was someone you could go toe to toe with and always know he would be the first to shake your hand after the final whistle. Rugby league is special like that, although occasionally you do come across people who bear a grudge.

I got through that semi-final without being sent off, but I was cited for hitting Graeme Bradley and I picked up a three-match ban. The only regret I have about that is that I didn't hit him harder. At the time, Bradley was the man I most disliked in Super League. I found him a really arrogant man on and off the pitch, though on the plus side he didn't get on with Jamie Mathiou. Whenever they had a confrontation, I never knew who to cheer for.

While I was serving my ban, Gary Hetherington came to me and asked what I thought about Leeds signing Iestyn Harris from Warrington. Iestyn is an Oldham lad, and though he wasn't a mate of mine I knew him to talk to and was aware of just how good a player he was.

When Gary said we were going to sign him I was thrilled to bits. I knew he would be a superb player for Leeds – and it would also mean I had someone to share the car with on journeys to and from Oldham! I phoned his house straight away and spoke to his mum, Sandra, to pass on my congratulations, and I offered to look after Iestyn in the big city.

Iestyn made his debut as a substitute in a one-point defeat by Wigan at Headingley on 4 April 1997, and it was obvious right from that first game that he was going to become a big hero at Leeds. He had been in dispute with Warrington, who were angry over him playing five-a-side football for a local team while he was out of their side through injury, and it took him a while to get back to full match fitness, but once he hit his straps he became one of the most influential players in Super League. Later on, in 1998, our then coach Graham Murray made him captain, and that was a masterstroke. Along with Andy Farrell, Iestyn is one of the best captains I have ever played for. He always leads by example and he's a fantastic attacking footballer with a great rugby brain, but he is also a fierce defender with a real will to win and is one of the best trainers I have ever come across. Being in the same team as Iestyn Harris was probably the best thing that could have happened to me at that stage of my career. I needed someone to guide me and make sure I was going in the right direction, and Iestyn fitted the bill perfectly.

Iestyn's signing perked us up a fair bit and we climbed steadily up the table; by the middle of the season we were second behind Bradford, who were the runaway leaders. I was in good form and enjoying my rugby, and I scored what I think was probably my best try in a game against Warrington at Headingley on 30 May. They had a light-weight pack and we were well on top. It was one of those games where everything goes right. I was just behind the line of attack, standing with my hands on my knees trying to get a bit of a breather, when Iestyn made a half-break, got tackled and hurled the ball back towards me. It popped straight into my hands, and because I had it in two hands, for some reason I dummied for a drop goal – lined the ball up, looked at the posts and swung my leg back as if to kick. It was probably the worst dummy ever seen on a rugby pitch, but Warrington's defence bought it and they all stopped dead, allowing me to run on an arc over the line to score next to the posts. The crowd were falling about laughing, but only about three or four of our lads came over to congratulate me. I think the rest of them knew they would be hearing all about that try for the next ten seasons.

We went on to win the game 50–12, and that set us up nicely for our trip to Australia in the World Club Championship. That season every Super League club went Down Under for two or three games, with the Aussies, plus Auckland Warriors, playing return fixtures over here. Unfortunately, the whole thing turned into a bit of an embarrassment as the Aussie sides wiped the floor with most of the British teams. The competition was arranged so that teams that had finished near the top of the league the previous year were drawn to face one another. As we had finished third from bottom, we were up against two of the lesser Aussie sides, North Queensland Cowboys and Adelaide Rams, and we really thought we had a chance.

We were away for the first leg, and we took it very seriously. We jetted out on the same flight as Oldham, who were treating it as a bit of a holiday. They were drinking and having a laugh on the flight, and when we had a stopover in Hong Kong, while we were training we could see them all mucking about in the jacuzzi, splashing around, drinking beer and having a whale of a time. We stayed in the same hotel as Oldham for the first week and it was the same again: us working really hard and them partying away. We were up at 8.30 a.m., training at nine and getting back for lunch a couple of hours later when they would just be getting out of bed. We had a good laugh at them, thinking they were really going to get their come-uppance, but as it turned out they didn't do any worse than we did.

Our first game was against North Queensland in Townsville and we were completely blown away. Their half-back Andrew Dunemann, who was later to become a team-mate of mine at Leeds, was the star of the show as they gave us a lesson in how to play the game. I clashed heads twice with different players during the match and got badly cut both times, which added injury to insult.

That result left us really dejected, but we were still confident we could get a victory in the final fixture against the Rams. That game was played at the Adelaide Oval, which had an astroturf patch in the middle of the field to protect the cricket wicket – another new experience. We started that one like a house on fire, taking the lead after about five minutes when Ryan Sheridan got over at the side of the posts. I said to Adrian Morley, 'Come on, we can beat this lot,' but as I turned back I saw Iestyn's conversion attempt hit the underside of the crossbar and bounce down and out. If you watched a thousand games you would probably only see that once, so from that moment the writing was on the wall. Adelaide scored the next thirty-four points, and by the time Leroy Rivett got our other try the game was well and truly gone. To make matters worse, Terry Newton got sent off for a high tackle late on. That really had him worried, because we were due to fly home the next day and he thought he would have to stay in Australia until a disciplinary hearing the following week. As it was, they held a special hearing for Terry and he got a one-match ban, which I think he thought was better than seven extra days Down Under with Gary and Kath Hetherington, who, as quite a shy teenager, he was terrified of.

Once the Adelaide game was over we were able to relax a bit and we had a huge booze-up at the hotel. We were all disappointed with the way the two matches had gone after we had put so much effort in, but that night was a chance to let our hair down and enjoy ourselves before we headed for home. We'd had a bit of a kangaroo court all the way through the trip, with fines for not wearing the right socks, turning up late and that sort of thing, so the cash from that paid for plenty of beer.

Damian Gibson had met a girl on the trip, and he was bragging about what a good time he was having, so I, Martin Masella, Moz and a couple of others came up with a plan to wipe the smile off his face. We decided to strip him naked, tie him to a chair, shut him in one of the hotel lifts and press all the buttons. We pinned him down and managed to pull his top and his socks off, but he was practically in tears by that stage, screaming like a baby and begging us to stop. We felt sorry for him and decided we were going a bit too far, so we untied him, but as soon as he was loose he leapt out of the chair with a big grin, shouted 'So long, suckers!' at us and raced off.

That night was also memorable for Dean Bell getting completely ratted. At first we had decided not to invite him because he had rightly given us a real roasting after the Adelaide game, but eventually we let him join us, and it wasn't long before he was absolutely steaming. All the young lads in the side, like Jamie Field, Phil Hassan and Francis Cummins, spent the night taking the piss out of the coach, tapping him on the shoulder and running off and that sort of thing. He was a great source of entertainment all evening.

When we got back to England we played Bradford on a Friday night at Headingley. I scored a try in a heavy defeat, and the following Tuesday, which was 2 July, we were at home to Halifax. Normally I have a set routine before a game that I don't like to stray from. For some reason, before that Halifax match I didn't do any of the things I normally do and in the changing rooms before the game I knew I wasn't right. About twenty minutes into the game I took an inside ball from Graham Holroyd, and Richard Marshall, Halifax's young front rower, came in to make the tackle. I fell awkwardly, dislocating my ankle and fracturing my lower leg. I don't stay down if I'm not injured, but I stayed down this time and I had to be stretchered off.

I was in a lot of discomfort, though in situations like that you don't get the fierce pain until the shock wears off. I knew I was badly hurt though, because when I was lying on my back with my knees together, instead of facing upwards my foot was pointing out at a right angle. Our physio at the time, Seamus McCallion, got me into the changing room, and then his wife Lesley, who helped out on matchdays, came in to try to get my boot off. As soon as she touched my foot the pain went rushing through my body and I was sick all over the changing-room floor. I wasn't too polite to Lesley, which I was upset about later, but I was in so much pain I turned the air blue. I have apologized to her plenty of times since and I hope she forgives me.

Eventually I was carried out and put into an ambulance, but what I didn't realize at the time was that it was a St John Ambulance, which is basically amateurs pretending to be proper medics. They had to take me to the BUPA hospital in Leeds, but they thought it would be nice to have a little tour of the city first. It was like a Benny Hill sketch. First of all they couldn't lift me into the ambulance and then they got completely lost. We spent what seemed like hours driving around the back streets of Leeds trying to find the hospital. One of them was in the back with me and my dad, and the other one was driving. I was lying there in agony and all I could hear was 'Are you sure it's left?' and 'Do you think we should turn right here?' Eventually the one in the back with me said, 'Don't worry, dear, we'll get you there in a minute.' I'd had enough by that stage. I told her, 'Never mind in a minute, get me to that bloody hospital now!' It worked. The woman in the back went and sat with her mate in the front, and they got me there quick smart after that.

Once in hospital I had an operation to fix my ankle and pin and plate my leg, which was in plaster for six weeks. And that was my 1997 season over.

10

BAD BREAKS

Dedicated to the spirit of the broken player.
If you think you will get back, you might. If you believe
and know you will, your road to recovery is easier.

There have been some ups and downs in my career, but the eighteen months after I broke my leg were the lowest by far. I was on top of my game when it happened, but the injury and what occurred afterwards didn't just cost me my place in the Leeds team and a chance to face Australia for Great Britain at the end of that season, it almost ended my career.

The physical problems were bad enough – a dislocated ankle and fractured leg are serious injuries in anybody's book – but I wasn't really prepared for the mental aspects of recovering and getting back to playing at the highest level again. I have always been able to cope with knocks, bumps, bruises and cuts. They are part of the game, and you can shrug them off. I have never been one for advertising the fact that I have an injury and there have been plenty of times when I've played and I probably shouldn't have. A lot of that is down to your mental approach and being able to block out the fact that you're not as strong physically as you should be. The mind is a very strong muscle, and mine has got me through a lot of adversity, but when you've had a long lay-off there's always a doubt: will I ever be as good again?

It was mid-summer when I got hurt against Halifax, but they were dark days. I was told straight away I wouldn't be able to play again that year, and that was devastating news as I had been determined to get my Great Britain place back. I had a spell in plaster, then I had to hobble on crutches up to the fourth floor of the Leeds General Infirmary to have the cast removed. There was no aftercare; it was just a case of off you go. I felt sick because the pain was that bad. The ligaments had been repaired and I had undergone a complete ankle reconstruction. The leg had been bolted and screwed to hold everything in place, but the moment the cast came off and there was a bit of movement, it hit me like a sledgehammer.

I had tears in my eyes. Jenny was with me and I had to grab her to hold me up. I couldn't make a sound because the room was full of other patients. Most of them were women or children and I didn't want to look like a big Jessie in front of them. I had to put on a bit of a show and make it look as though I was made of iron, when in fact I was in absolute agony. To rub salt into the wounds, I had to borrow a walking stick off a nurse, otherwise I wouldn't have been able to get out of the room. Eventually I managed to get outside the hospital, but then I had to sit down on the pavement and send Jenny to get the car, while people walked around me on the street.

That was just the start of it. Rehab is the big part of any injury and I spent a lot of late nights and early mornings with the Leeds physio Seamus McCallion in the gym at Headingley working on getting a bit of strength back into my leg. He had every faith I could get myself back to where I had been before the injury, but he kept telling me, 'You'll need bucket-loads of grit and determination and no one else is going to be able to do it for you.' At that stage just getting back onto a rugby pitch seemed a long way off, but

I kept myself going by thinking about 1994 and the feeling I had when we beat the Aussies at Wembley.

If you get an injury which means you have to have a period of complete rest, you will need to spend as long again on rehab before you can play again, plus the same amount of time regaining your match fitness. So, if you're laid up for three weeks, that will mean another three doing rehab and then half a dozen matches before you're back to where you started from. My right leg was badly wasted away, so I had to do a lot of work to regain strength and movement. I was back on my feet by the autumn and I set my sights on being back in action for the start of the 1998 Challenge Cup campaign. Leeds were playing friendlies on Boxing Day and New Year's Day, but I was told by the coaching staff to sit them out because they wanted me to be 100 per cent right when I came back.

At the end of the 1997 season Dean Bell decided to step down as coach to take over as head of Rhinos' youth development system, and the club appointed an Aussie, Graham Murray, as the new team boss. That put a little bit more pressure on me, because as well as proving to myself that I still had what it takes, I also needed to show Graham how good I was. I trained the house down, and when the Challenge Cup began in mid-February 1998 Graham named me among the substitutes for our opening game, which was against local rivals Castleford in front of the BBC *Grandstand* cameras at Headingley.

I had been working for more than half a year towards this game, but to tell the truth I was nowhere near ready to play either physically or mentally and the entire afternoon turned into a disaster for me and the team. In fact, I cost us the game. Physically I was actually in reasonable shape, but the mental scars were much worse. After a serious injury things you would normally do automatically, like stepping and twisting in a tackle, become a big worry. In any game your ankle gets bent about a bit; it's something that happens on a regular basis during a match and usually you wince a bit and get on with it. But when I came back I was so worried it would dislocate again that I just crumpled into a heap and dropped to the ground every time I got into contact. That diminished the power game I had. Before I hurt the ankle my pumping leg action was a bit of a trademark, taking me into the opposition's defensive line and gaining another five or six metres through a tackle.

Still, I'd been thrilled when Graham named me on the bench, which was a bit of a gamble for him in his first game, and I was determined to come on, make a big impact and prove to him I was going to be a major part of his team. I got on in the second half, with the scores quite close. Straight away Dean Sampson, the Castleford prop, took the ball up and I stopped him with a head shot, which was more clumsy than anything else but contained a definite element of 'look out, I'm back'. So that was one penalty conceded. A couple of minutes later I gave away another penalty, for offside this time; my first hit-up was OK, but the second one I offloaded, the ball went to the floor and we knocked on to put us back on defence. I soon gave another penalty away for lying on, and at that point Graham must have been sitting in the stand thinking, 'Which team is he playing for? He's a one-man wrecking crew.' I made yet another error and then that was it: the big shepherd's hook was on and I was hauled off and banished to the bench where I couldn't do any more damage.

All that might have been forgotten if we had gone on to win the game, but we didn't. We were hanging on right into the final minute, but then Adrian Vowles, who had a spell at Leeds a few years later, put up a perfect high kick and Andrew Schick touched down to give Cas a dramatic 15–12 win. I was distraught. I knew I had cost us the game and I think Graham probably felt the same way. He had obviously watched tapes of me in action and thought I was a good player who would contribute to the team, but after that there were more than a few doubts in his mind.

Our first Super League game wasn't until April, so we had six weeks or so to lick our wounds. The club arranged a friendly for the end of March at Second Division York to give a few of the lads a run-out. We fielded mainly a reserve line-up with a few experienced players in there as well, and I was made captain for the night. Unfortunately, what happened that evening cost me a season's work and meant I missed out on the first Super League Grand Final and another Great Britain Test series, this time against New Zealand.

We should have won easily, but it was a typical game against a team from a lower division with high shots and late tackles raining in all over the place. Going in at half-time we were behind and York were starting to think they could beat us, which would have been a big feather in their caps.

I had kept myself out of trouble, despite a series of incidents throughout the game with our experienced big-name players coming in for most of York's attention. But at the end of the second half one of the York props, Craig Booth, who had caught me with a high shot a few minutes before, started fighting with Daryl Powell. I went in to help and an all-in brawl exploded. I let rip on a few of their players, and the second the red mist cleared I started thinking about the consequences that were bound to follow. It was only a pre-season friendly, but the red card came out and I was off to Red Hall again for my regular date with the RFL disciplinary committee, though this one was much earlier in the season than normal.

I usually go into those hearings in a positive frame of mind; in this case I was thinking, 'It's only a trial game.

They might take pity and let me off with a fine or a couple of matches.' No chance. I got a five-match ban, four for the fight and one for a 'careless throw' which was placed on report earlier in the game, and after that Graham had severe reservations about whether I was ever going to be any good to him. To make things worse, I later found out there had only been eight seconds of the game left when I got sent off.

I had a meeting with Graham and he told me I was nowhere near where he thought I should be in the lead-up to the start of the season. And then he dropped the bombshell: 'What do you think about going on loan to Bramley for a month?'

Bramley have since dropped out of the professional game, but at the time they were a Second Division side that was ground-sharing at Headingley, playing in front of one man and his dog. They were probably the least glamorous team in the country. Leeds had scrapped their A team, the reserves, as a way of saving money, so they sent quite a few of their highly rated young players on loan to Bramley to gain a bit of experience, as well as senior lads who were out of favour or who needed a few games to get back from injury. I had been in line for a place in the Great Britain side against Australia a few months before, and now I was being asked to play for Bramley. I wasn't happy about it, but I wanted to show a good attitude so I agreed. I thought I could be a role model for the younger players there, and it was also chance to exploit a loophole in the laws to clear my ban a little more quickly.

Bramley were coached by Paul Fletcher, who was sort of on loan from Leeds himself. Fletch is a good mate of mine, and he told me years later that he hadn't wanted me to go to Bramley because he knew how hard it would be for me to play in front of 600 people when I was used to

15,000. I played four games for Bramley and didn't exactly cover myself in glory; in fact, I was a shadow of my former self. The people involved with the club were great to me and I felt a bit sorry for them. They thought they would be getting a Great Britain-standard player, but they didn't.

My first game was away to Workington on 9 May, and I had an absolute nightmare. I was badly off form. I couldn't catch the ball, the passes I threw out went to ground or to the opposition, and I kept missing tackles. The next one was at home against Batley, which wasn't a lot better, but I remember it because it was the last time I saw Roy Powell alive. Roy was one of rugby league's most popular players, a lovely man. He played at the top level for Great Britain, Leeds and Bradford before dropping down a tier, and he was helping out at Batley at the time. At the end of that season he went to join Rochdale and collapsed and died at a Christmas training session, aged just thirty-three, which was a terrible loss for his wife and young family and for rugby league as a whole.

I played a bit better in my third game, which was Barrow away, and then I completed the loan spell with a home game against York and another uninspiring performance. A friend of mine from Oldham, Ian Smith, was the referee. He was working his way up through the ranks and has since gone on to become one of this country's top Super League officials, but I'm sure when he looked at his appointment list at the start of that week he must have been thinking, 'Oh no, Barrie will be playing. I hope I don't have to send him off.' Although you might not believe it after reading about all my red cards and assorted misdemeanours, I'm a big believer in not making the same mistake over and over again. I knew what York would have in store for me, and I did indeed take plenty of cheap shots and high tackles, but I kept my focus, scored a try and we won the game, so at least my Bramley adventure finished on a reasonably high note with a record of two wins and two defeats from four matches.

After that I returned to Leeds, who had made a great start to the 1998 Super League campaign winning their first nine games, including victories at home to Wigan and away against Bradford and St Helens. I was on the bench for the ninth game, which was at home to Huddersfield on 5 June. We won 54–4 and I played well enough to keep my place for the next match, away at Hull. Leeds never did well at the Boulevard, and it was no surprise when the winning run came to an end there. I scored one of our tries, but to keep my spell of bad luck going I picked up a shoulder injury that bothered me for the rest of the season and meant I wasn't as effective in defence as I should have been.

Graham was looking for more from me, but I couldn't impose myself as much as I or he would have liked. I've always been a bit of an enforcer; I'm not someone who scores tries or kicks goals to win games, but I do play a vital role in the team. But when I returned to the Leeds side I just could not get that commanding presence back, no matter how hard I tried.

Darren Fleary and Martin Masella were both in front of me in the pecking order and I just couldn't force my way past them. In all, I only started five times that season with another eight appearances off the bench, which was a pretty miserable record for a fairly experienced international player.

It was a real test of character, and there were times during that year when I thought about walking away. I have always liked to be in the thick of things so it was hard to adjust to being on the fringes. The Leeds assistant coach Damian McGrath was a good friend of mine and was always there with useful advice and a sympathetic ear. He told me to hang on and keep plugging away. There was always a chance one of the front rowers would get injured, and the way the team was going I might even end up with a Grand Final spot.

As we got towards the end of the season it was becoming more and more obvious that Graham was not planning to use me in his first seventeen, but I still had to turn up every day and keep training, and that was really hard. Our last game of the league season was away to Halifax. We had already finished in second spot, which meant we were in the play-offs and would start with a home tie, also against the Blue Sox. Graham rested a few of his first-choice players for the league match, so I got a start. We got hammered 42–0, and that was my final appearance of the year.

That season was the first time Super League had used play-offs to decide the championship. As runners-up to Wigan in the league table we were expected to get through to the Grand Final at Old Trafford, so the pressure was on. After the Halifax league game we went off for a players' get-together in Blackpool, to do a bit of bonding before the play-offs. We did a bit of training and then had a few beers, or in my case far too many beers. We went to a nightclub and I ended up having a fight with Jamie Mathiou, who was the one player in the Leeds squad who always irritated me. It was more of a scuffle than a full-blown punch-up and was entirely due to frustration over the way things were going, but it put me in a foul mood and that led to me getting into another set-to, this time with Terry Newton.

It's something I have always regretted, because we are great mates and I have got a lot of respect for Terry. He broke into the Leeds team as a teenager in 1996 and went on to become one of the best hookers in the game, eventually gaining a lot of success with his hometown club Wigan. I have always got on really well with Terry, but we fell out in a big way because of the frame of mind I was in after a miserable season and my run-in with Jamie Mathiou. Terry gave me a real crack that night and knocked me on my backside. He ran off as fast as I have ever seen him move, but when I got up I thought he must have had a sledgehammer in his hand.

The following morning I woke up feeling totally ashamed of myself, and I quickly made a point of apologizing to Terry, who accepted. I wasn't going to bother with Jamie, though, but to my astonishment he came to my room and said we should keep what had happened quiet. I agreed, and later I found out that he thought he had marked my face, when in fact our 'fight' had just been a case of me knocking him down and getting dragged out by the door staff.

I was left out of the side for the Halifax game in the play-offs, though I was eighteenth man, which meant I would be in if anyone dropped out on the day. Damian told me I wasn't far off and that I might get a chance later in the series, but that was pretty hard to take. We battered Halifax, then lost away to Wigan before taking on St Helens at Headingley in the qualifying semi-final, with the winners going through to Old Trafford. I spent the last two weeks of the season on tenterhooks because Martin Masella had picked up an injury. Right up until a few minutes before kick-off at Wigan he wasn't going to play, but he got the all-clear and had an absolute blinder. He was a bit of a doubt for the Saints game as well, but came through once more, and Leeds had a big win to reach the Grand Final and another clash with Wigan.

So it was an awful season all round for me, but being eighteenth man for the Grand Final was rock bottom. I would have preferred not to go to the game, but Graham told me it would stand me in good stead for the future if I did, so I was travelling reserve and was in charge of relaying walkie-talkie messages from Graham, who was sitting in the stand, to the coaching staff on the bench. That was heartbreaking, being involved but not where I wanted to be – out on the pitch. I also got the booby prize of sharing a room before the game with Anthony Farrell, who smokes like a chimney and snores like a buffalo. I went to the players' meeting before we set off for the stadium, but while they were all getting mentally prepared for the biggest game of their career, I was restricted to sitting in my hotel room watching TV. I said to myself there and then, 'This is never going to happen to me again. Next time we get to a final, I'll be playing.'

It was bad enough being left out of the Leeds side that day, but to make matters worse I was also told, on the day of the final, that I wouldn't be figuring for Great Britain in the end-of-season Test series against the Kiwi tourists. The squad was due to be announced shortly after the game. Wigan assistant boss Andy Goodway was the national coach, and as we were walking to the dugouts before kick-off I asked him, 'Will I be getting a letter tomorrow?' He told me, 'I'm sorry, Barrie. You know what I think of you, but if you're not even in the seventeen I can't pick you.'

We lost the final narrowly after taking an early lead. Richie Blackmore scored for us in the first half, but Jason Robinson hit back for Wigan with a wonderful solo try and they held on to take the title 10–4. The game, played in torrential rain which didn't really suit our style of play, went by very slowly and all the way through I was thinking, 'I could be making a difference out there.' The following year, Graham came to my wedding reception and admitted, 'Looking back, we needed to play some football and open them up a bit, so if I had that time again I would have picked you for the team.' That made me feel a lot better!

We had an after-match function back at Headingley, which had been organized win or lose. I stayed away from that, but the players had a big social day out the following Monday, which I joined.

Great Britain were in camp in Leeds at the same time, and Terry O'Connor, who had played for Wigan in the Grand Final, arranged to meet up with me in a pub in Leeds to try to cheer me up. I was half asleep at the bar when he arrived, but he propped me up and we started knocking back the booze. I ended up in a terrible state. Franny Cummins was there too, and he told me I'd had enough, so I decided to crash out at Neil Harmon's house in Leeds.

When I got there the house was empty, which shouldn't have been a surprise because Neil was in France and Adrian Morley, his lodger, was in camp with Great Britain. I had a bit of a sleep in the front garden, then decided to try to get a taxi back into Leeds city centre. It was about four a.m. by this time so there weren't any taxis about, but I managed to flag down a passing bus. The driver was great. I tried to explain my plight and he said, 'I'm heading for the city centre. Have a sleep on the back seat and when we get there I'll wake you up.' I only had 12p with me, which I gave the driver. Very kindly, he gave it back, in case of emergencies later on. You never know when 12p might come in handy.

I went to sleep at the back of the bus, but all the drink was coming back to haunt me by then and – I am deeply ashamed to say this – I threw up all over the floor. I felt bad about that for ages. He had done me a favour and that was how I repaid him. I was writing a weekly column for the *Yorkshire Evening Post* at the time and when I did a list of people I wanted to thank at the end of the year, the bus driver was on it. Eventually I managed to get a taxi home to Oldham and spent three days with the world's worst hangover. I haven't touched Jack Daniel's since.

That column in the *YEP* turned out to be another fiasco.

In fact, I was beginning to think it was cursed. Neil Harmon was the columnist for a while, but he only lasted a couple of months before Leeds got shot of him. Then Gary Mercer took it over, and they got rid of him. I did it for a season but I couldn't get in the team. For most of the time in the column I was just explaining to people why I wasn't in the side. It got to the stage where players were refusing to be the *YEP*'s new columnist. Now they pass it around different players, though whoever does it always seems to get injured or dropped the following week.

The star of my column was definitely Dean Lawford, or Donk as we all called him. Donk was a great lad and a very talented player who was one of the best passers of a ball I ever saw. The pack loved to have him at hooker because he could hit you in the breadbasket with a pass every time. His problem was that he was a bit too laid back, and he liked a bacon butty and a beer a bit more than he did getting up early for training, which was a real shame.

Donk was famous at Leeds for his daft sayings. He once ordered a pizza and told the waiter to cut it into four pieces because he couldn't eat eight. Another time, Damian McGrath needed to ring him on his mobile. Dean didn't give his number out to many people, but obviously Graham Murray had it in his book and Damian got it from there. When Donk answered the phone he said, 'Damian, how did you get my number?' Damian said, 'I didn't, I just guessed.' Donk replied, 'Blimey, that was lucky!' And once, during a pre-season training camp in Tunisia, Donk told us of his plans to hire a bike and go and explore the island. We said, 'You'll have a job, Donk. We're in Africa.' He thought we were in Tenerife.

11

'ELLO, 'ELLO, 'ELLO

It's nice to be important, but it's more important to be nice. With special thanks to my wife Jenny and kids Billy, Sophie and Jessica.

As well as writing the odd piece, I'm used to reading about myself in newspaper sports sections. That comes with the territory, but at times I have also found myself splashed all over the front pages, and that's never good news.

I like to think of myself as a fairly law-abiding person, but sometimes trouble just seems to follow me around. As I have already mentioned, I went off the rails a bit after I lost my eye and there was a spell when I got into quite regular late-night brawls around Oldham town centre. Fortunately I never seemed to get anywhere near a police van or a policeman, though that was probably more due to luck than judgement.

The first time I began to attract the attentions of the local constabulary was when I started working as a door-man in Oldham. I was trapped in a bit of a vicious circle at the time because I was easing back on my work to concen-trate on training, but Oldham were paying me virtually nothing, certainly not enough to live on, so I had to find some way of keeping body and soul together. The licensing trade are big sponsors of the game, and I got to know various people in Oldham's pubs and clubs. Eventually a bloke I knew asked me to work on the door of his club in the town centre. My parents and various other people didn't think it was a great idea, for obvious reasons, but it was good money and it would give me enough time to spend on the track and in the gym.

The downside was that there were a lot of distractions, and I saw plenty of action, of all sorts. There were plenty of women to take my focus off what I was supposed to be concentrating on, and when you're on the doors there's always someone who wants to have a go and prove how hard he is. When you are also someone who's beginning to get a bit of a reputation, you become even more of a target.

The lads I was working with were good, tough blokes, and probably the hardest I ever met off the pitch was a guy called John Connor, an Italian who worked as a doorman in Oldham. He wasn't much to look at, and if he was on his own in a pub and started shouting the odds you wouldn't think twice, but he was a little bit of everything and anyone who tangled with him regretted it. He could do wrestling, kick boxing, boxing, karate, martial arts, the lot. He was a real athlete, as strong as an ox, and I was glad he was on my side. It was John who showed me the ropes, and one of the pieces of advice he gave me was if trouble starts, count to twenty until they have blown off that first bit of steam, then get in there and try to sort it out and pull people away. My problem was, my natural instinct was completely the opposite.

A fight in a nightclub is a very frightening thing, and when you're supposed to be in charge of calming events down and making sure people don't get hurt, it's a bit intimidating.

As soon as any trouble began I couldn't help myself: my automatic reaction was just to pile in and try to pull people off each other straight away. John kept telling me that was the easiest way to get hurt, even though the trouble causers were usually drunk and I was sober. I got into quite a few scrapes that way, and eventually I was hauled in by Oldham for a ticking off.

That came after an incident with a few off-duty policemen. There were about a dozen of them on a works do and they wanted an after-hours drink. The lads on the door wouldn't let them in and I had to back my colleagues up. It all got a bit messy, with the off-duty coppers and the doormen fighting in the street outside the club. The whole thing ended up in court. I hadn't been involved, but one of the blokes wanted me to be a character witness. The Oldham chairman, Jim Quinn, pulled me up and told me that sort of thing wasn't doing me or the club any favours, so, even though I was only working on the doors because Oldham didn't pay me enough, I had to jack the job in.

Away from door work, being part-time at Oldham meant I didn't have much time for going out. We played every Sunday, so I stayed in on Friday and Saturday nights, though we would have a social get-together after training on a Thursday. Sundays, however, were a different matter. It was usually a whole week to the next game, so we would all be out straight after the match, which was normally done and dusted by five p.m. We would go around a few bars in Oldham, then on to a particular pub we all liked to visit, and it was a case of last one out switch the lights off. Fortunately, in the sort of environment we had at Oldham I didn't get exposed to many violent situations and I generally kept my nose clean.

But then I signed for Wigan, and that was a completely different matter. I suddenly had more money in my pocket and more time on my hands. Tuesday was always my night out because we used to have Wednesdays off, and I began regularly getting myself into scrapes with the law and the club.

The first time I found myself in court was when I was

banned for drink-driving, which is something I'm still ashamed about. My car was a new Nissan Primera with my name plastered all over it. It wasn't exactly inconspicuous and it seemed to hold a special fascination for police speed guns. One year I got done for speeding on the same bit of road three months on the trot. I was caught on 19 May and 19 June, so on 19 July I left the car at home and caught the bus. I got done again on the 20th.

One particular night I had played for Wigan against Hull and we'd had a good win. After matches we used to go to the Riverside Club in Wigan to celebrate, which was always a great night. It was a fantastic club and there was always a bit of a cabaret on after games with Wigan director John Martin acting as compère and singer. Everybody used to get up, dance on the chairs and sing along, and the atmosphere was something a bit special. After the Hull game I had a few drinks to celebrate, only a couple of bottles of lager, and I was sure I was OK to drive.

There was a house near the Central Park ground where some of the younger lads lived which players used to crash at if they couldn't or didn't want to drive home, but I thought I was all right so I opted to drive myself back to Oldham in order to pick up my training gear for the following day. There was always a bit of an envious attitude in the surrounding areas when it came to Wigan players, and I don't know whether the police were watching out for someone to stop, but I got pulled over and given a breath test and I was just over the limit. I was taken back to the police station and charged, and I ended up losing my licence for a year, which got reported in the local press. Jack Robinson, the Wigan chairman, was quite strict on things like that and he pulled me into his office. 'Everyone makes mistakes,' he told me. 'I know you're a young lad, but this is your life, so one more and you're out.' The whole thing shook me up. I was quite disgusted with myself, and I vowed never to do it again. Since then I have never driven after having a drink. I will either have soft drinks and I'll drive, or I'll have a pint or two and leave the car behind, so in that case I learned my lesson.

That was the second time I had upset Jack Robinson by drinking and driving, though the previous occasion had involved pop rather than beer. I often like a can of soft drink on my way home from training. This particular time it was a beautiful sunny day, so I was driving home with the windows down and the music blaring. I was doing seventy or eighty miles an hour on the motorway when I spotted a clapped-out old Saab in front of me, so I flashed my lights, he pulled over and I zoomed past him. I finished my can of pop and, without even thinking, threw it out of the window. As I let go I realized what I had done, and I watched in the mirror as it bounced once, then twice before landing smack-bang on the Saab's windscreen. I put my foot down and shot off home, hoping the driver hadn't clocked my number plate, or my name, which was splashed all over the side of the car. Nothing happened all week, until I got on the coach to the away game the following Sunday and Jack pulled me to one side. 'I saw you on the motorway the other day,' he said. 'I've got a tip for you: next time you decide to throw a can of pop out of the window, make sure I'm not driving the car right behind you.' He had seen the Wigan car in his mirror and pulled over to see who it was, and he wasn't too happy to have his latest signing pelting him with a pop can. Fortunately it didn't smash the windscreen or I would really have been up shit street.

The next time I got into trouble at Wigan came after we had won the top team honour at the BBC's prestigious *Sports Review of the Year* in London. I don't suppose too many rugby league players get invited to glittering show-biz parties, and that evening is probably why. The *Sports*

Review of the Year is always broadcast live on a Sunday night, and it's a bit of a national institution. We had played Leeds at Headingley that afternoon and the BBC had flown us down from Leeds-Bradford airport so that we could be at the show. I didn't play in the game, but Wigan lost and everyone was in rather a sombre mood on the flight south, which was a bit of a nightmare in itself. It was a filthy night in the middle of December and we flew down in two separate planes, trying to ignore the fact that these little propeller-driven aircraft were being battered all over the place and were going up and down like rollercoasters. Even the hostess who was looking after us was a bit worried, but it was macho time for most of the players. I've never been very keen on flying, though it's a lot better than crashing, so I wasn't really bothered about how I looked, but some of the rest of them were trying to appear cool and unconcerned and weren't making too good a job of it.

We eventually touched down safely and got to the show about half an hour late, but we sneaked in just in time to pick up the award. It was a huge honour for the club and the sport, which is usually either ignored or patronized at events like that. It was a great experience to be there and to meet some of the world's best sportsmen. I had been at Wigan for six months, but it wasn't too long since my days on the building sites in Oldham, so to be in the same room as all these stars was something special.

The event itself was quite formal, but the party afterwards turned into a monumental piss-up. They had laid on accommodation for us and there was a bit of food at a hotel afterwards, plus a free bar all night. The evening of the show became quite notorious because of allegations that a rugby league player had stolen a charity collection box. As it turned out, the box had just been accidentally damaged when a prank went wrong, but when I woke up the following morning and read the headline RUGBY LEAGUE

STAR ACCUSED OF STEALING CHARITY BOX. I was terrified it might have been me who had done it. If it had been, I wouldn't have been able to tell anyone any different because I couldn't remember much of what had gone on.

Everyone who was anyone was at the after-show function, and they were nearly all blind drunk and making complete fools of themselves. When we first got there it was all quite quiet and formal. Jonathan Davies and the Welsh rugby union lads were all there, so we started to mingle and things began to get going. We had a great time swapping stories, and as the night went on and the alcohol really began to flow the things that were happening got more and more outrageous. Paul Gascoigne had been in the charts with his version of the Lindisfarne song 'Fog on the Tyne'. There was a band on, so Gazza got up to perform his hit single and all the rugby union lads and the Wigan players pelted him with Christmas decorations. Gazza obviously thought better of it and got off the stage smartish, so Andy Farrell, the Wigan captain, got up and finished the song for him. Faz has always been a bit of a demon on the karaoke, and as I remember it he was a much better singer than Gazza. Jonathan Davies knew Gazza and he introduced us, so I had a chat with him and his mate Jimmy Five Bellies. When Jimmy asked where I came from, he told me he had never heard of Oldham.

Eventually it was time for bed, but even that became a bit of a fiasco. I was sharing a room with Terry O'Connor, and in the middle of the night I got up to go to the toilet. Tez heard me get up, open the door and shut it again, but he didn't hear me come back out of the toilet, so he just assumed I had fallen asleep on the loo. The following morning he got up, went into the toilet and I wasn't there. There was no sign of me anywhere in the room either, so Tez and a few of the other Wigan lads launched a full-scale search of the hotel. What had happened was, in my dazed state I had got up, opened the wrong door and wandered out of the room into the corridor, then not been able to find my way back. One of the maids found me staggering around in a confused manner and shoved me into one of the unused rooms. I slept there for hours while everyone else – Tez, Faz, Martin Hall and Neil Cowie – were out searching high and low for me. Eventually I woke up, wondering where on earth I was. I phoned down to reception and they put me through to Tez's room, but there was no reply. I got back on to reception and asked them if there were any rugby players down there, big lads with bent noses and cauliflower ears. The receptionist said, 'Yes, there's four of them here and they've lost the other one.'

Because of all the mucking about while I was AWOL, we missed our train back to Manchester, so we decided to go to the station and have a few beers while waiting for the next express. A few drinks turned into a few more, and as we were just topping up from the previous night it wasn't too long before we were back to being dazed and confused again. Martin Hall was known as a bit of a champion spewer, and as we stood up to make our way towards the train he decided it was time to treat us all to his impression of the girl from *The Exorcist*, all over the table in the station bar. And this was peak time on a Monday evening, just as all the commuters were coming in for a quick coffee before catching the train home.

We beat a hasty retreat, got on the Manchester train and out came the cards. The more we played, the more I lost; I ended up a couple of hundred quid down to Andy Farrell, so my mood wasn't particularly good when the conductor turned up.

I'm not sure why, but he seemed to take an instant dislike to us, especially when I couldn't find my ticket. After a quick search I managed to dig it out of one of my pockets, but the conductor, who had already warned us that gambling on the train was illegal, refused to accept it because it was torn. We had made a bit of a mess, but we hadn't damaged anything and we weren't offending anybody, but the conductor was having none of it. Things got a bit heated, and when we arrived at Manchester the police were waiting. The conductor had radioed ahead telling them there was a group of drunken yobs on the train and they had wrecked the carriage. The police inspector took a quick look around the train and he obviously saw we hadn't caused any damage, but he wanted to keep the conductor sweet so he said we would have to go with him back to the police station, just as a formality. All this didn't go down too well with Tez's wife Jane, who was waiting to give him a lift home. As soon as he told her he was going off to help the police with their enquiries, she knew I had to be involved somewhere along the line.

Neil Cowie has a bit of an arrogant manner, and as we were speaking to the police he told them, 'Either arrest us or piss off, because I'm really late and I want to get home.' That was like a red rag to a bull. The police officer took out his handcuffs, flicked them open and cuffed him, so that kept us smiling while the coppers did all the paperwork.

They kept telling us it was just a formality and it was no big deal, so we didn't think too much of it, but when we got to training on Monday we were splashed all over the front of the Wigan evening paper. There were head-and-shoulders pictures of the five of us under a huge one-word headline: DISGRACED. Of course all the lads blamed me, because it was my ticket that had started all the trouble in the first place. We ended up in court, charged with something like being loud and losing badly at cards in a public place, and we were bound over for twelve months. We were all hugely embarrassed about the whole business, especially Tez, who got a right roasting off his mum Teresa.

He wouldn't tell her who was to blame, but for some reason she knew I had been involved.

We had to wait in the dock while the charges and the statements were read out, and all the conductor's evidence basically involved 'the man in the dark jumper'. Every time 'the man in the dark jumper' was mentioned, the other four lads turned to me and started shaking their heads. The longer the statement went on, the more ridiculous the whole thing got, until eventually they got to the bit where 'the man in the dark jumper' had told the conductor, 'If you don't stop mithering me, I'm going to throw you off this train.' When the lawyer read that bit out, everyone burst out laughing, and the magistrate had to tell us all to shut up. Then I got a bit fed up with what the conductor was accusing me of saying and I told the magistrate, 'That's not true, I didn't say anything like that.' I turned and said to the other lads, 'Did you hear me say anything like that?' They were all shaking their heads and saying no as the magistrate was telling us to shut up – it was complete chaos. We were probably lucky we didn't get locked up for contempt of court.

Jack Robinson took a dim view, again, but because there were five of us involved he didn't blame me.

The worst incident I have ever been involved in off the field happened just after I had left Wigan to join Leeds, and this time I found myself on the front pages of the national papers as well as the local ones. It all began innocently enough with a trip to see my old amateur club Waterhead play. I met up with one of my mates at the game, and as both our girlfriends were pregnant we decided to have a bit of a celebration after the game in a few clubs around Oldham. In those days I could get into the clubs without paying, so I used to see if I could get round them all in an evening, just to see who was about and what was happening.

We ended up in one club at about 1.30 a.m., just in time for a last drink. I was standing at the bar when one of the doormen tapped me on the shoulder and said the police wanted me outside. When I got outside a policeman was waiting and he told me a taxi driver had accused me of kicking his car. It was completely untrue, but it was very late at night, there was no one else about and my only witness was still inside the club. I'd had a few drinks and I knew the police wouldn't take me seriously, so I told them to come and see me about it at home the following afternoon, and I went back inside the club.

Ten minutes later, the policeman came back again and said the taxi driver was adamant it was me who had kicked his cab. It was a bloke in a dark jumper, and I was the only bloke in a dark jumper who had entered the club in the last half an hour. I went back outside again and there were a few coppers gathering by this time: a big, tall policeman, another one and a special constable. The taxi driver was getting more and more aggravated and the police were telling me to give him £20 and the whole thing would be forgotten. Someone had kicked his cab and he just wanted me to cover his costs, because he thought I would be able to afford it. I hadn't done anything, though, and I wasn't going to give the driver £20 just because I was someone he recognized.

That weekend was the first time police in this country had been issued with CS gas sprays for subduing suspects, and this lot in Oldham obviously had itchy trigger fingers. I'm not sure why, but the next thing I knew I had a mouthful of CS gas and several policemen were jumping on top of me trying to pin me down. Now I know police get riot training, but my job depends on me not being put in any position I don't want to be in, and there was no way these coppers were going to be able to get me on the ground. They say CS gas is an irritant, and it is. It really irritated me; it made me act like a maniac. The coppers radioed for back-up and another van arrived, but they still couldn't pin me down. This went on for a couple of minutes, then the batons came out. I got whacked on the leg a couple of times, clouted on my side and then hit on my snooze button on the top of my head, and that was me out for the count. Everybody was piling out of the nightclub by that stage, so they had a big audience. The police wanted to be seen to be doing something, so after they had knocked me out they dragged me up the street by my feet with my head bouncing along the floor.

I spent the night in the cells, and the following day it was all over the newspapers. It turned out I was the first person ever to be arrested by police using CS gas. It was very embarrassing, and the fact that I hadn't kicked the taxi in the first place made it even worse, though I knew the way I had carried on after they tried to arrest me wouldn't look good in court. Because I'm a big, aggressive lad, it's a little like the boy who cried wolf: when you haven't done something no one believes you.

I had just made a clean break to join a new club and the last thing I wanted was to upset Leeds straight away, so I phoned the Leeds coach Dean Bell and told him what had happened. He gave me the week off training to lie low a bit while all the fuss died down, so Jenny and I went to Blackpool just to get away from it all.

The first court hearing was adjourned, and the second came on a Friday, the same day I was due to play for Leeds in Paris. I told my solicitor that would be difficult, because the team were due to set off on the Thursday, play the following day and return on the Saturday. He assured me there would be no problem; he would just get the case adjourned again. On the Friday we were training in France before the game when Dean Bell came up to me and asked if I had forgotten anything, like the fact that I was supposed to be in court back in England. It was all over the news back home that there was a warrant out for my arrest. But I genuinely thought everything had been sorted; I had been told the case would be put back due to my work commitments. I was furious with my solicitor. There was absolutely no way I would have missed the court date unless I thought we had got an adjournment, but obviously the magistrates back in Oldham thought I wasn't taking the business seriously and they decided they would teach me a lesson.

We won the game and flew home the next day, and sure enough, as we walked through passport control there were three coppers waiting for me. They had a police van parked at the airport and they wanted me to go in the back, but I told them, 'I'm not a mass murderer and I'm not going to cause any trouble. I'll sit up the front with you. Take me home so I can get some stuff and then I'll jump in the back when we get near to the police station.' They said fair enough, so I rode up front until we got to Oldham, then nipped into the back to complete the journey. It was a Saturday, so all the police officers who had been involved in my arrest were on duty again, and they were pretty pleased to see me.

I spent the whole weekend in the cells, and every time I started to nod off there would be a bang on the door and some abuse shouted at me along the lines of 'You're not so tough now, are you, McDermott?' just to wake me up. It was a miserable few days, but I knew I would get the last laugh because I was innocent. Eventually it went to court and I was found not guilty, which was gratifying because I knew I was not the yobbish idiot everyone had been saying I was. It was ironic, though, that when I was arrested there were big pictures of me in the papers under headlines like SHAME OF RL STAR, and when I was cleared that rated only a couple of paragraphs in the middle of the papers.

The incident is something I will always regret, although I was genuinely the innocent party and the only thing I did wrong was to have a bit of a reputation. It was an awful experience, not least because Jenny was pregnant and the last thing she needed was all that worry. It was a very stressful time for my whole family, and that's one of the reasons why I made the decision to go back to church.

I have never been a bible basher, but when that happened and I saw what my family went through and what people thought of me, I realized that was not how I really was, and it certainly wasn't how I wanted to be perceived. I had lost a bit of trust in the church after my accident and I honestly couldn't see the point of going, but shortly after the CS gas business I went back. If people spot me in church, that's a much nicer thing than them seeing me on the front of a newspaper.

I have had plenty of dealings with the media throughout my career and on the whole they have been pretty fair to me, even after my various red cards and other misdemeanours. You learn to cope with the occasional critical report, and obviously not all reporters rate you highly, but you have to take the rough with the smooth. Generally most of the stuff written about me has been fairly truthful – apart from certain articles concerning the CS gas court case, of course, and one other occasion when a men's magazine led me up the garden path. My interview was supposed to be for a lifestyle feature, with me talking about my family and hobbies away from rugby. But when the magazine was published, seven-eighths of the article concerned the court case, with a massive headline reading IT TOOK 10 OF THEM TO PUT ME DOWN, which is what I was supposed to have said about the police when they tried to arrest me. It was quite a prestigious magazine and I'd felt proud that they wanted to interview me, so I had told everybody about the article. I was hurt when it came out. Maybe I was being a bit naive, but basically I thought I had been shafted. I spoke to the club about it and they talked about taking legal action, but we contacted the magazine and they claimed they had everything on tape. I told the editor that most of it had been taken completely out of context, but he put that down to 'journalistic interpretation'.

That was a lesson learned. The reporter had lulled me into a false sense of security, and once I'd relaxed a bit I'd slipped into my normal, jokey self and made a throwaway remark about it taking ten police to get me into custody. The journalist had set a trap, and I'd fallen straight into it. I have been a lot more careful ever since.

12

IN FROM THE COLD

*Thanks to Damian McGrath, for your words
of encouragement and advice.*

After all the traumas of 1998 it was beginning to look like Leeds no longer wanted me, but St Helens did. I came close to waving goodbye to Headingley and hightailing it back across the Pennines to Merseyside, but thank God I didn't because 1999 turned out to be one of the best years of my career.

Missing out on the 1998 Grand Final was a huge blow to me, although not a massive surprise. It was clear that Graham Murray didn't see me as one of his first-choice props, but I was still confident I could do a job at Leeds, and if not there, at some other top club. I didn't want to leave Leeds, but I did want to be playing regular first-team rugby. I was willing to fight for my spot, but there's no point in doing that if the coach is dead set on not picking you.

What I needed to do at the end of 1998 was find out where I stood, whether or not I had a future at Leeds. The first thing I did was phone Damian McGrath, the assistant coach. He had always given me sound advice, so I asked him, 'Do you think there's a future here for me?' He told me, 'I think Graham Murray rates you and I think you can still rescue the situation. All you have to do is go in, confront him like a man and ask him, "What do I have to do to get in the team?"'

So I did. I hadn't exactly seen eye to eye with Graham up to that point, but he was straight with me and he told me exactly what he wanted, which was for me to work on my discipline, my fitness and my lateral movement, which is basically defence around the smaller blokes. It might sound strange, but I would rather tackle a six-foot-tall forward than a small, whippet-type half-back, which can be like chasing shadows. 'If you work on those things,' Graham said, 'there is definitely a place here for you. You are too good a player not to be in the team and I will make the side fit around you. Let's wipe the slate clean.'

I went away and had a chat with Jenny about it. I had two choices: I could leave and maybe regret it for the rest of my career – and with the Wigan situation still a painfully fresh memory that did not appeal – or I could stick it out, knuckle down and take Graham at his word.

In between talking to Graham and speaking with Jenny, I had received a phone call from a player at St Helens who had said they were interested in me. They were hoping to recruit an Aussie forward, Phil Adamson, but they weren't sure if he would get work-permit clearance, and if he didn't they would like to sign me instead. I told them I had spoken to Graham and I was keen to stay at Leeds, but if that became impossible then Saints would be the next team I would like to go to, especially as they were coached by Ellery Hanley.

We left it at that, but after talking to Jenny I got stuck into a good off-season's training with Leeds' conditioner Edgar Curtis, and I really began to feel part of things at the Rhinos again. I was so determined to have a good build-up to the new campaign, Jenny and I went on our honeymoon before we actually got married. We had been planning the wedding for a couple of years and when we first started hunting around for dates I asked the then coach Dean Bell when would be a good time and he said January would not be a problem.

We booked the wedding for 9 January 1999, but as time moved on, the season began earlier and earlier and so did pre-season training. By the end of the 1998 season it was obvious that if I went away on honeymoon in January I would miss an important part of our preparations for the new campaign and after the year I had just had, that was not really an option.

We both wanted to have a honeymoon so the solution was obvious, we decided to go away in November and get married, as planned, two months later. Graham Murray said that was fine as far as his plans for the team were concerned, so that's what we did. We had a great time in Barbados and when we returned I could get well and truly stuck into pre-season training.

Jenny was happy to go along with the whole business. She has always supported me 100 per cent in my rugby career. She was aware how important 1999 was going to be for me and she knew I would never have been able to relax if we had gone away in January.

We got married on the Saturday, I had the Sunday to recover and I was back in at training on the Monday morning. We also went on a pre-season trip to Lanzarote, which was a big success and probably the start of all the good things that happened that season at Leeds. I roomed with Terry Newton and Adrian Morley and we had some great laughs, as well as putting a lot of pretty tough training in. I know people think these trips are a bit of a holiday, but honestly they aren't. The club pays a lot of money to send the players away and they don't want to see you lounging around by the pool.

In these days of summer rugby, off-season and the pre-season build-up comes in the depths of winter when it's difficult to train in cold and wet conditions. Warm weather allows you to spend longer out on the pitch or the track and you get a lot more done. That year we went to the Club La Santa complex, which hosts a lot of top sports teams and boasts fantastic facilities. It's good to get away from all the distractions and get a really solid week's training under your belt, but it's also a great opportunity for all the lads to get to know one another better. The year before we had been in Tunisia, which was a dismal experience. There was absolutely nothing for us to do away from training, but we had had a bit of fun with Phil Cantillon. About half a dozen of us shaved our heads but we left great tufts of hair on Phil's head. He was also the victim of a few games of spoons, which basically involves bashing someone over the head with a spoon.

Moz and I decided shaved heads would be the team look for the start of the 1999 Challenge Cup. Leroy Rivett had some clippers with him, so Moz and I did each other and then went on the rampage, pinning lads down, shaving chunks out of their hair and then moving on. Karl Pratt didn't want to do it because he said he had a modelling contract with a salon in Leeds. We didn't believe him and we didn't care anyway, so he was scalped with the rest of them. Iestyn fell victim too, much to the horror of Tissot, who had just done a big poster campaign featuring him modelling their expensive watches. He had spent two or three days having his picture taken, but when the posters came out they didn't look anything like the Iestyn who was running around on TV. Daryl Powell refused because he was worried short hair would look even greyer than his did already, and Franny Cummins and Ryan Sheridan managed to escape by locking themselves in a room until we got fed up and went away.

Graham Murray encouraged that sort of thing. He was very sound technically, but he was also big on team spirit and he was keen on anything that brought the players closer together. He had the knack for organizing a good do, where you were encouraged to have a couple of beers so that you would stop being the professional rugby player on duty and start being the ordinary bloke relaxing and having a good time with his mates.

While we were away in Lanzarote I started to think about where I wanted to be and where I wanted to go, and I decided there was no reason why I could not get back into the Leeds team and stay there. All the vibes from Graham were good, I was working hard in training and, as an added bonus, two of the other front rowers, Martin Masella and Jamie Mathiou, had both somehow upset Graham a bit. It looked pretty much like Darren Fleary and I were going to be the starting props, with Martin and Jamie fighting it out for the other spot.

Our key signing for the 1999 season was Lee Jackson, who had just won an Australian Grand Final with Newcastle Knights. Jacko was a great bloke to have around the club. He's a real joker, and he made everyone smile. A mate of mine was driving back from work in Hull one day and he found himself behind a car that was veering from lane to lane. My mate thought the driver must be drunk or falling asleep, but when he got level with him at some traffic lights it turned out to be Jacko, with his eyes shut, conducting classical music on his car stereo. He was into Classic FM all day, every day. Graham Murray used Jacko mainly off the substitutes' bench, throwing him on to exploit his pace after Terry Newton had worn the opposition down early doors. Jacko was one of those players who always did the unexpected. We never knew what he was going to do next, and most of the time neither did he.

As a team we sat down and set some goals for 1999, and the first of those was to win the Challenge Cup. Leeds hadn't lifted the trophy since 1978 and everybody in the city and all those connected with the club were desperate to put that right. We adopted a rallying cry of '78', and it worked a treat. That week in Lanzarote we also sorted out the bonus scheme for the competition, and for the first time we decided we would make it win or bust. We were on £12,000 a man to win it, but nothing if we didn't. After tax, and once you had paid for your family to go down to the final and that sort of thing, it would be £7,500 each, but only as long as we won it. That seemed like a good idea at the time, but more or less at the same moment as we were having our bonus meeting the draw for the fourth round of the Challenge Cup was made and we got Wigan at home, which was a bit of a spanner in the works.

I was determined to keep my nose clean in the build-up to the mid-February game, but even so I upset Graham just a few days before the match. The papers had latched on to my friendship with Terry O'Connor and the fact that he had been my best man, and that was the angle a lot of them used to build their previews around. There was a bit of banter in the rugby league papers about each of our wives fancying the other's husband. It was just a bit of fun, and it's how we talk to each other, but Graham came up to me and said, 'You have got to act your age, you two. All you're doing is playing into the media's hands.' Which was fair enough, but the only problem was I had done another interview with the *Sun* that had yet to appear. Terry had had a bit of a poke at me and I had done something back on the Monday morning, just before Graham came to tell me to knock it off. I said, 'I'll have to be straight with you, I've done one back.' He wasn't too pleased, but I added, 'Don't worry, it's only a bit of fun. It won't affect me mentally and you don't have to worry about me being any less committed because Tez is my mate. My loyalties are to the people I'm playing with, and most of all to myself. I represent myself every time I go out on the pitch. If that means I have to step over Tez or anyone else to get into the next round of the cup, I will. He knows that, and it's the same the other way.'

The piece duly came out in the *Sun* and it was another full page of banter, with us taking the mickey out of each other. I shouldn't have done it, because you have to be careful what you say to the press – if you aren't you can leave yourself open to a bit of ridicule – but at the time it was just a bit of fun. It was published on the Saturday, which was the day of the game. The tie was on *Grandstand*, and that seemed to be all they talked about during the commentary.

Leeds against Wigan is always a big game, and this was one of the biggest. I will definitely never forget it. The first few minutes were probably as good as I had played all the previous season. I was enjoying my football and I was getting stuck in. I particularly remember a challenge on Mick Cassidy. I hadn't liked what he'd done to Moz the previous season, when he had smashed him in the face during a game at Central Park. The two of us made a tackle on Cassidy together and we really whacked him, and that probably set the snowball rolling.

Throughout my career I have heard voices in my head saying, 'Hit him, hit him!' Now I can ignore them, but that afternoon they certainly got their message across. After about twenty minutes Simon Haughton came on a crash ball and I took him quite high. Now when I watch it I have to hold my hands up and admit it was high, but at the time I thought he made a meal of it. There was me and Daryl Powell in the tackle, and Simon dropped like he had been shot. He's a tough lad, but he can be a drama queen sometimes and I don't think he was anything like as hurt as he made out. Daryl was telling him, 'Get up, Simon, you soft git,' but Andy Farrell, the Wigan and Great Britain captain, was standing there saying, 'You've got to go for that, Barrie, you've really hurt him.' Russell Smith was the referee. He reached into his back pocket and, yet again, I was sent off. Disaster.

I have watched the video, and on it you can see the look on my face change straight away from anger to regret, and that's how it has always been whenever I have been sent off.

It hit me like a ton of bricks as I walked off. I went into the changing room and started kicking things around out of sheer temper. On top of the anger, I honestly felt like crying.

After everything that had happened over the past year or so I really thought this was the end of my Leeds career, just as something similar had put paid to my time at Wigan. All the pre-season effort and all the hard work I had put in had been ruined inside twenty minutes of the first game of the year.

I got into the shower fully clothed, then I went into the sauna, simply because I was too ashamed to look anyone in the face. In the Headingley changing room there's a place where you get changed, then there are the showers and a sauna. I was in there when the team came in at half-time and they were leading 13–12. I could hear everything they were saying and it was all really positive. I will always remember Marc Glanville getting the lads together and telling them, 'Listen, I don't want the fact that we have had a man sent off being used as an excuse for losing this one. We can go out and win this.' That was exactly the right thing to say, and it made me feel a bit better. When they went back out for the second half I put my suit on and went out and watched the rest of the game from the players' tunnel.

Somehow the boys managed to get on top of Wigan and they held on for a great win, 28–18. I think that really set the team up for the season. It showed that whatever happened, Leeds could come through in the end. There were many times that year when we went behind early on in a game but came through because of what the players had gained from that day against Wigan.

I felt numb all through the second half, and at the end I basically hung my head in shame. I didn't go into the changing room to congratulate the lads, I just stayed outside and tried to be as inconspicuous as possible. I kept thinking, 'I'm in shit street now. That could be me off to Saints.' I was pretty upset and embarrassed about what had happened, but I was angry as well. My thoughts were, 'That Simon Haughton's cost me my job. My family are all depending on me and he has ruined it by taking a dive.' Now I accept I did hit him, but I couldn't see that at the time.

Things almost got a lot worse after the match. In rugby league all the players eat together following a game, and this time I was sitting with a few of the Leeds lads when Andy Goodway, the Wigan assistant coach and a good friend of mine, came in. He said I was looking at a long ban and asked me what I was doing picking on poor Simon. That started to get under my skin. Then Andy Farrell and Denis Betts came in and had a bit of a go. It was just a bit of banter, but because of the frame of mind I was in I was getting angrier and angrier.

Then Simon walked in. As soon as he came in I stood up and said, 'You, you soft bastard, you took a dive there.' He said, 'I didn't, Barrie, you knocked my legs from under me.' But I persisted: 'You're a soft bastard. Pick your bag up and get out of here before I really do you some damage.' Farrell, Goodway and Betts were all laughing, and that just made things worse. If I had taken a step towards him I would have gone all the way across the room and smacked him, but I didn't. I stayed rooted to the spot, and a couple of our lads, Iestyn Harris among them, came up to me and told me to calm down and not make a fool of myself. Luckily, Simon picked up his bag and walked off. He obviously thought he should quit while he was ahead, and I'm glad that he did, because otherwise I would have done something both of us would have regretted.

Looking back now, I admit I was out of line during the game and after it, but I was caught up in the emotion of it all at the time. I thought Graham Murray would be steaming about me getting sent off, but he wasn't. In fact, he came up to me afterwards and said, 'That's the best twenty minutes you have ever played for me.' I apologized for letting him and the team down, but he told me, 'These things happen, don't worry about it. We'll see what happens at the disciplinary on Tuesday.'

I made my usual trip to headquarters at Red Hall and got a two-match ban, which wasn't too bad. It meant I missed the next cup game, ironically at home to St Helens, but a fantastic team performance got Leeds through that one and I was back for the quarter-final at Widnes on 14 March, a month to the day after the Wigan game.

We had already beaten the two top sides and we didn't have too much trouble getting past Widnes, who weren't a Super League club at the time. We were always in command, but they competed pretty well until Kevin Sinfield, who was only a young fringe player then, came off the bench and got a couple of tries to kill them off. I enjoyed the game, played reasonably well and even popped over for a try, which was good because I wanted to repay the team and the coaches and everyone who had been really good to me, as opposed to the year before when they had washed their hands of me.

So fortunately, the sending-off didn't really set me back at all. I was back in the side for the start of Super League and then we played Bradford Bulls in the cup semi-final at the McAlpine Stadium in Huddersfield. I had already lost to them there in one cup semi-final and I was determined that wasn't going to happen again. After all we had been through, we were determined to go to Wembley and lift the Challenge Cup, but again it was not plain sailing. Bradford came at us like an express train and got a couple of early tries to lead 10–0. It could have been worse, but they had a try ruled out for a forward pass and we managed to get level by half-time, thanks mainly to an amazing touchdown by Ryan Sheridan. Danny Peacock was running the ball out from his own twenty-metre area when Shez moved in to make a tackle, wrapped his arm around the ball, tugged it loose and scampered over for the score that really got us back into the contest.

We were thrilled to bits to be back in the game at the break, and Graham said to us, 'We've got them on the ropes, they're rocking. They didn't expect you to survive the onslaught, they didn't expect you to come back, and now they're running out of ideas.' It was tight for most of the second half, but we always felt we had the upper hand and Marcus St Hilaire and Iestyn both got over for tries near the end to send us to Wembley. That was something special, because Bradford have come out on top in games against teams I have played for on too many occasions throughout my career.

We celebrated in appropriate style afterwards, in the changing rooms and elsewhere. I had said to Jenny beforehand, 'If we lose the game I'll be straight home. If we win, I'll see you after training on Monday afternoon.' And I did. We had a fantastic night. We had a good drink round the pubs in Leeds, then we went to a casino, which wouldn't let Iestyn and me in. We turned up in a confused state and asked the doormen to let us in. We told them, 'It's Barrie and Iestyn, we played in the semi-final today.' But the manager came over and said, 'Look, we know who you are, but the fact is you're not members and you're blind drunk.'

It's a good job they did keep us out, because I would probably have lost my house, my car and everything else. We ended up going to a club in Leeds and we stayed there until the wee small hours, creating a bit of havoc on the karaoke. In the morning we did a bit of rehab and I went home on Monday afternoon, as promised.

The time between the semi and the final brought five of the strangest games I have ever played in. It was just a case of getting through with no injuries. The mental and physical stress took its toll and quite a few of the boys missed the odd game, but most of us played right through. When you have watched as many games as I have through suspension, you don't want to miss any more. If I can hobble out onto the pitch, my adrenalin and anti-inflammatory tablets will get me through. Without anti-inflammatory tablets, there wouldn't be much Super League played at all in this country. They are a God-send and keep a lot of us going.

It was a big relief when we got our last league game before the final out of the way, and the build-up to Wembley itself was fantastic. There was so much anticipation and excitement around the place. Everybody in and around Leeds suddenly became a Rhinos fan and everywhere we went people were wishing us good luck and saying how much it meant to them. The final saw us up against London Broncos, who had beaten Castleford in a fantastic game in the semi-final at Headingley, snatching a place at Wembley with a try in the very last second by Steele Retchless. London were a good side, but we had beaten them in Super League between the semi and the final and it was a game we thought we could win, and win well. We had already played three 'finals' before we even got to Wembley, so we knew nothing was going to stop us lifting that trophy this time.

We travelled down to London on the Tuesday to go into camp and we had a walkabout at Wembley the day before the game, which brought back great memories of 1994 for me. The walkabout is a chance to have a look at the pitch, decide what boots you are going to wear, inspect the changing rooms and that sort of thing.

The atmosphere in the hotel before the game was really focused, with not much laughing and joking. I'm normally quite loose before a game, but this time it was all business. As normal, I woke up early and went down for a bite to eat. I follow the same ritual before every game: steak the night before and scrambled eggs in the morning. Then it was a case of reading the papers and trying to relax before we set off for the ground.

The coach journey over to Wembley was very quiet, with just the radio on in the background. We got into the changing rooms and, as usual, I was the first to get strapped.

I am probably the most superstitious person I know. There must be a dozen things I have to do before every game. I got my ankle strapped, elbow pad taped on, and knee strapped, and I was ready fifty minutes before we were due to warm up, which felt like a horribly long time. I drive people mad in the changing rooms because I walk up and down bouncing the ball on the floor until it annoys somebody enough to make them stand up; then they start to pass the ball to me. I do that for fifty minutes, and though I try not to, it probably irritates the hell out of everyone. But that's just how I am before a game. Over the years people have got used to me. Franny Cummins is always cursing me because wherever he sits I seem to be passing the ball six inches in front of his nose, but he has grown accustomed to it now. This time, for some reason, I had 'Abide with Me' ringing round in my head and I was singing that out loud as we were getting ready. The hairs on the back of my neck were standing on end.

We weren't allowed on the pitch before the walk out, so

we had to warm up in the Wembley tunnel. You could have heard a pin drop. After the rollercoaster ride of the past twelve months, to get to a Challenge Cup final, and one we knew we could win, was very emotional, and I had a big lump in my throat. After the warm-up Graham gave us a few words of encouragement and then we all went round one another, giving everyone else a handshake or an embrace and wishing one another good luck, all the best and enjoy the day.

Then it was time to go out. I always like to be second in the line coming out of the changing room, and as we walked up the Wembley tunnel my son Billy came running towards us. I had arranged with the club that if we got to the final he would be the team mascot for the day. I was a bit worried about what Graham might say, considering our relationship at the time, so the week before the game I asked him if he would mind if Billy was the mascot at Wembley. I told him it wouldn't affect me at all; if anything, it would probably inspire me. To his credit, Graham said he thought it was a brilliant idea, so we got Billy kitted out with a Leeds jersey with the number 10 on the back and the name Daddy.

I thought I had got my angry head on and I was ready for battle, but when Billy came running down the tunnel, though I tried to hide it, there were tears in my eyes. I was thinking, 'This is the best day of my life, and I haven't even got out on the pitch yet.' The song as we walked out was 'Search for a Hero' by M People. Our Billy was only three at the time, but even now if he hears the song he says 'Wembley'. Fortunately, Iestyn was captain and Billy had known him all his life, so I knew he was in good hands when he led the team out and I didn't have to worry about him.

As for the game itself, I didn't think I had contributed as much as I had in previous weeks. I was carrying a bit of a shoulder injury, but I wasn't going to risk missing out so I hadn't told anyone about it. Our game plan had me playing for the first twenty minutes or so and then being replaced by Jamie Mathiou. That went according to plan, and I came back on as a blood-bin for Darren Fleary just after half-time.

London started strongly and got the first two tries through Martin Offiah and Robbie Simpson to go 10–0 up. As we had done in the semi-final, we hit back, and we were in front 12–10 at half-time, Leroy Rivett and Brad Godden having got over for touchdowns. London scored again through Greg Fleming straight after the break to go back in front, and they were leading 16–12 when I returned to the action.

Not long after that we got a penalty near their line for a late challenge, and Iestyn was getting ready to take a quick tap. I nodded at him and said, 'Yes, I'm ready.' I remember looking at their line and thinking there were three players I knew were poor on their feet standing in front of me. I knew I could at the very least catch them off guard, enough to get an offload or a quick play-the-ball in to set us up for the next play. Iestyn took the tap and gave me the ball. Matt Salter flew out of the line to smash me, so I stepped off my right foot; someone else came across and I stepped off it again; and suddenly the line opened up in front of me. Like the typical front rower who doesn't know anything other than to put his head down and go, I ran at the line with as much power and pace as I could and managed to get over for what turned out to be the try that changed the game and the one I will probably be remembered the most for.

More than the try, the thing people always talk to me about is my reaction afterwards. It was a combination of everything that had gone on throughout that day, that season, and in fact my whole career. It had all come to a head with that one try, on the biggest stage in the world, playing in the greatest competition in the world. I remember hurling the ball up in the air. Lee Jackson was behind me and he got a bit over-ambitious. He's only about thirteen stone and I was eighteen stone at the time, but he tried to lift me up. He barely got my feet off the ground before he dropped me, then Iestyn came from ten yards back to jump on me. He took off just as Jacko dropped me, so he shot straight over the top and landed on his shoulder. How he didn't dislocate it I will never know. Something that sticks out in my mind is the fact that every single Leeds player on the pitch came up to me and either shook my hand or embraced me. They were thrilled to bits for me, and I will always remember that.

We went on to win the game 52–16, which set all sorts of records. Leroy Rivett got the first four-try haul in a Challenge Cup final and Iestyn kicked eight goals, with Brad Godden, Marcus St Hilaire, Iestyn and Franny also getting touchdowns. Leroy was man of the match, but I thought Moz and Shez must have been pretty close – they were both outstanding. As for me, I had scored a try and contributed to the victory, and I could not have been more pleased.

Before the game we had been told by the Wembley authorities that they would not let any of the players' kids onto the pitch after the final hooter. That had become a bit of a tradition, and they were determined to stop it this time. We had a chat about it and we decided that if we won no one was going to prevent us from celebrating with our families. At the end, everyone was passing kids over the fence to us on the running track at the side of the pitch. Even players who didn't have kids were lifting them over for others in the team. That was a really touching moment, and to be on the pitch at the end enjoying the occasion and the achievement surrounded by our children crowned a truly wonderful day. Rugby league is a tough game, but I think that was a good image for the TV viewers.

Someone at the club had the bright idea of making a banner that read RHINOS FANS, THIS IS FOR YOU, and we unfurled that during the lap of honour. We all knew how long it had been since Leeds had won the cup and just what it meant to the supporters, and I think they appreciated that.

After the reception at Wembley we went back to the hotel for a celebration dinner and everyone had their picture taken with their family and the Challenge Cup. That picture has got pride of place in my front room at home.

The following day we travelled back to Leeds and then we got on an open-top bus at Hyde Park for the journey to Headingley. The streets were lined with people and there were 17,000 fans in the ground to welcome us home, which was brilliant. We did a lap of honour, then we made a few speeches and had a bit of a sing-song on a stage that had been built on the pitch. There was a local radio guy doing the introductions, and he kept sticking the microphone in my face when we were singing 'Let Me Entertain You'.

At the time we had a little trick: if someone's shorts weren't tied properly, someone would distract the victim and somebody else would whip their pants down. That was always a great cause of amusement, and we did it to the poor bloke who was singing on stage. Unfortunately he wasn't wearing any underpants, so he was standing on the pitch at Headingley in front of thousands of people with his meat and two veg hanging out!

The homecoming was a memorable end to an unforgettable weekend and a great cup run, one that kicked my career on to bigger and better things. I'd had many low points before it and I have had many high points since, but that was the best.

13

TROUBLED TIMES

*To the odd man out. Nobody goes through life unscathed,
but God never shuts a door without opening a window.*

When we won the Challenge Cup in 1999 Leeds Rhinos
looked ready to dominate British rugby league for years to
come, but unfortunately that didn't happen. Perhaps unsurprisingly, because there are only two major trophies for
Super League clubs to win and we had already picked up
one of them, the rest of the season fizzled out. Our hopes
of doing the double came to an end when we finished
third in the league and lost both our play-off games, at
St Helens and against Castleford at Headingley. That was
the first time we had been beaten in successive games
under Graham Murray and it was a sad end to his reign.

At the start of the year, Graham had announced that he
would be returning to Australia after the 1999 Super League
season to take over as coach of North Sydney. That was a
big blow for the club as Graham had become a folk hero
in Leeds after guiding the Rhinos to a Grand Final and
their first Challenge Cup success in twenty-one years. He
had always been planning to go home eventually, but the
opportunity had come along much sooner than anyone
expected. It was probably the right move for him at the
time, but it didn't work out as expected. Before Graham
even got to take up his new post, North Sydney merged

with Manly and someone else was appointed coach. All that happened towards the end of our 1999 season, so when he left Leeds he didn't have a job to go to. He fell on his feet, though, by being named coach of Sydney City Roosters, and he guided them to the Aussie Grand Final at the first attempt, though Brisbane Broncos pipped them in the big game. The Roosters didn't have such a good time the following year and Graham was sacked part of the way through. He then had a spell of unemployment before taking over at North Queensland Cowboys, who were traditionally one of the poorest sides in the National Rugby League, so all in all he had a tough time after leaving Leeds. I think he must wonder now whether he made the right decision, when things had been going so well for him over here.

After Graham had gone back to Australia we were confident we could win more silverware under his replacement Dean Lance, who had captained Canberra when they were one of Australia's top sides and who also had spells coaching Perth and Adelaide. Maybe that wasn't such a good omen, though: both those clubs went out of business shortly afterwards.

Dean had come over to have a look at us midway through the 1999 campaign and he must have been impressed with what he saw because we had some great victories while he was here, winning at Wigan and hammering Bradford on a very memorable Headingley evening. I was quite pleased when Dean was named coach because he was someone I had a lot of time for as a player. I had seen him star in a couple of Aussie Grand Finals and he was a hard, no-nonsense character and a very tough competitor. Just the sort of player I admire. I thought if he coached like he played I would probably have a good time with him in charge. I spoke to a few of Gateshead Thunder's Aussies who had played under him at Adelaide, and they said Dean was a great bloke and a player's coach, so the signs were very positive.

Before the start of the 2000 season I went with Great Britain on the Tri-Nations tour to New Zealand and Australia, which at best was a learning experience, but when I came back I was ready for a really big year. We had retained most of the Challenge Cup-winning side, but Marc Glanville had retired and Brad Godden wasn't kept on, which didn't go down too well with him or the fans. Keith Senior was signed as Brad's replacement, and he had made his debut in the final league game of 1999. That meant Goddo got left out of the side and didn't get a chance to say goodbye to the supporters, which wasn't the smartest move the club has ever made.

David Barnhill, whose dad had banned me when he was on the judiciary in Australia during my spell with Wyong, joined us from Sydney Roosters, and we also signed Paul Bell, who had been Dean's club captain in Australia. Bell didn't last long: he got injured after about four games and was forced to retire. Barny stayed the season, but didn't really establish himself and went home a year early. That was a shame, because Barny was a bloke I really admired and got along very well with. He was a player's player. He wasn't your traditional type of tough guy because he wasn't particularly aggressive, but he was a strong competitor, he set high standards for himself and he turned up when nobody else would.

We started the year with a couple of wins in the Challenge Cup, including a great victory over St Helens at Headingley, coming from a long way behind to snatch the win with a last-gasp try by Adrian Morley. We beat Dewsbury at Headingley in the quarter-final and then saw off Hull in the semi at the McAlpine Stadium on 26 March 2000. That game is famous for what happened on the pitch, but only after the rugby had finished.

I have always had problems with the Hull fans, who absolutely hate me. Every team has a player who's loved by his own supporters and detested by the opposition's. I have held that role all through my career and I try not to take it to heart, but I always seem to come in for special treatment from the crowd when we play Hull. Maybe it's not personal, because they seem particularly vindictive towards anyone who happens to play for a rival team. I played alongside Iestyn at their old Boulevard ground, which was one of the most atmospheric in rugby league, and some of the chants they threw at him were especially disgusting. Rugby league has always been known as a family game and it's a shame when a few idiots spoil that. To their credit, Hull have started to clean up their act over the last few years and a lot of that is a legacy of that infamous year 2000 cup semi-final.

We were only at half-pace, but we won the game 28–22, despite Matt Daylight scoring a hat-trick of tries for Hull and Wayne McDonald, who later joined Leeds, getting over for a late touchdown. There were all the usual celebrations afterwards, but when we got into the changing rooms the stewards were rushing about and people were saying it had all kicked off on the pitch. The Hull fans had invaded the field at the end of the game, started fighting with police and stewards and were trying to get at the Leeds support- ers at the other end. Eventually the goal posts were pulled down and it was complete chaos, all broadcast live on BBC's *Grandstand*.

It was an ugly day for rugby league and it did the code's image a lot of harm. I am very passionate about my sport. I love to win and I hate to lose, but you have to keep it all in perspective and there's absolutely no excuse for that sort of mindless thuggery. Hull have a lot of genuine supporters who deplore that sort of thing as much as everyone else. They too were bitterly disappointed with the result, but they didn't go on the pitch after the game and start attacking people and throwing things. I felt sorry for them, because their name was being dragged through the mud.

Of course the crowd trouble stole all the headlines, which was a pity as we could have done with some positive publicity. Though we were doing well in the cup, the start of the league campaign was a disaster. We just couldn't get our league form going. We lost our opening five games, and it looked like we would be the first team ever to play in a Challenge Cup final while bottom of the league table.

Dean Lance, understandably, wanted to be his own man and to bring in his own ideas, but it took us a long time to get used to his tactics and way of doing things. We began the 2000 Super League campaign with a last-minute home defeat at the hands of Wakefield on 3 March and then lost to Wigan, Halifax and St Helens. Our fifth Super League game was at Warrington, and when we came off the field at the end of yet another defeat we heard that Huddersfield had beaten Wakefield, so we were rock bottom. We played Huddersfield the week after that and squeezed to a 20–10 victory, so we were tenth when we took on Bradford in the first cup final played at Murrayfield on 29 April.

That almost didn't take place as Edinburgh was hit by a massive storm a couple of days before the final and the Waters of Leith, the river that runs past the ground, flooded leaving the pitch under five feet of water. The Rugby Football League called the military in and, along with the groundstaff, they somehow got the field cleared and the game went ahead as scheduled. Sadly we couldn't repeat the heroics of the previous year, but we weren't far off; if the final had gone on ten minutes longer, we might have won it.

Adrian Morley had a fantastic game, and man for man we pretty much matched Bradford, who had started as red-hot favourites, but in the end they had a little bit too much class and Henry Paul's kicking proved the difference. He terrorized Leroy Rivett with his high bombs to earn them a couple of tries, which was a huge shame for Leroy after he had been the hero at Wembley the year before. That shattered his confidence, and he never played for Leeds again. Bradford were 14–2 up at half-time and 20–4 in front eight minutes after the break, but tries by Andy Hay and Marcus St Hilaire got us right back in it. Our second try made it 22–18 with seven minutes left. Henry Paul then kicked a penalty to give them a bit more breathing space, but we were pounding their line at the end, and if Jimmy Lowes hadn't been able to take Iestyn's bomb in the last seconds we might have snatched a draw. But Bradford held on to win 24–18.

It was the first time since the war that the Challenge Cup final had been staged away from Wembley and it's an occasion I will always remember, even though we lost. One of the sad parts of that afternoon was the fact that Kevin Sinfield was left out of the side. He had played in every game up until then, but Dean had decided he wanted more size on the bench to combat Bradford's big pack, so Jamie Mathiou got a place among the substitutes and Sinny had to watch from the stands. Personally, I thought Kevin should have got the nod. He was playing well and I thought he offered us something extra with his versatility. He was desperately upset when he heard the news, and, having been through a similar experience for the 1998 Grand Final, I knew how he felt. The worst thing you can do in a situation like that is take it out on the coach. You've got to take it on the chin. Dwell on it for as long as you need to, but then use it as a tool to motivate yourself and make sure it doesn't happen again. Sinny could have let it get to him, but he responded in the right way and came back stronger. It was always obvious he was going to be a special player and he has fulfilled that potential now. That would have happened anyway, but I think the experience of being left out at Murrayfield gave him something extra. Rugby league is a rollercoaster sport and you have to endure the bad times to appreciate the good ones.

After the final we began to get our league form together and built a thirteen-game winning run in the middle of the season, which was remarkable considering how we had started the year. The most memorable victory in that sequence was against Castleford Tigers at the Jungle on 31 May, when Ryan Sheridan got over for a try to level the scores with twenty seconds left and Iestyn kicked a wonderful touchline goal to win it.

We finished fourth in the table, which was disappointing but not too bad considering the circumstances. A win over Castleford in the play-offs was revenge for the previous year, but Bradford were too strong for us at Odsal and that was our season over.

The Bradford defeat was Adrian Morley's last game for the club, along with a few others like Daryl Powell and Paul Sterling. Moz was from a similar background to me. He lived in Salford, which is a tough area in Manchester, and his mum and dad were staunch Catholics. Like me he went to church as often as he could and he tried to make the best of his life, but he had a similar mentality, that he was fighting the world and everyone was against him. Moz is a great lad off the field, but a really fearsome competitor on it. He always plays the game with passion and pride and it was a pleasure to be in the same team as him. I would definitely rather have him on my side than against me. We used to say we had managed to fool the world between us, because when we were in the same team people didn't fancy tangling with us. Moz would admit he's not the best scuffler around, but people always thought he was because he had such a fearsome presence on the pitch.

Graham Murray was a big admirer of Moz, and when he started at Sydney Roosters one of his first priorities was to get Moz on board with him. Adrian eventually signed for them towards the end of 2000 on a three-year contract, which at the time made him the only Englishman playing top-flight rugby in Australia. He had a difficult start, with a few injuries and some on-field disciplinary problems, and when Graham departed it looked like he might come home. But he stuck at it and went on to earn a Grand Final winners' ring with the Roosters at the end of the 2002 season, which was a huge achievement and something only a handful of British players have done. He got to the final again the following year, and though he was on the losing side that time against Penrith, he had another outstanding game and was easily Roosters' man of the match. He also got their player of the season honour, which was a deserved accolade. Moz is keen to stay on Down Under, and he definitely made the right decision to test himself in Australia. I have nothing but admiration for the way he took the risk and came out on top.

Sometimes I wonder if I should have taken the same opportunity when it came along. I have always done OK playing against Aussies at club or international level and I think I've got a pretty good reputation over there. I lined up an off-season stint with South Sydney during my Wigan days, but a dislocated shoulder put paid to that. Then I had a chance to play for Newcastle Knights when Warren Ryan was coach. I spoke to Ryan and to a few of the Newcastle players, including Matty Johns. Ryan said he was keen to sign me; if I was interested they would hammer out a deal. I was desperate to go, but in the end I decided to stay put.

It was a tough decision, but I wasn't sure it would work

out financially, and with a young family it would have been a massive upheaval. I only wanted to go out there to prove myself for a season or two, but I would have needed to be there for ten years to make it worth my while. I was sure I would be able to hold my own in the National Rugby League, but it's a very cut-throat competition and if I ever fell out of favour I would be a long way from home or from anyone with any sympathy. In the NRL, if you lose your spot there are another five or six blokes queuing up to take over. I also knew that if I did go I would be taking with me a reputation as a Pommy hardman and I would be a target not only for the opposition but also for the judiciary. They have a points system over there for on-field indiscretions, and I think I would probably have spent more time sitting in the stands watching than I would have done out on the field. Generally over here I get the benefit of the doubt, but that would not have been the case in Australia. I don't regret not going, but I do regard it as a missed opportunity. It would have been good to play against some of the best players in the world and to prove to myself, and to them, that I could mix it with them.

It would have been nice for Moz to bow out of Leeds with a Super League Grand Final appearance in 2000, but that was never really on the cards considering what was going on behind the scenes at Headingley at the end of that season.

When Dean Lance arrived he obviously brought his own ideas with him and had his personal opinions on who he did and did not want in the team. One of the players he wasn't keen on was Paul Sterling. At thirty-five at the start of the campaign, Sterlo was the oldest player in Super League that year and he had been a big hit over the previous couple of seasons, scoring a hatful of tries. But Dean wanted to give some of the younger lads a chance, and he also felt Sterlo's attitude wasn't right, especially after he missed the pre-season trip because he wanted to attend a wedding. Dean thought Paul was an unpopular player and that by getting rid of him he would gain the respect of the rest of the team. Now, I'm a big believer in putting professionalism before personal feelings. Although Sterlo could be a bit abrupt and a bit opinionated, I didn't have a problem with him and I knew he was a decent player. I think Sterlo felt Iestyn, Daryl Powell and I had been trying to get him the sack, which couldn't have been further from the truth. Throughout my career I have had to play with lads I didn't like personally, but you've got to look at the big picture, and the team has to come first.

Dean made it clear from the outset that Sterlo was not in his plans, and that didn't go down too well with Paul, who felt it was personal. When Dean tried to get rid of him, Sterlo took the club to a tribunal, claiming he was being racially discriminated against because Dean had told him he would not be selected whatever his perform-ances in the reserves were like. The dispute rumbled on all through the 2000 season and the hearing was eventually held in the week leading up to the Bradford play-off game, which wasn't exactly ideal preparation for such a crucial tie. Sterlo won a partial victory and the club was ordered to pay him a settlement. The tribunal decided that Sterlo had been a victim of 'unconscious' racial discrimination and ruled that he had been victimized by club officials because they hadn't investigated his complaints more thor-oughly. Unsurprisingly, the whole business brought the Rhinos some very bad publicity. I don't for one minute think Dean Lance was a racist, and there are certainly no racists in the Leeds team, but unfortunately Dean got himself into a situation he didn't know how to get out of.

That definitely affected the way he coached, and it was one of the reasons why things didn't work out for him at Leeds. Although I thought Dean was a decent bloke, not everyone got on with him, and he didn't do himself any favours with the way he treated Damian McGrath. Damian was popular with the players and had been a big part of our success under Graham Murray, but Dean saw him as a reminder of the old regime and wouldn't use him properly, which was a waste of a good talent. Eventually Damian moved on to be assistant coach at London Broncos, and then he switched codes to join Leicester Rugby Union Club and the England set-up, alongside another ex-league man, Joe Lydon. That was devastating for Damian. He's from Bradford, but he was a Leeds man at heart and he didn't want to leave. I felt sorry for him because I believed he was harshly treated by Dean and other people who should have shown him a bit more loyalty.

14

THE GREATEST GAME

Dedicated to the game I love. Rugby league has shown me the world. Long may it prosper.

As far as I'm concerned, rugby league is the best team sport in the world and the best game. I'm a big sports fan in general and I have a lot of time for boxing in particular, but for pure entertainment value rugby league surpasses everything else. It is fast, tough and skilful, and that's what makes rugby league so good to watch. It is also one of our sport's big problems. It's not an easy game to play at any level, and that's probably why it will never match the popularity of soccer, which just about anyone can have a go at whether they are any good or not.

A lot of people seem to think rugby league is just bash and barge, but in fact it's a very difficult game to master. Not everybody can pick a ball up, pass both ways, tackle with both shoulders or step off both feet. It takes a lot of practice, dedication and skill to make it at even a decent amateur level. In soccer there are different strengths in different positions. In rugby union, if you're a tall lad you can be a lineout specialist; if you're fast you can be a try-scorer or a ball handler. You don't need to worry about other positions on the field. In rugby league, whatever position you play you have to be able to run, pass and tackle and you need a certain amount of skill and knowledge in every facet of the game.

I will be honest and say I am jealous of the popularity of football and rugby union, which I love to watch, because I really believe as far as the product on the field is concerned our game is streets ahead and we have got much more to offer.

What makes rugby union so strong is the fact that it is an international sport that toys with the club game, whereas we are a club game that toys with internationals. There are maybe half a dozen nations playing rugby league seriously, and three of them, Great Britain, Australia and New Zealand, can play it to a good, competitive standard. Sadly, from a British point of view, we have been a poor third for a long time, and that's something else that has held the code back.

Personally, I would love to see rugby league expand, both domestically and internationally. It would be fantastic if we could set down some roots in sports-mad countries like South Africa, Russia, Canada and the United States. If those countries can play and watch union, they can enjoy rugby league as well. The opening game of the 2003 union World Cup saw 80,000 people watch Australia play Argentina, so the audience is definitely there. In 2001 I went with Leeds on a pre-season training camp to Jacksonville, Florida, and we got a crowd of about 8,000 for a couple of exhibition games against Halifax and Huddersfield. The people who came to watch loved it, and efforts are being made to get the game going over there, but so far nothing much has come of it.

I think rugby league could be hugely popular in the States because its physical nature makes it a natural for the Americans. I really believe there could be a gap in the market. In the USA there's nothing much below the elite levels of gridiron, ice hockey, basketball and baseball. The lads who don't make it as American footballers play rugby union, and if they can't get to grips with union there's nowhere for them to go. Rugby league could step in and become their sport.

People have been making efforts to establish the game in South Africa for years without much success, but Russia is somewhere rugby league could really flourish. I have seen a few Russian teams and they aren't technically the best yet, but physically they have some big, tough lads, and if they get their skill levels up they could give the established nations a real run for their money. They have had some good crowds for student and exhibition games in Russia, and if people are willing to watch they are willing to play. Apparently the game is being played at youth level in Russia now and that's a positive sign for the future. It's hard to teach an old dog new tricks, but if you get players involved from an early age it gets into their blood.

The potential is definitely there for expansion all over the globe, but rugby league always seems to miss the opportunity. Being part of the Ireland team in the 2000 World Cup was hugely enjoyable, but not enough is being done to promote the sport over there. When we do play in Ireland the people who come along to watch love it, but it doesn't happen often enough. There doesn't seem to be enough people willing to take a risk and put the hard work in, which will pay off a few years down the line. Too many people in rugby league are motivated only by self-interest, or interested only in a quick fix. What rugby league needs is a visionary, someone with a bit of cash and a lot of clout who really believes in the game. Rupert Murdoch looked as though he was going to take on that mantle in the early 1990s, but it never really happened. If someone of that stature could get hold of rugby league and make people sit up and take notice, the game could really take off because, as I said, we have a great product.

When rugby union went professional a few years ago a lot of people were predicting the end for rugby league.

They thought if you could get paid for playing union, no one would be interested in playing league. They were wrong. There is room for both codes. What those people didn't realize is just how much rugby league means to people in the heartlands, areas like Yorkshire, Lancashire and Cumbria. I think the sport has a big future in its traditional hotbeds in this country, and in places like New South Wales and Queensland in Australia, parts of New Zealand, the south of France and Papua New Guinea. But until we work hard and put the time, effort and money into developing the game in places where we think it could take off, it will always lag behind union and soccer.

I would like to see a European Super League, which was the idea when we switched to playing in the summer in 1996. There was a team in Paris and talk of sides in places like Dublin, Rome and Barcelona, but Paris lasted only a couple of years and the others never got off the drawing board. It could still happen, and the introduction of Perpignon into Super League in 2006 is a good move, but it's going to take years of hard work. I would like to see the authorities being brave enough to take a big Super League game, such as Leeds against Bradford or Wigan against Saints, to somewhere like Rome or Dublin. If they announced it a year in advance that would give the fans time to save up and there would be ample opportunity to publicize the fixture and raise interest at home and abroad.

I think one of the biggest mistakes rugby league ever made was not pushing ahead with mergers of clubs, which were planned in the early 1990s. When Super League was first discussed Maurice Lindsay, the former Wigan chairman who was then head of the Rugby Football League, announced a massive shake-up that would have seen many of the traditional teams combined to form new super clubs. Castleford, Wakefield and Featherstone were all going to merge to become Calder, and Oldham and Salford would have been reinvented as Manchester. Other planned mergers were Cheshire (Warrington and Widnes), Cumbria (Barrow, Carlisle, Whitehaven and Workington), Humberside (Hull and Hull Kingston Rovers) and South Yorkshire (Doncaster and Sheffield Eagles). There was uproar about it and big protests from the fans, and the idea got dropped, which I think was a shame.

None of the clubs that would have been involved in mergers has made much headway since, on or off the pitch, and a lot of them are in financial trouble. Almost a decade on they are really struggling. Had the mergers taken place, by now people would have got used to the idea and all the old allegiances would have been forgotten. I'm sure that Calder, Manchester and the other merged clubs would now be playing to healthy crowds in purpose-built stadiums and really challenging the established big guns like Leeds, Bradford and Wigan. I love tradition, but our game has so much more to offer than parochial pride. The administrators got cold feet over the proposed mergers because of the fans' anger, but where are those supporters now? Virtually all the clubs that refused to merge are struggling to pull in the crowds. The nearly ten years since the merger row could have been put to really good use; instead they have been wasted.

One merger I would not be in favour of is between union and league to form a single code of rugby. It's an idea that gets mentioned quite often, but I really can't see it happening. I do understand the attraction of a truly nationwide game, with fixtures like Leeds Rhinos against Bath or Bradford Bulls against Saracens, but the problems are probably insurmountable. The codes can learn from each other, but they are literally very different ball games. What I want to see is the two games continuing separately with each fully appreciating what the other does.

Union has certainly improved as a game since the

barriers that prevented free movement between the two codes came down. Until union went openly professional anyone who fancied a go at league would be banned for life from the fifteen-a-side game. Now, if someone wants to try the other code he can, in the knowledge that he can always go back if it doesn't work out. As far as I'm concerned, that's a good thing.

When union first went professional they were miles behind league in terms of fitness and skill levels. The gap has closed now, and a lot of that is due to league players and coaches going across and passing on their knowledge and experience. In recent years all the rugby union Six Nations, apart from Italy, have brought league guys into their coaching structure. People like Phil Larder and Joe Lydon have become a key part of the England set-up, my old Leeds team-mate Alan Tait is involved with Scotland, there's a big league influence in the Welsh RFU through Clive Griffiths, and Mike Ford, an Oldham lad, went off to be Ireland's defensive coach.

Quite a few big-name league players have also been tempted to have a go at union, most of them on massive contracts. Jason Robinson has been a huge success with Sale and England, but a lot of the others have struggled, which just goes to show how different the codes are. Iestyn Harris is a natural rugby player, but at first even he had problems adjusting from league to union, and it was the same in reverse for Jonathan Davies when he switched codes, though the in-built talent they both have ensured they did make a success of it after time.

I honestly do not think the loss of the players who have gone to union has done league any permanent harm. It would be great if Jason Robinson was still playing the thirteen-a-side game, but we have managed without him and others have come through to take his place. The idea that people would go from league to union just for the money was rubbish. A lot of the league lads play it because they prefer it as a game. Cash doesn't really come into it.

At Leeds we share our training facilities with the Tykes union club, and that has given me a chance to appreciate what they do day in and day out. It was a bit of a shock, but I found out that they are decent blokes, not stuck-up, toffee-nosed snobs from public schools. They are just like me, keen to learn and willing to listen about training methods and different aspects of our code.

As I said, I do envy union's national profile. League gets virtually no recognition in places like the Midlands and in Wales, Ireland and Scotland. Our best players, people like Andy Farrell (though that may change now he has switched to union), Kevin Sinfield and Paul Sculthorpe, could walk down the street in Birmingham, Glasgow or Dublin and no one would recognize them, which is a huge shame. Jason Robinson became a household name when he started playing for England and the British Lions at rugby union, but he hadn't suddenly become a better rugby player overnight. Jason is a wonderful player, but he does nothing in union that he didn't do in rugby league. He had been terrifying defences and making monkeys out of big blokes years before anyone in the national media really started to take notice. We have plenty of players in league who could be as good as Jason, but they don't get any recognition.

Rugby league desperately needs better coverage on television and in the national newspapers, so that our superstars start to get the credit they deserve. When was the last time you saw a rugby league player on television, other than during a game? Rugby league is full of characters and they deserve to be promoted. Things need to be better for the young kids coming through into the sport. I have a reasonably high profile in Yorkshire and Lancashire, but I'm probably better known in Newcastle, New South Wales, than I am in Newcastle, Tyne and Wear. I have had to work hard to build my profile and to get myself noticed. No one has helped me along the way, but I hope that the next player who comes along who's a little different or a bit of a character will have people queuing up to promote him and to give him the profile – and the money – he deserves. Rugby league is a rough, tough game. You take a lot of punishment over a career and the top players deserve every penny they earn, but that will never be a fortune in the vast majority of cases.

I'm sure rugby league would expand if it got the media coverage it really deserves, but on the other hand, if we had a team in every big city in the country the sport would be national news, so it's a chicken and egg situation. In Australia, especially Sydney where rugby league is the undisputed number one sport, the TV and newspapers are full of it and the coverage is just like soccer gets over here.

The game has changed plenty since I first started playing in the early 1990s, and probably the biggest difference, at the top level at least, is full-time professionalism. Wigan began the trend during their glory years, Leeds were the second top club to go fully professional, and now all the Super League clubs are full time. Until Wigan took the plunge all players were semi-professional, working during the day and training at night. That's certainly how I started, and though it was really tough at the time, it was probably the best thing that could ever have happened to me. Having started out as a joiner, I know that there is more to life than rugby, and it has been motivational for me. I didn't want to go back to the building sites where I came from, with all the stress that involved, the long, hard hours, and the worry over whether there will be work available. That's a tough lifestyle and one I never particularly enjoyed. I love the way of life being a professional rugby league player has given me and that's what has made me the person I am today.

Since the mid-1990s things have begun to change. Now kids are being picked up by clubs as eleven- or twelve-year-olds, going straight from school into apprenticeship schemes and then on into full-time rugby. Rugby league has been the only job most of the youngsters coming through now have ever known, and I think they are missing out. They are definitely better rugby players for it, but they don't know what life is like in the real world and it will be a big shock to them when they have to find out at the end of their playing careers, which in professional sport are relatively brief. However, I did pick up some bad habits during my days on the building sites that the modern youngsters don't need to worry about. When you are in a 'proper job' it's often a case of going to work, getting on with whatever it is you are doing and then going home at the end of it. You don't need to spend your free time being around your work mates and putting effort into building up a relationship with them. Full-time sport is very much about the unit and about teamwork, and you have to put a big effort into making sure everyone gets along. If I didn't like a bloke on the building site I would tell him and then make sure I stayed away from him. In a team environment you have to put up with people you don't like and it's important to make an effort to appreciate them for what they can bring to the party, rather than letting personal feelings take over.

I think rugby league is a much better game now than when I first started playing, and no doubt it will be better again in five or ten years' time. For a start the sport is a lot faster than it was when I began my career, and the main reason for that is the switch from winter to summer in 1996. When I was just starting out at Oldham the chairman, Jim Quinn, was a big advocate of summer rugby and I thought he was living in cloud-cuckoo-land. When Super League started in 1996 the season was switched from August–May to February–October and it has transformed the game, for the better.

The first summer season was a bit of a torment because we had all basically been playing non-stop rugby for two years, but everyone got a break at the end of 1996 and from Super League II onwards the standard has just got faster and better every year. In the winter era rugby league struggled to compete with soccer or union, but moving to summer opened up a whole new market, and I think it has been an unqualified success. If you don't believe me you only have to go along and watch Bradford Bulls playing at Odsal. Odsal is absolutely unique. The ground is an old council tip and you go in at street level and drop down to the pitch in the valley way below. In winter Odsal had its own climate, and there were times when you would be standing under one set of posts and you couldn't see the halfway line because of thick fog. It really was a miserable place to watch or play rugby and Bradford never seemed to be able to pull in the crowds because of that. But in summer, with all the pre-match entertainment the Bulls put on, it has been completely transformed and has gone from literally a dump to a cauldron of rugby league, a home fortress that has played a huge part in Bradford's success in Super League.

I think even the staunch traditionalists would have to admit that rugby league is a much better product now it's a top-of-the-ground sport. Instead of all the rolling around in the mud you used to get in the winter era, we are a fast-flowing, speed-orientated power game totally suited to lush pitches and dry, hard conditions. The skill factor has definitely come on 100 per cent since we started playing in the summer. I have always been a big fan of the Aussie game, and in the early 1990s I was in awe of the skills they had and baffled by the fact that I couldn't do the same, until we turned to summer rugby. The ball sticks now and you don't have to cling onto it with both hands. Now you can hold it in the palm of one hand and offer it to your support. The new offloading game summer rugby encourages has made the sport quicker and more exciting to watch.

Something else I believe has improved the game over the last few years is the use of technology. The video referee, who operates at all televised games, has been a great innovation and one I am all in favour of. If a match is being televised and someone scores a dubious try, the man in the middle doesn't have to guess, he can hand the decision on to the video referee. There has been plenty of controversy about video referees over the years and during the course of a season decisions go for you and against you, but far more often than not the video referee gets it right. It's a system I would never like to see scrapped. In fact, I would like to see it expanded so that there's a video referee at every game, not just the ones being broadcast live on Sky Sports or the BBC. Sports like soccer are still arguing over whether or not to use technology, but in rugby league it has only made the game better.

Of course fans and players do sometimes get frustrated over the amount of time it can take a video referee to come up with a decision. When we played Bradford at Odsal in 2003, Steve Cross took four minutes to decide whether or not Lesley Vainikolo had scored a try from a kick when he and Mark Calderwood seemed to have got the ball down at exactly the same time. But there was no way the referee would have been able to make an accurate decision in real time; the half a dozen slow-motion replays from three or four different angles were crucial. I don't mind if the video referee takes an hour to make a decision, as long as he gets it right in the end. In 1996 a video referee decision virtually decided the Super League title. Saints were running neck and neck with Wigan at the top of the table, but they almost came unstuck in a game at London Broncos. In the end they got a crucial victory thanks to an Apollo Perelini try, which was awarded by the video referee. The match ref would not have given it because he was unsighted, but various camera angles proved that Perelini had got the ball down. Saints went on to win the game and the Super League crown.

Those were the days when the team that finished top of the table was crowned champions. Since 1998 we have had a Grand Finals series to decide the championship, and that has been another huge success. The title used to get decided in a championship final until the 1970s, when two divisions came in and rugby league began to use a first-past-the-post system. What happened under the old format was the league leaders won the title and then the top eight clubs played off for the Premiership crown. I always thought that was a bit of an anticlimax. It came just a few weeks after the Challenge Cup final, and that was always regarded as the big finale to the season. Now your most important game of the season is your last one. The Grand Final series means that even if one team is running away at the top of the table, most other sides still have something to play for. Anyone who finishes in the top six has a chance of going on to win the Grand Final and being crowned champions, but the higher up the table you finish, the better the odds. The league leaders need to win only one play-off to get to the Grand Final and they are guaranteed home advantage, whereas if you finish sixth you will be away to teams who finished higher up the table in every round.

The Grand Final system was accepted very quickly, and the title decider at Old Trafford is now the biggest day in the British rugby league calendar.

15

INTERNATIONAL BREAKDOWN

The pinnacle of any sportsman's career is to
represent his country. It has been an honour for me.
Thanks to Ellery Hanley, who gave me the
strength and belief to rise to my finest hour for
Great Britain, and to everyone involved with
Ireland's World Cup campaign – a great lesson,
and a chance to spread the gospel.

Right from my amateur days I have always regarded playing for my country as the biggest honour I can receive in
the game, but it's fair to say that my international career
has had its ups and downs. My Test debut in 1994 was
definitely an up, even though we lost the series, but I had
to endure five years of frustration before I got back on to
the international stage, and once I was there it was not a
happy experience.

My Great Britain comeback began in the 1999 Tri-
Nations series, which saw Great Britain fly Down Under
to take on Australia and New Zealand. That was a sort of
replacement for the old-style Ashes tours, which were a
victim of the split that happened in the game in Australia
when Super League came along, something which is a great
pity in my opinion. Andy Goodway was the Great Britain
coach at the time so I knew I had a good chance of being
called up, but I was still pleased and relieved when I heard

I had been selected. I thought the way Goodway played the game, used his forwards and motivated his players would benefit me.

I was happy with my form for the Rhinos at the time, but this was a good opportunity to show what I could do on an even bigger stage. In addition, going overseas with Great Britain was a huge thing for me because it meant I was finally a British Lion, which is an honour you only get if you have gone on tour. Although Leeds had finished the 1999 season disappointingly we were well represented on the plane Down Under, with myself, Francis Cummins, Iestyn Harris, Andy Hay, Adrian Morley, Keith Senior (who had just joined us from Sheffield) and Ryan Sheridan all selected.

We flew out cattle class, but we stayed in a nice hotel, trained very hard and were confident of beating Australia and New Zealand, qualifying for the final and winning that as well. We were due to play one warm-up match against an Australian country side called the Burleigh Bears, followed by Tests against Australia at Brisbane's Lang Park – or Suncorp Stadium as it has been renamed – and the Kiwis at Auckland's Ericsson Stadium. Then, we hoped, we would feature in the final, which was also being played in Auckland.

But things started to go wrong right from the practice game. We should have absolutely hammered the Bears, but we ended up scraping home 10–6 after trailing 6–4 with twenty minutes left. Coming off the field at the end we couldn't understand how it had been so close, because we were sure we hadn't been playing that badly. We discovered the answer when we watched the tape. Every time one of our lads made a break, the Bears would manage to find a scramble defender to cut us down. It was almost like they had extra men, and the reason for that was that they did. Whenever there was a break they were making unauthorized interchanges; our coach driver said at one stage he had actually counted fifteen Burleigh players on the pitch!

The next game we played was in the tournament proper against Australia, who had been battered and beaten 24–22 by New Zealand in their first match. We had prepared well and we really thought we would beat them, but the game was a minor disaster. We got hammered, I picked up an injury early on and it was not a happy experience. The crowd was less than 13,000, so there wasn't much of an atmosphere, and we never clicked into gear, though Moz had a storming game. Encouragingly, we were still in it at half-time. We were probably the better team for the first forty, but Denis Betts was harshly sin-binned and they ran in two tries while we were down to twelve men. Even so, Iestyn scored a try just before the hooter, which he also converted, so we were only 10–6 down. But the second half was one-way traffic. They added five more tries and we never looked like getting over their line. It finished 42–6, which was Great Britain's heaviest defeat in Australia and the second worst ever. An unwanted piece of history.

New Zealand were next up, and they too wiped the floor with us. The final score was 26–4, which was Great Britain's worst ever defeat by the Kiwis. As a front rower, I can't remember ever playing a game like it. Every time I caught the ball there would be three tacklers straight on me and I got absolutely smashed. The Kiwis are a very enthusiastic team and when they are on top against you they will certainly let you know, which is what happened that day.

Like it or not, sledging is part of the game, but I don't enjoy being patronized and I didn't appreciate some of the remarks being made by the Kiwis, and in particular by Henry Paul. I tend to remember things like that, and the chickens came home to roost when we played Bradford Bulls at Murrayfield in the Challenge Cup final the following year. Henry Paul flashed across the back of the ruck and I hit him quite high – and was not very remorseful afterwards. The reason was that Kiwi game in the Tri-Nations. Henry stands three or four places wide of the ruck where not much happens, and he had been making plenty of noise and making me feel really small. I made a promise to myself at the time that I would pay him back, which is what happened in Edinburgh. I apologized to him after the game, but I also told him why I had done it and warned him not to do that sort of thing again. Henry had not been badly hurt and he was all right about it afterwards, and so was the referee, Steve Presley. He asked me after the game what had been going on. Referees are human, after all. They know that not everything that happens is spur of the moment, that sometimes there's a bit of payback involved.

That day in New Zealand was uncharacteristic of Henry, who is a fantastic player, a good bloke and someone I have got a lot of time for. I had just broken into the first team at Wigan when Henry joined us from Wakefield. We were on the bench together for his debut, and as the old stager – I had played all of two or three senior games for the club at the time – I thought I had better give him some advice. As we were waiting to go on, I told Henry, 'This is a bit different to Wakefield and it will take you a bit of time to adjust, so take it nice and steady and make sure you ease yourself into the game.' Henry, playing at full-back, must have taken my words to heart because the first time he got the ball he chipped over the defensive line, regathered, made a twenty-metre break, drew the opposing full-back and then shipped out a perfect pass for Martin Offiah to score a wonderful try. So much for easing himself into the game!

There weren't many players who came back from that 1999 tour with their reputations enhanced. Moz and Keiron Cunningham were two who did, and that was one of the reasons why Adrian ended up playing in Australia for Sydney City Roosters. Our two defeats meant New Zealand faced Australia in the final, but there was still more humiliation to come when we were told we would be playing New Zealand Maori in a curtain-raiser to the main game.

That didn't go down too well with the players or coaching staff, but I put my hand up and said I would play. We didn't want to be part of the warm-up for the big show, especially after two spankings on the back of a very long domestic season, but an international is an international, plus I didn't want to end the season with a game like the one we had endured against New Zealand. Goodway felt it was a bit degrading, but he picked a strong team and we won 22–12, so the tour was not a complete fiasco, but it was a big disappointment.

Despite the results I enjoyed the experience, and it was good to spend time with players from different clubs and to learn a few new things off them. We had a pretty good squad and there was a definite structure in place, but things just didn't work out for us. Nothing went our way and we ended up playing the games as a group of individuals rather than as a team. Most international sides are made up of players from a handful of clubs, in our case Leeds, Wigan, Bradford and Saints, and when things start to go wrong you tend to drift back to what you know, so we were playing like four or five different groups instead of one unit.

We got a lot of criticism from the media both Down Under and back home. A lot of it was justified, but some of what was written and said was over the top. No one went on that tour for a holiday. We prepared properly and we gave our best in every game, but we just weren't good enough when it mattered.

The next international rugby on the agenda was the 2000 World Cup. That was meant to be an opportunity to showcase rugby league as a major international sport, but sadly it turned into an embarrassing fiasco.

After a traumatic year with Leeds it was a relief to switch off from club rugby and join Ireland for their first World Cup campaign, but though we did well as a team the tournament as a whole left rugby league with egg on its face. The competition was probably the biggest event rugby league has ever staged, but unfortunately it proved to be a huge flop. There were sixteen teams taking part, but the tournament never caught the public imagination, and crowds for most of the matches were pitiful. The weather didn't help. That year turned out to be probably the wettest autumn on record: it never stopped raining right from the very first match through to the final. The 1995 World Cup had been staged mainly in the north of England, where they were more or less guaranteed to get decent crowds, and had been a massive, unexpected success. This time the organizers decided to be a bit more adventurous and took matches all over the UK.

At first I thought it was great that places like Gloucester, Wrexham, Llanelli, Glasgow, Dublin, Belfast, Reading and Edinburgh would get a chance to see top-class rugby league in action. It seemed like a golden opportunity to expand the code, and I thought it was fantastic that they were trying to develop the sport in new areas, but they didn't invest any time or money in marketing or promoting the games. When we played Samoa in Belfast in our first fixture on 28 October, the only people who knew about it were those staying in the same hotel as us and the occasional person who had found out by accident. For some reason, they chose Ireland against Samoa as the opening game of the entire tournament, which was a pretty low-key way to start. England played Australia at Twickenham, the first rugby league game ever staged at rugby union's head-quarters, in an evening kick-off later that day.

It should have been a tremendous tournament. There were some fantastic teams and a lot of the games were high-quality, but it just never took off. It's heartbreaking for a genuine rugby league fan to see so many empty seats. I have played for Great Britain in front of 58,000 at Wembley so I know people will pay to watch good rugby league if it is marketed properly, but some games attracted crowds of only a couple of thousand, which was embarrassing for such a prestigious tournament.

Despite all that, being involved with the Ireland squad was a tremendous experience. I have always been very proud of my Irish roots and I was totally committed to the cause, even though I had already played one game for England back in 1996 before the Ireland team was formed. I made the decision to opt for Ireland in 1997, and it's something I have never regretted. I saw it as a chance to spread the gospel, because I felt that with the right team and the right people involved we could do something positive for the game. The World Cup organizers had decided to split Great Britain into England, Ireland, Wales and Scotland for the purposes of the tournament, so I could play for Ireland without having to worry about jeopardizing my future Test prospects with GB.

The people I have met in Ireland are genuinely enthusiastic about rugby league. I bumped into some of the Ireland rugby union squad at a hotel after one of the World Cup games and they had loved it. They couldn't understand why we weren't a bigger game when we had so much to offer.

Turning out in the World Cup with Ireland was special because it gave me a chance to play alongside Terry O'Connor, which is something I always enjoy, as well as great players like Kevin Campion, Luke Ricketson, Danny Williams, Tommy Martyn, Steve Prescott and a lot of others. But more than that, it was just a great time. There was a terrific atmosphere in the squad, which really did feel like a close-knit family. One of the best social nights I have ever had was in a back-street pub in Belfast when our sponsors, WKD, laid on a bit of a party for us. We drank Guinness and sang songs literally all night, and that was one of the things that brought us together. Part of our build-up to the World Cup was spent in a training camp at La Manga, in Spain. The main aim was to develop an understanding on the pitch, but having a few drinks together and enjoying each other's company is a big part of rugby. You have to have that camaraderie, because you need to know you can rely on the guy next to you when the going gets tough out on the field.

While we were in La Manga we trained really hard, but we had a good time away from the practice ground as well, and that inevitably led to trouble. Before the World Cup began we decided to adopt 'Ireland's Call', a rugby union anthem, as our official song, mainly because we wanted to avoid any political problems. We were just there to play rugby. There were Catholics and Protestants in the team, but that wasn't an issue for us; we simply wanted to do a good job and to represent the game and our families. Whenever we'd had a few beers we would always end up singing 'Ireland's Call', and that's why we sang it with so much passion at the games, because it took us back to the social side of things before the actual tournament began.

After we had been in La Manga for about four days a few of the lads went off to play golf as a way of relaxing after some very intensive training. They arranged to meet the rest of us later for a team meal. We all arrived at the restaurant as planned, but the golfers were late. They eventually rolled in an hour after the appointed time, smiling, laughing and falling over their own feet but still trying to be as inconspicuous as they could, which was not very. Brian Carney, the only player in the squad born and bred in Ireland, came to sit with us and he explained that the golf course had been fully booked, so they had spent the entire afternoon in the bar. By the time they got back they were absolutely steaming. The coaches, Steve O'Neill and Andy Kelly, were against anyone having more than a couple of beers because we were there to do a job, so they obviously weren't going to be best pleased when they found out.

The lads might have got away with it if they had managed to keep quiet, but after a few minutes one of them started singing 'Ireland's Call' and that set the rest of them off. Even Steve and the rest of the management joined in. They thought it was fantastic that the players were so proud of the team they wanted to sing about it in a packed public restaurant. They didn't realize it was the beer talking.

Everyone went out for a few drinks that evening and Tez O'Connor and I promised the management we would make sure everyone behaved themselves. When we reported for training at seven o'clock the next morning Steve O'Neill turned up with a face like thunder. It turned out that the lads who had been on the beers all afternoon had been a bit rowdy in the hotel reception and had upset some of the guests. This all came a couple of months after a Premiership soccer team had made front-page headlines for some trouble they had caused in the resort. The Ireland management were desperate to avoid similar bad publicity and they made us go and apologize to the hotel manager. We discovered that things had got completely out of hand. There had been a live band on in the hotel bar and when they had put their instruments down to go and have a break some of the Irish lads had invaded the stage and started a performance of their own. One of the squad was playing the piano with his fingers and toes and the rest of them were out in reception swimming in the fountain!

We calmed the manager down and fortunately it stayed out of the newspapers, but it didn't take Steve, or Squarie as we called him, long to get his revenge. He flogged us at training that morning and again in the afternoon, then ordered us down to an early session at seven a.m. the following day. We all turned up on time, but there was no sign of the coaching staff. Half past seven came, then eight a.m., and eventually I was delegated to go to Squarie's room and find out what was happening. When I got up there I found the team management enjoying a room-service breakfast and pissing themselves laughing at us. Squarie told me, 'Go and get your breakfast, we'll train at nine.'

The World Cup itself was a tremendous experience. We spent the first week in Belfast before moving on to Dublin, and it was an eye-opener. One night I was in my hotel room chatting with Ryan Sheridan, watching a film and listening to what we thought were fireworks going off outside. The next morning we saw on the TV news that there had been a mini-riot quite close to where we were staying. The Belfast people really looked after us, though, and it was a great experience to look round a city most of us thought we would never get a chance to visit. We had a drive down the Garvaghy Road to look at the murals on the walls. We asked the guy who was showing us around if they ever got vandalized. 'Nobody ever touches them,' he replied. 'They are as sacred as gravestones. If anyone did touch them they wouldn't be walking around for long afterwards.' We weren't too keen to get out of the bus and have a look. We were happy enough going along in third gear at twenty miles an hour, taking it all in.

We beat Samoa, who were captained by Willie Poching, in our first game at Windsor Park and I got the man of the match award, which was a huge honour. I should have grabbed the opening try of the World Cup when I made a bit of a burst, used some footwork and offloaded to Chris Joynt, who scored. When I watched the tape later I realized I had been almost on the line when I passed, so all I would have had to do was reach out and put the ball down.

The next tie was against Scotland on a Wednesday night in Dublin, with only 1,782 spectators turning up at Tolka Park. That was an ordinary sort of game. The one I really enjoyed was against the New Zealand Maori the following Saturday.

I always enjoy playing against Kiwis because they are big, strong opponents with plenty of skill, and I love the haka they do before every game. All South Pacific teams have their own war dance, but the New Zealand Maori haka was spectacular, with them running from their own goal line to confront the opposition face to face on halfway. The game was really tough and physical and I had a good old tussle with the Maori's big forwards. They had some great players in their team, people like Tawera Nikau, Tyran Smith, Paul Rauhihi and Gene Ngamu, so it was a real feather in our cap to beat them.

We'd gone into that game knowing that if we won we would go through to face England at Headingley in the quarter-finals. That was the big incentive from the start, especially for the Leeds lads – me, Ryan Sheridan, David Barnhill and Jamie Mathiou. The quarter-final on 11 November drew a big crowd for once and was broadcast live on BBC's *Grandstand*. We gave England all the trouble they could handle before losing out 26–16. I thoroughly enjoyed playing against my Leeds team-mates Chev Walker, Keith Senior and Moz, even though Chev and Keith both scored, but it was a bit strange going into the away changing room for the first time in six or seven years.

Losing in the last eight was a shame, but we had done well to get that far, and from an Ireland point of view it had been a worthwhile exercise, certainly on the field.

England went on to lose heavily to New Zealand in one semi-final, while Australia beat Wales in the other. Iestyn was one of the stars of the Welsh team, and for a while it looked like they might create the biggest shock in rugby league history. Australia led early on, but Wales turned things around to go 22–14 up early in the second half before the Aussies finally got going to run out comfortable winners. New Zealand had been in good form all the way through the tournament and a lot of people thought they would win the final, but Australia cruised in 40–12 in front of a decent-sized crowd at Old Trafford.

At least that was a positive end to a disappointing tournament. It took rugby league a long time to recover from the World Cup, which, with the poor marketing and sparse crowds, made the game a bit of a laughing stock. But personally I would not have missed the experience. Being part of the Ireland squad was something I will always treasure, and I think it helped make me a better player. We didn't get the coverage or support we had hoped for, but I have met a lot of Irish people who have said what a great boost it was and how nice it was to see rugby league being promoted in Ireland. I don't think there were many negatives to come out of our involvement in the tournament. All the mistakes that were made were down to the commercial and marketing side rather than the players, who took it very seriously and played with a lot of pride.

To put it all into perspective, people think rugby league is a highly paid job, that the players must earn a fortune at international level. Believe it or not, my wage packet for the entire tournament was £30.10! We got £10 a day meal expenses, but we had to pay for things like our family's tickets and I was heavily out of pocket after another of my little spats with Bradford Bulls' Stuart Fielden who is one of my biggest rivals in Super League. He was propping against me for England in the quarter-final and I caught him with a bit of a high tackle, which landed me on report. I was found guilty by the World Cup disciplinary committee and suspended for a game, as well as fined £500. I was the only player banned during the World Cup, which was another claim to fame I could have done without.

The following year, Australia came over to play three Tests against Great Britain. It was their first tour of any sort since 1997 and the first time the full Aussie team had been here since my international debut back in 1994. They were originally due to play three Tests, plus club games against the top sides, including Leeds. But all that fell by the wayside after the 11 September terrorist attacks in New York. Unsurprisingly, a lot of people weren't keen on air travel at the time and there was a fear of more attacks in Europe and Britain. The Aussie players had a series of meetings about it. Originally the players voted in favour of coming, but then the vote was split evenly and eventually they said they weren't going to come over. One of their top players, Robbie Kearns, said they didn't want to come to Great Britain because they thought English landmarks like the Eiffel Tower might be a terrorist target! The British Rugby League, however, were banking on the tour to recoup some of the cash they had lost because of the previous year's World Cup; they were looking at a £2 million loss if it was called off. After a lot of negotiations the Aussies announced they would be coming after all, but the games against the club sides were called off.

I was delighted, because I couldn't wait for another crack at them after the disappointments of 1994 and 1999, and, as usual, I really thought we could win the Ashes back. The British game generally suffers from a lack of respect, particularly from the Australians. My career goal at first was to get the respect of people around me and then people I played with and against, but ultimately, when you get to the top you want to be respected by Australians and to have them fear you. That was always a goal of mine, and whenever I have played against Australia I have thrived on my desire to make them sit up and take notice. People often ask me why the Aussies are so much better than us. My reply is they aren't, but they have the belief we sadly lack.

As Leeds' player of the year in 2001 I knew I would be going into the Test series in good form, so it was a golden opportunity to really stake my claim as one of the top front rowers in either hemisphere.

The 2001 series was the first time Great Britain had been coached by an Aussie, David Waite, who had come over from St George after a successful spell at Newcastle Knights. He had played for Australia a number of times and had toured Britain with the Kangaroos so he was someone who deserved respect. My first meeting with David was very positive, and I was impressed with his tremendous knowledge of the game. There was a lot of criticism over the fact that an Aussie was coaching the British team, but I was more concerned about judging him on his ability and desire than his accent, and I think most of the other players felt the same.

Straight away I was bowled over by how much ambition he had and how much he wanted to bring the British game forward. It was a pleasure to work under him and I learned a lot off him technically, though I sometimes struggled with some of his man-management methods. I was never quite sure whether he was pleased with me or what he expected from me. David had Brian Noble, the Bradford Bulls coach, and Castleford Tigers boss Graham Steadman working alongside him, and that made for a nice blend in the GB set-up.

We prepared well with a very tough week-long training camp in Spain. We did technical training in the afternoons, but every morning was devoted to physical contact stuff.

For the whole week all Stuart Fielden and I did was continue where we had left off in the Super League season. Everyone else was doing the normal sort of contact work, but we spent the week bashing each other.

Our warm-up for the Ashes series was a game against France in Agen, and before that Brian Noble called a forwards meeting to have a chat about a few things. Stuart and I were both there and Brian made a point of telling everyone at the meeting, 'I don't want you to take your personal differences with each other out on to the pitch. You are wearing the same colour shirt now and you have got to have respect for each other.' There were eight or nine other forwards in the room, but everyone knew just what Nobby was driving at. I put my hand up straight away and said, 'There's nobody in this room I don't want to play with and nobody I won't back to the hilt in any kind of situation, whether that's a physical confrontation or any-thing else.' I think that broke a bit of ice, and everyone else followed by saying that they were fully committed to the side and anything that had happened in the past would be forgotten while we were all together with GB.

The practice game against France was played just a week after the Aussies announced their tour was back on, and it went pretty well. We were 24–0 up after just nine minutes and went on to win 42–12, which was pleasing, but we knew Australia would be much, much tougher.

The first Test was at the McAlpine Stadium in Hudders-field on 11 November and I was named in the starting line-up alongside Keith Senior, Kevin Sinfield and my mate Terry O'Connor. It was my first Test on home soil since the decider against Australia seven years earlier, and Andy Farrell, Gary Connolly, Chris Joynt and I were the only survivors from that series. Just like my GB debut, we got off to a great start with a shock win. The togetherness we had developed in France and during our preparations really stood us in good stead, and I think the Aussies, who had only just arrived and hadn't played a warm-up game in this country, were shocked at how well we played. We beat them on the scoreboard, 20–12, and we beat them up too. I really enjoyed it, and I was pleased with the way I performed, though I would have liked a bit more game time. Paul Sculthorpe had a fantastic match for us, scoring a couple of tries, including the winner four minutes from the end, and landing two drop goals, but the whole team went really well and we were on top right from the start, with Jamie Peacock getting the opening try after less than two minutes. We were 12–0 up at half-time after Scully got our second try of the game and we held on in the second half, though they hit back with a couple of tries around the hour mark to make it a tense final quarter.

One of the incidents from that match that sticks in my mind involved Terry O'Connor and the Australian prop Jason Stevens. The game hadn't been going long when Tez put a big hit on Stevens, but when the Aussie got up to play the ball he caught the side of Tez's face with his boot, causing quite a nasty injury. He wasn't sent off, though he got a ban at a later disciplinary hearing, but the sight of blood gushing out of Tez's face really fired us up. From then on I had plenty of fury to spur me on, and the next time I tackled Stevens I jarred the ball loose to put us back on the attack, which was very satisfying.

David Waite used me in fairly short bursts, but whenever I was on the field I was determined to make an impact and let people know I was out there. After the game I was happy to think I had done that. It wasn't as special as my first game against Australia, but I was with people I cared about and had a lot of respect for and it was a different situation to 1994. I was just happy to be out there on the pitch.

That was Australia's first defeat in thirteen games, and

it worried them. From our point of view it restored a lot of pride after the Tri-Nations and World Cup disappointments, and I felt I had made a point. I always knew I was a quality player and that I could match it with anybody. I knew that if I was playing in the right team under the right circumstances I would make people sit up and take notice.

Unfortunately, Australians don't give you any credit if you are playing in Super League. Adrian Morley is one of the best players I have ever played with, but the Aussies didn't rate him at all until he went over there and showed what he could do in their own back yard. In a way, that sort of attitude has helped us, and it's maybe one of the reasons why we seem to do well in the first match of a series. We are always fired up for it when the Aussies are probably expecting us just to roll over. They underestimate us, and they have to see us face to face before they realize we are good players and they discover they are going to have to play at their best to beat us. Great Britain do have a habit of winning the first Test, and I have heard some people suggest that it's some sort of fiddle to increase interest and sell tickets for the other two games. What a load of rubbish! That is an insult to all the Great Britain players who have been involved in some great Test wins over the years, as well as to the Aussies. Rugby league is not the sort of sport you can fix. No game I have ever played in has been arranged. Nobody can ever take the Wembley first Test away from me – and I would be happy to speak with anyone who wants to try. All this talk of letting GB win the first game diminishes our victories, all of which have come on the back of a lot of blood, sweat and hard work. People who say it's a con are trying to steal from me something I have worked hard for and I really deserve. It makes me angry, and I don't understand why people think like that.

Anyway, going into the second Test, to be played at

Bolton six days after the opener, we were in a fairly familiar position, just a win away from the Ashes, but I think psychologically we talked ourselves into a defeat. We'd had meetings before the first Test and talked about what it takes to win a three-game series. We knew winning one game wasn't a problem, but what we could never seem to do was get the other victory that would wrap up the series. Australia came out a much better side at Bolton and they played us off the park. Obviously after we had outplayed them at Huddersfield we thought we were in with a great chance, and so did the fans, but we were never in the contest. They were 24–0 up at half-time and 40–0 ahead before we scored a couple of late tries, which wasn't much consolation.

That set up a decider at Wigan on 24 November, at the end of what was a traumatic few days for the Australians. Their coach Chris Anderson was ill in the lead-up to the game and he actually suffered a heart attack in the stand in the first half and had to be rushed off to hospital, though fortunately he made a full recovery. Paul Fletcher, who works at Leeds Rhinos, was acting as a liaison man for the Aussies and he told me all about it later. We scored first and were still well in the contest at half-time, when they were only 12–6 ahead. Apparently their skipper Brad Fittler gave them a rousing speech during the break. He said it was a real Test match and we were giving it to them, and if they didn't step up a gear they could be about to lose the Ashes. The last thing he said before they went back out was, 'Let's win it for Chris.' It worked, because they came out and got on top of us in the second half. We never gave in, but they pulled away and finished 28–8 winners to retain the Ashes. At least we had made a game of it, and personally, I went down fighting – literally.

After the second Test David Waite had held a video session during which he really got stuck into the forwards. He told us we hadn't muscled up and basically we had let

THE try. Scoring the
crucial touchdown against
London Broncos in the
1999 Challenge Cup final
at Wembley.

Sheer delight.
Celebrating with
Lee Jackson.

The proudest moment
of my career, I celebrate
as Rhinos skipper Iestyn
Harris lifts the Cup.

On top of the world, with my man of the match trophy, following the opening game of the 2000 World Cup for Ireland against Samoa.

Ireland calling. Chris Joynt (far right) and I lead the singing after our win over New Zealand Maori in the 2000 World Cup.

The red rose blooms. Lifting the Origin Trophy after Lancashire's series win in 2001. I am wearing Nick Fozzard's Yorkshire top after swapping shirts at the end of the game.

The hard stare.
I try to psyche-out
the Aussies during
the national anthems
before the first
Ashes Test at
Huddersfield
in 2001.

Cheeky. I show a
little bit more leg
than usual in the
same match.

Collision course.
I come up against
Bradford Bulls' giant prop
Paul Anderson.

Two Big Macs.
I take on Bradford Bulls'
Brian McDermott.

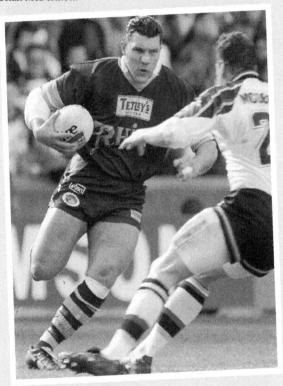

In the thick of it.
A little disagreement with
Bradford's Stuart Fielden
(No. 29) led to yet another
red card.

A familiar sight.
The red mist descends,
the red card comes out
and I'm off for another
early bath.

Rhinos teammate
Keith Senior and I show off
the Baskerville Trophy,
after Great Britain's win
over New Zealand in the
third Test at Wigan in 2002.

Made in Oldham.
Leeds teammate
Kevin Sinfield and I
celebrate another victory
for Lancashire over the
old enemy Yorkshire.

Flagging. Rhinos teammate
Willie Poching and I come
to terms with defeat in
the 2003 Challenge Cup
final at Cardiff.

Jenny with (left to right) Jessica, Billy and Sophie.

Leeds Rhinos players let our hair down at a benefit night for Francis Cummins. Left to right: Richard Mathers, me, Dave Furner, Chev Walker, Kevin Sinfield, Wayne McDonald, and Gary Connolly.

Thanks. The fans really do mean a lot to me. Here I am signing autographs on a lap of honour following our final Super League game in 2003.

The best feeling. Along with Kevin Sinfield, I get my hands on the big prize at long last, moments after our Super League Grand Final victory over Bradford Bulls at Old Trafford, October 2004.

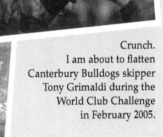

Crunch. I am about to flatten Canterbury Bulldogs skipper Tony Grimaldi during the World Club Challenge in February 2005.

Bubbling up. The champagne flows as we celebrate our World Club Challenge triumph on the pitch at Elland Road.

them do to us what we had done to them in the first game. Tez was my room-mate, and we talked about this the night before the decider. I said, 'I'll tell you what I'm going to do: I'm going to cause a fight at the first scrum and that really will get people fired up – and it will make my intentions crystal clear to David Waite. I'll show him I'm not going to get outmuscled this time.'

As it turned out we got off to a great start in the third Test, Paul Johnson scoring inside the first couple of minutes, so I never got a chance to start my punch-up. I was given a breather after the opening exchanges and I didn't get back on until the second half. At half-time I said to Tez, 'Here we go again. If I can get something on now, I will.' We got down to the first scrum and I said to the Aussies' front rower Jason Ryles, 'What did you call me?' He had no idea what I was on about – because he hadn't actually said anything. Andrew Johns, Brad Fittler and their other prop, Petero Civoniceva, didn't know what was going on either, but they knew what was coming and the scrum erupted into a huge fight. That really lifted the tempo, and for about ten minutes we were attacking their line non-stop. Johnson and Gary Connolly both went close to getting the try we needed, and if we had scored then it would have been all on, but they held out, and in typical Australian fashion they took the game beyond us in the final ten minutes.

That Wigan Test was a great occasion in front of a sell-out crowd, and we had done ourselves justice, but it was frustrating to go so close to sporting immortality and just miss out again. That may sound like an exaggeration, but when Great Britain finally do win the Ashes back, the players who achieve that will become legends of the game, just as the 1970 team are.

The 2001 series showed the Aussies yet again that we can compete at their level, but unfortunately the next time we played them was a complete disaster and without doubt the most embarrassing day of my sporting life.

It was Friday, 12 July 2002. I didn't have to look that up; I will never forget the date because it was an awful day. The idea was for us to play a one-off Test against Australia in Sydney midway through our Super League season, which must have seemed like a good idea at the time to whoever thought of it.

Whenever you are asked to play for your country you put your hand up without question I would never turn down the chance to pull on the red, white and blue jersey that means so much to me. As I've said before, when I'm playing for Great Britain I am representing everyone who has ever had anything to do with my career or with rugby league in this country. It's a big responsibility and a great honour. So when I was picked for the mid-season Test I was pleased to be going, even though I knew it was going to be a big ask, jetting halfway around the world and then taking on Australia on their own turf, all within the space of a week.

The round of Super League matches before the Test was brought forward a day, so we played Warrington on the Thursday night at Headingley and flew out a few hours later. Warrington beat us with a last-minute Lee Briers drop goal, so I was stewing over that for the entire twenty-four-hour flight, which was not ideal preparation. It was the first time I had ever flown in business class rather than in economy, so that was a bonus, but things went pear-shaped from the moment we touched down. We had all played the night before we set off, so it had just been a case of chucking kit into a bag and rushing to the airport hotel. None of us had even had a chance to clean our boots, which led to the first problem. There was a big foot-and-mouth disease scare on at the time and the Australian authorities were desperate not to import it into their country. So when we got off the plane in Sydney they made us clean our boots at the airport before they would let us through immigration.

The management and medical staff did everything they could to minimize jet lag, but we were all over the place. For the first three or four days after we arrived in Australia I would be up at three or four in the morning. I'd go down to the hotel games room and there would be a dozen other players there all saying they couldn't sleep. The doctor handed out sleeping tablets to solve that problem, but the side effect of that was you were constantly thirsty, and when it was time to go and train you were knackered. On top of that, the sleeping tablets played havoc with our taste buds: when we drank the water it tasted like dog piss.

Expecting us to beat Australia under those circumstances was a tall order, but we can make all the excuses we like, we still had a good enough game plan, a good enough structure and enough belief in what we were doing and why we were there to give a good account of ourselves.

The game was played at Aussie Stadium, and as we were warming up there was a big gang of about thirty Australian supporters, dressed in green and gold T-shirts, abusing us. The stadium went quiet for a while and I heard one of them shout, 'McDermott, you've got nothing.' Tez O'Connor turned to me and said, 'Has he been looking at your bank account?' I should have known then that as usual they obviously had no respect for anybody in our team and they didn't give us a chance.

Unfortunately, they were right. We started off poorly and things got steadily worse. If you let any Australian side get a roll on they are going to destroy you, and that is exactly what happened. They wiped the floor with us, and it finished 64–10, Great Britain's worst ever defeat. I always want to make history when I'm playing for GB, but not like that.

It's hard to describe how you feel after a game of that

nature. I honestly felt that most of us had played well and got stuck in, but it just hadn't been enough on an international stage against a team as good as Australia. They out-fought us, out-thought us and out-enthused us, and they turned it all into points.

The Australians didn't rate us very highly before the game, but after it their press were predicting the death of international rugby league. In the space of a few months, with virtually the same team, we had gone from a side on the brink of winning the Ashes and becoming legends in the sport to one in the record books for all the wrong reasons. That sums sport up. Just when you think you're at the top of the tree someone appears at the bottom to shake you off and you have to start climbing all over again. It's how you react to things like that that really counts.

To make matters worse, Leeds opted to play their fixture against Castleford the same day, even though five of us were on Test duty. When we phoned home for the result we found out that the Rhinos had been well beaten, so that capped a miserable week all round.

A few months after the Sydney débâcle we were back in action against the New Zealand tourists in another three-Test series, which turned out to be a bit of a mixed experience for me and the team. Leeds had a poor season in 2002, so going on to play a Test series at the end of it wasn't easy. But what I always want to do after a poor performance, or even a poor season, is to get back out and play again straight away, to put things right. The morning after the disaster in Sydney, I wanted to pull on a GB jersey and go out and wipe that memory away. The defeat at the hands of Australia bothered me for a long time, and by the time the Kiwis arrived I was champing at the bit to get out onto the field and have a go at them.

Unfortunately, during Leeds' final game of the season I injured my wrist. I should probably have declared myself unavailable for the Test series or waited until the second or third Test, which would have given the injury time to heal, but if I get the chance to play for Great Britain it would take wild horses to stop me and I was particularly desperate to put a disappointing year behind me and give myself something to smile about. We had a training camp in Marbella, and to make things worse for me I picked up a knee injury as well, one that blighted me for a long time. With the two injuries I was carrying I was ordinary at best in the first Test on 9 November and I was left out of the side for the second game a week later. New Zealand won that opener, in Blackburn, and were the better side. I made a mistake right at the start of the second half which gifted them an important try, after we had been leading at the break, and I blamed myself, but not because of that. I blamed myself for the fact that I was underprepared, I was generally in bad nick and, worse, I wasn't mentally right.

The second Test at Huddersfield was a difficult experience. I was travelling reserve so I had to warm up with the team before the game and go through all the preparations, then go off and watch from the stand. It wasn't nice, but I looked on it as a test of character. It was a bit similar to the troubles I had endured during Graham Murray's first season at Leeds. I knew it was David Waite's way of asking me how committed I was to the international team. I was devastated to be left out, but I kept quiet and just tried to influence the players in a positive way. I did what was required of me and I think that played a part in me getting my spot back for the third Test on 23 November.

I was in the same situation physically as I had been for the first Test, but mentally I was much more focused and I was determined not to let the injuries affect me in any way. I didn't want to go out and play an international and then feel the way I had after the game in Blackburn.

The second Test was drawn, so we went to Wigan 1–0

down with one to play. New Zealand had agreed that whoever won that Test would take the trophy, even though the best we could do was share the series. We won the game, and I thoroughly enjoyed the celebrations afterwards. It was the first time I had won something at international level. In fact, it was the first time I had played in a series that Great Britain hadn't lost. We should have won the second game, but we played them off the park in Wigan, which was as good as we had played under David Waite. Importantly, we had improved throughout the series and we had shown we were a much better team than the one that had been humbled in Sydney, so it was a positive end to the year.

Winning the trophy against New Zealand put us in good heart for another crack at the Aussies, who came over to Britain for an Ashes tour at the end of the 2003 domestic season.

They were without some of their biggest star names, including their inspiration Andrew Johns, and lost to New Zealand in a one-off Test just before the tour began, so the media were building up our chances and saying we were ready to reclaim the Ashes for the first time in thirty-three years.

Once again preparations went well, but the three Tests were agonizing from a team point of view and bitterly frustrating for me as an individual. We went down to a 3–0 whitewash, but there was nothing between the sides in any of the games. We lost the first one on 8 November at Wigan 22–18 after Moz was sent off after just twelve seconds for a swinging arm on Robbie Kearns. It was shades of 1994 as we hung in there, defended magnificently and got our noses in front in the closing stages, only for Australia to edge it in the final few minutes. That was heartbreaking for Moz, but no one in the team blamed him for the defeat. Moz plays the game hard and sometimes things like that happen, as I know only too well. He was distraught for quite a while afterwards and he felt he had let the rest of the team down, but I tried to help him through it and eventually we were able to have a joke about what happened.

I had been named as a substitute for the first Test, but I didn't get on until the seventieth minute and was pulled off again about four minutes later, which just rubbed salt into the wound. As I have already mentioned, I love playing against Australia and I enjoy getting stuck into the Aussies, but there's no personal animosity and most of the Aussies I have come across in international series have been good blokes.

The Brisbane Broncos prop Shane Webcke is one of the best front rowers around, as well as a gentleman off the field, as I discovered after that first Test. Shane asked the Aussie tour manager to get in touch with our camp to ask if I would swap shirts with him, which I did. Later he got in touch again asking if I would sign my shirt, and saying that he would do the same in exchange. That was a great gesture, something I really appreciated.

Obviously I was pretty upset about my lack of game time in the series opener. I spoke to David Waite about what had happened and put my case forward, and he named me in the starting line-up for the second Test at Hull's KC Stadium. I was pleased about that, but again I didn't get long on the field and the result was equally upsetting. We were leading 20–8 midway through the first half, Gary Connolly scoring the third of our tries, which was his first GB touchdown in thirty-one Tests. At that stage we were playing really well and were in total control, but Australia got a try either side of the break and levelled with a penalty goal, before a late drop goal and another penalty secured them a 23–20 victory to win the series.

I was back on the bench for the final Test, in Huddersfield on 22 November, and once more I had only a limited taste of the action. We led twice and were 12–6 up with four minutes left, but Michael De Vere touched down in the corner and Craig Fitzgibbon landed a touchline goal to level the scores. To make matters worse, from the restart Australia surged back up field and Brett Kimmorley and Darren Lockyer carved out a try for my Ireland World Cup team-mate Luke Ricketson in the last move of the match to give them an 18–12 win.

After the heavy defeat in Sydney only sixteen months earlier we had reduced the gap to just thirteen points over three games, but that was very little consolation. It was a series we felt we could and should have won, and with no more Aussie tours on the horizon I was left, at the age of thirty-one, to realize that I would never be part of an Ashes-winning squad.

16

THE NEARLY MEN

To sport's battlers. Ultimately you will be judged on your victories, but triumph over adversity is just as sweet.

Adversity brings out the best in all players at some stage, and that is what happened to me in 2001. Leeds had a disappointing season as a team, but I was named player of the year, which was a great honour. That was my tenth season as a professional, and I think it was the year I really stepped up a gear and started to take on some leadership qualities, rather than just being a member of the team. We were badly hit by injury that year with most of our senior players having to spend time on the sidelines. That meant quite a few young kids got a crack at the first team, and it also ensured that, as one of the more experienced players in the squad, there was more responsibility on my shoulders.

Overall 2001 was a below-par campaign for us, though there were some memorable games. We set a new club record when we won a Challenge Cup tie 106–10 at Swinton on 11 February and we also won away to Hull and Castleford, which are traditionally tough places for Leeds to get a result. But inconsistency let us down. We couldn't beat any of our main rivals, Bradford, Wigan and Saints, and finishing fifth in the Super League was a big anticlimax.

But in terms of my own personal performances, the fact

that I had to stick my hand up and take on more responsibility definitely helped my game. Until then I had never thought of myself as a leader, but that started to develop that year. I had always been a bit of a follower, but I knew the young kids were looking to me to take the ship forward. What I did influenced others at the club on and off the field, and I took that very seriously. It wasn't a natural attribute, but I deliberately tried to mould myself into a leader. I had always been a person who liked to enjoy himself, to be a bit of a joker, though that never meant I didn't take my rugby seriously. I have always been the sort of person people turn to when things aren't going well for them, mainly because I've been there myself and I usually know what they're going through. But in 2001 I started to take the initiative and say, 'I think we should do this.' Sometimes I might have been wrong, or it wasn't what people wanted to hear, but in those circumstances I always think honesty is the best policy.

Our preparation for the 2001 campaign broke new ground, in the United States. We went over to Jacksonville, Florida, for a week-long training camp that culminated in an exhibition tournament against Halifax, Huddersfield and the American national team. The whole week was a great experience. We trained hard, but we also got to taste a bit of a different way of life. We spent some time with the Jacksonville Jaguars, the local American football team, and they gave us a tour of their stadium where the exhibition matches were played. We won the Sunshine State Challenge tournament, which set us up for a storming start to the season, but then injuries kicked in and by the time we got to the Challenge Cup semi-final, against St Helens at Wigan's new JJB Stadium on 31 March, we were down to the bare bones.

The thing I remember most about our preparations for that game was a training-ground spat with Jamie Mathiou.

By the time he left at the end of the 2001 season Jamie was the club's longest-serving overseas player in the modern era, but we didn't have a good relationship. I got on all right with Jamie at first, but that soon went sour. I thought he was only interested in himself and had an inflated opinion of his own abilities. He felt he was a better player than me, that he should be starting most games in my place. Of course I didn't agree, and that was the main bone of contention between us. Jamie spent most of his time at Leeds as a substitute, so I wasn't the only one to hold that opinion.

I have played with a few blokes I don't have much in common with, apart from the game, and usually it's not a problem, as long as they are good at their job. With Jamie, I didn't respect him as a bloke or as a player, and eventually things came to a head before that semi-final.

The coach, Dean Lance, decided to leave the players alone for the final training session so it was our call as to what we did or didn't do. Karl Pratt used to get a lift to training with Jamie and they had got into a conversation about who was pulling their weight in the team. Pratty said he thought I was doing my best to take the side forward, but Jamie said he thought I was a shithouse. Karl is a mate of mine, and he reported this conversation to me. I didn't pay much attention at first, but when I thought about it I began to think Jamie was two-faced, because he wouldn't dare say something like that to my face.

Tonie Carroll, who was always winding people up, had been reading something on a website where a fan had written that Jamie and I were both useless and Danny Ward was the best prop at the club. We were stretching before training when Tonie told Jamie, who was due to be a substitute as usual, about this article. Jamie turned round, looked at me and said, 'It's not my fault we're always losing by the time I get on.'

There was already some bad blood between us after our altercation in Blackpool in 1998, and on top of what Pratty had told me, I just blew my top. I went for Jamie, who was standing about twelve feet away. The first few steps I took I was intending to whack him, but by the time I got a bit closer I had realized that we were at Headingley the day before a cup semi-final and there were dozens of people watching. In the space of twelve feet I made the decision that it wouldn't be the best move to go and stick one on him, satisfying as that would be, so I got Jamie by the scruff of his neck and told him to keep his opinions to himself, but if he did have anything to say, to say it to my face. Jamie kept quiet, but as I threw him off he said I had broken the chain he was wearing around his neck. I told him, 'Never mind your chain, I'll break your nose as well if you don't shut up,' and that was the end of it. Later, I started to regret what had happened. On the team coach going to the game I could see Jamie fiddling with the broken chain, and one of the other players told me the reason he had been so upset was because he had been given it by one of his kids. That tugged at my heart strings because I know how you treasure presents from your children. We never really spoke to each other after that, and I wasn't sorry when Jamie went back to Australia at the end of that season.

That set-to did not affect our performance, and our under-strength team put up a great fight before losing narrowly after Saints scored a late try. The match was a bit similar to our semi-final defeat by Bradford in 1997, and just like after that game, I ended up sitting out the next four matches. At one point during the game I caught a shot from behind, turned round and saw Saints' second rower Peter Shiels looking at me, so I clouted him. He had to go off with a bad cut, and though I didn't get sent off, I was placed on report and got suspended after the disciplinary committee looked at the video. When I watched the tape I found out it was Paul Sculthorpe who had hit me in the first place, and he apologized to me a few weeks later.

That defeat was almost the final straw for Dean Lance, who survived just one more match before getting the push, with Daryl Powell taking over as coach. I always liked Dean. He often came to me for advice or to see what the mood of the team was and I thought he was a good bloke, but I know some of the players didn't appreciate his style of coaching and didn't really know how to take him. He wasn't prepared for such a big job. I think he came over with the idea, which a lot of Australians share, that we are a small sport and we don't know as much about the game as they do Down Under. But Leeds is a huge club and the city is rugby league through and through. When you are part of it, there is no hiding place. And Dean really struggled to cope with the pressure. He tried to introduce his own ideas and methods when he first took over, but when they didn't work he gradually drifted back to what had been so successful under Graham Murray. Dean had a lot of good qualities and he didn't do as badly as coach as a lot of people think, but I'm sure that if he could have his time again he would do nearly everything differently.

The backroom change on top of all the injuries we were suffering meant we found it tough all season, and though we comfortably qualified in the top five we never really looked like making an impact when it came to the end-of-season play-offs.

The year was not all doom and gloom, though. The most pleasing aspect of that season was the emergence of some Leeds players who I think will go on to become big names in the game. Rob Burrow came into the side halfway through the campaign and did so well he was named Super League young player of the year, while Mark Calderwood established himself as one of the best try-scorers around.

Anyone who thinks rugby league is a game for giants has never met Rob. At five feet four inches he's among the shortest players in the British game. When he ran out for his debut with Leeds' Academy side I honestly thought he was the mascot! Rob is probably the best impact player Leeds have ever had. He's as near to Jason Robinson as I have seen for a long time. Rob has electric pace and a great side step, and he has turned the fact that he's tiny into a big advantage. When he runs at the big fellas, he terrifies them with his footwork and agility. It must be like chasing shadows, and I'm glad he's on my side. When Yorkshire play Lancashire I always pull him to one side and tell him, 'You make sure you stay away from me and don't make me look stupid and I won't belt you when someone else has got hold of you.'

Mark is originally from London but moved up to Leeds as a kid and played amateur rugby in the city before joining the Rhinos. He was actually working in a KFC takeaway when he asked Leeds for a trial. Dean Bell gave him a chance, and he has never looked back. Calders averaged two touchdowns a game in two seasons in the Academy and has scored tries for fun since he was promoted into the first team. He's a freakish finisher and has got the best kick-chase game I have ever seen. He's a lovely lad, has bags of enthusiasm and probably more pride in the Leeds shirt than anyone else I have ever played with. He's still young, but I think he could go on to great things.

Rob and Mark probably wouldn't have been given an opportunity so early if experienced players had been able to stay clear of injury. The biggest disappointment in 2001 was the form of our imports, particularly Bradley Clyde and Brett Mullins, both of them Australian ex-Test players who came over here with massive reputations. They spent most of the season injured and cut their contracts short to go home after just a year at Leeds. I know a lot of fans were angry about that and thought the two of them had just come over for a holiday, but I don't believe that was the case.

Clydey is a legend in Australia and I liked him a lot. He had been voted the best back rower in his country in the 1990s and he was an excellent player, but I think if he was honest with himself he would admit he underestimated how tough it was going to be over here. He didn't think the competition in this country would be as difficult as it was. He was a good influence in the dressing room, and when he was on the field he was fantastic, but he simply didn't play enough games to keep the supporters happy. A certain section of the fan base at Leeds demands success and they didn't think he was pulling his weight. I went to Clydey many times for advice and he was happy to give it, but because of the stick he was getting he liked to keep his opinions to himself and he went into his shell a bit, which was a pity.

Brett Mullins suffered all sorts of injuries while he was over here and never got a long run in the team. Mullo had something of a reputation for being difficult, but I never saw that. I think he genuinely wanted to do well; he just didn't get the chance because of injuries.

I felt sorry for both of them. I think they came over here with good intentions, and at another time, under different circumstances, they would both have been sensational. Clydey retired at the end of the year, but ironically Mullo got himself fit back in Australia, joined Sydney City Roosters as a triallist and went on to win an NRL Grand Final, in the same side as Adrian Morley.

The third Aussie we signed that year was the hooker Robbie Mears, and he was dogged by injury problems as well. He suffered a broken collarbone against Swinton on his debut in the Challenge Cup and then, near the end of the season, had his jaw broken by a late tackle from

St Helens' Sonny Nickle in what turned out to be his final game. We actually won that game, which meant we went back to Knowsley Road in the play-offs in reasonable spirits, despite having lost 62–18 at Bradford the week before. It turned out to be a cracking game, with Saints just pipping us 38–30 after a fair bit of controversy involving my old Oldham and Ireland team-mate Tommy Martyn. We were attacking Saints' line late on when Tommy spotted a spare ball on the pitch and kicked it infield towards where the play was. The referee had to stop the action for the second ball to be removed, and that gave Saints' defensive line time to regroup. We weren't sure what had happened at the time, but it was clear from Sky TV's replays. When Sky asked Tommy about it afterwards he said it wasn't gamesmanship, it was 'the foot of God'.

In 2002 we began the year with another trip abroad, this time to South Africa, which was a great experience. We played Widnes in a torrential thunderstorm in Johannesburg, and even though we lost, the week out there did us a power of good. We proved that by coming back and pulling off one of the best results I have been involved with at Leeds. The Challenge Cup draw sent us to Bradford, who had won the previous season's Grand Final and were the newly crowned world club champions after a fantastic victory over Newcastle Knights. They had beaten us four times the previous season, including the rout at Valley Parade in our final league game, so absolutely nobody gave us a chance when we had to go there again on 9 February.

But sometimes you get a feeling about a game, and this was one of those occasions. Looking around at the people alongside me, like Matt Adamson, our new signing from Penrith, Adrian Vowles, Kevin Sinfield and Keith Senior, I remember thinking we were ready to give somebody a real hiding.

Wigan played Hull the same afternoon, and both ties

were being shown live on the BBC. The Wigan game was on the big screen at Valley Parade as we were warming up, but nobody was watching it. I could feel the intensity of the atmosphere during our preparation and I knew it was our day. We bashed them from pillar to post, dominated from the start and came out deserved winners 17–4, which was a great victory and had people once more saying that this might be Leeds' year.

We got through to the cup semi-final yet again, and yet again we had to go over to play St Helens at Wigan. The previous year our below-strength side had put up a great fight and gone down with honour, but this time we had everybody available and we were blown off the park. Saints at their best are hard to stop, and we caught them on a really hot day. All you can do on occasions like that is dig in. We fought to the end, but it was an embarrassing defeat and the Saints fans really rubbed our noses in it. We got a late try when I sent Willie Poching over, and as we returned to our positions for Saints' kick-off all their fans stood up and cheered us back to our marks. They were taking the piss, and it hurt, but it's all part and parcel of the game.

Losing in the semi-final was a case of so near and yet so far that set the pattern for the rest of our 2002 campaign. We had some good wins and showed flashes of our best form, but we lacked consistency.

I missed four games late in the season after getting involved in a punch-up with my old sparring partner Stuart Fielden, which earned me a red card and a ban. That only fuelled media talk of my supposed feud with Stuart, so I suppose this is a good time to set the record straight. The fact is, there is no feud. I have absolutely nothing against Stuart, and though I wouldn't count him as a close friend, he is someone I have a lot of respect for as a player. Stuart got into the Bradford first team as a teenager, which is very young for a prop, and the moment he did, we clashed, and we have carried on clashing ever since. We have got into more than our fair share of scuffles, but it has never been personal. As a prop forward you are the engine room of a team and the rest of the players are looking to you to take them forward and to stop the opposition's front rowers doing the same for their side. You have to get on top physically, whoever you are up against, and sometimes that might mean throwing the odd punch and bending a few rules, or even breaking them. Believe it or not, it does not mean you've got anything against the guy opposite you; you're both just doing whatever you can for the team. If Stuart Fielden is propping against me I know I have to get on top of him or the rest of my team will really have their work cut out to win the game. I'm sure he feels the same about me.

What most people think is a feud is in fact just two very competitive athletes who like the fact that neither of them is prepared to back down. We enjoy getting stuck into each other, but it's based on mutual respect, not personal dislike. We have played together quite a number of times for Great Britain and I always enjoy having Stuart on my side. He's someone I am pleased to have alongside me in the trenches.

Whenever Leeds play Bradford, most of the people in the ground are waiting for Stuart Fielden and Barrie McDermott to get stuck into each other, and we rarely disappoint them. It's usually just a case of lighting the touch paper. On that particular August night at Valley Parade we had quite an inexperienced side and I decided it was up to me to set a lead and get the lads fired up. I shot out of the line to get a big hit on Stuart, he reacted, punches were thrown and I got dismissed.

Funnily enough, we had a Great Britain squad meeting a few days later, which was a bit awkward. I had been thinking about the incident, and when Stuart turned up, still sporting a black eye, for the meeting at Kirkstall, which is also the Rhinos' training headquarters, I decided to try to smooth things over. As soon as he got out of his car I went up to him and said, 'I'm sorry for what happened. As far as I'm concerned we've had a ding-dong but I've got the shitty end of the stick because I've been banned and I have to pay a £500 fine. We've got a Test series against New Zealand coming up and we both want to play, but if the management thinks there's a problem, one or both of us will get left out.' Stuart agreed and said there was no problem, that whatever happened on the pitch would stay on it. And that was the end of that, though my sense of humour being the way it is I couldn't resist cracking a joke, asking him if he would pay half of my fine. His smirk and deafening silence spoke volumes.

My ban didn't help our cause that season and we eventually finished fourth in the Super League table, which was below our expectations; we also went out of the play-offs in the second round, away to Wigan. The club had been hoping for a top two or three finish, and when we didn't achieve that they decided that heads had to roll. Tonie Carroll and Ben Walker returned to Australia, and Karl Pratt, Ryan Sheridan and Andy Hay were all told they wouldn't figure in the first team the following season, even though they were all still under contract.

I will always remember the morning Gary Hetherington told us he would be sacking players, because it was the day of our Mad Monday end-of-season blow-out. We had planned to go out in fancy dress around Leeds and I had decided to decorate myself with a shocking pink moustache for a laugh. I knew we were due to have a team meeting, but I didn't have a clue what it was about. Gary had said in the press that he would take action if we didn't finish in the top three in the table, but I don't think anyone was expecting what was about to happen. I was sitting right at the front, and as Gary made his shock announcement

I found myself slowly sliding further and further down in my chair and trying to cover my mouth.

Karl signed for Bradford, and Ryan and Andy went to Widnes. Karl in particular was angry and upset about the whole business, and though the club later said the door might be open for him to return, he had made his mind up that he would not play for Leeds again. As it turned out, he did well out of his move. Just over a year later he had Challenge Cup, league leaders', Grand Final and World Club Challenge winners' medals on his sideboard.

The sacking business caused a huge stink in the media and among the fans, and the club didn't come out of it in a very good light. It's always sad when team-mates leave and we all felt for the ones who were forced out, but Daryl Powell and Gary Hetherington obviously thought that what they were doing was for the best, so the rest of us just had to be professional and get on with things.

To replace the players who had left, the club signed Aussie Test player Chris McKenna from Cronulla, Dave Furner from Wigan, Andrew Dunemann from Halifax and Wakefield's young front rower Chris Feather, and Gary Connolly joined us a little later after turning down the chance to finish his career in rugby union with Orrell. The rebuilding process began at the start of pre-season training in November when we all joined the army for a week in Germany, with the Great Britain lads flying straight out at the end of the Test series against New Zealand. Basically, we lived like squaddies the whole time, and it was an interesting experience to say the least. I had always wanted to join the army when I was a kid so I quite enjoyed it, but I think a few of the other lads found it a bit of a culture shock, especially when we had to sleep in tents out in the middle of nowhere and got woken up at five a.m. one morning by the real soldiers staging a mock attack on our camp.

I had to fly home a day early, on government business! I was invited to a reception at No. 10 Downing Street to mark the work sportsmen and women do in the community. That was a great honour, and it was a privilege to be rubbing shoulders with top stars from a whole variety of different sports.

That week in Germany was one of the toughest things I have undertaken as a Leeds player, but it did the trick and set us up for a positive season in 2003. We had a week away, in Lanzarote this time, to put the final touches to our preparations, and when we got back we were straight into one of the best runs of my career at Leeds, winning our opening ten league and cup games. There was a great spirit in the team, and during the trip to Germany we had developed a tremendous togetherness and will to win. Youngsters like Ryan Bailey, Chev Walker, Matt Diskin, Danny McGuire, Mark Calderwood and Rob Burrow were all a year older and more experienced, and their enthusiasm rubbed off on the rest of us. With a handful of top-quality experienced players having been brought in as well, we had a winning mix, and we felt we could finally bring some silverware back to Headingley.

With ten straight wins behind us we were well on our way, but typically, when our hot streak came to an end it was in the Challenge Cup final, and to our fiercest rivals, Bradford Bulls. Losing yet another final was a cruel blow, but at least we had an epic semi-final win over St Helens to look back on.

A lot of people have said that the 12 April showdown was the greatest cup semi-final ever and one of the best games the BBC have shown. It was certainly the best game I have ever played in. Saints were the reigning league champions, and by a strange twist of fate, for the second successive year we played them in a Super League game at Knowsley Road the week before the semi-final. In 2002 we had lost the league match to a last-minute try, but in 2003 we turned the tables and had a great win, capped by Wayne McDonald racing almost the length of the field for one of the best tries I have ever seen by a front rower. We were hanging on to a lead in the closing stages when Wayne got the ball near his own line, brushed off a couple of tacklers, fooled the cover with an outrageous dummy and just kept on going.

That victory, especially the manner of it, gave us a real lift going into the semi-final and we were well prepared for the game mentally and physically. We stayed together the night before and then had a team meeting before setting off to the McAlpine Stadium, which is one of my favourite grounds. The meeting was at the George Hotel in Huddersfield, the birthplace of rugby league, and we had our get-together in the very room where the sport was founded way back in 1895, so that was a nice touch from Gary Hetherington and it put everybody in the mood. We all sat around a big table and talked about what the game meant to each of us. There were players with tears in their eyes, and I knew then that we had the passion and desire to win it, so all it was going to take was a bit of structure and direction, and maybe a bit of luck.

The game itself was a real thriller. They scored first, we went into a big lead, and then they hit back to go two points in front going into the final few minutes. With two minutes to go they scored a try in the corner, but Paul Sculthorpe couldn't convert, so we were six points behind. We managed to get the ball back from the restart and young Danny McGuire forced his way over with about sixty seconds left. He touched down right by the corner flag on the right-hand side of the field. That gave Kevin Sinfield the hardest possible conversion attempt, but Sinny landed the goal – the greatest kick I have ever seen – to send the game into an extra twenty minutes. Saints had a try ruled out by the video referee right at the start of extra time, Sinny booted us in front with a drop goal, and then he linked with Dave Furner to send Danny weaving over in the final minute to complete a wonderful win.

The emotion afterwards was incredible. If that game had been a heavyweight boxing match, the ref would have stopped it long before Danny got his first try because several times we were dead on our feet. I have been physically and mentally drained after games plenty of times during my career, but never as utterly exhausted as I was at the end of that one. It took me a good four or five days to get the stiffness out of my body, which wouldn't have been so bad if we'd not had a game at Castleford the following Thursday. From the kitman Roy Adams and timekeeper Billy Watts right through to the chief executive Gary Hetherington, there were tears in everybody's eyes after those emotionally traumatic hundred minutes.

I remember staggering into the changing rooms afterwards ready to start spraying the champagne around, but there was none to be seen. It wasn't that the directors lacked confidence in us, rather that everyone had been so focused on the game itself no one had thought about what to do afterwards. Fortunately, someone turned up with a couple of bottles and we celebrated in appropriate style.

After that high, maybe it was inevitable the final, played fourteen days later, would not live up to expectations, even though we went into the game at Cardiff's Millennium Stadium as slight favourites. We just didn't get the rub of the green on the day, though it was a great occasion and the first time a Challenge Cup final had been played under a closed roof. Iestyn Harris was playing for Cardiff Rugby Union Club at the time and I asked him to come to the team hotel to calm a few of the lads down and give us some tips on what to expect in the stadium, where he had played with Wales. So we were totally prepared, but on the

day a few things went against us and we came up two
points short, Bradford winning 22–20. We thought a few of
referee Russell Smith's decisions were questionable and the
club launched a protest after the game, but the horse had
bolted by then. Given the bounce of the ball, we could have
won that game. It was definitely one that got away. We
certainly felt it was a case of us losing the game rather than
Bradford winning it.

Daryl caused a bit of controversy before the game by
leaving out our semi-final hero Danny McGuire. Danny had
come in for the Saints game in place of Rob Burrow, and
his two tries secured us our place at Cardiff. But when it
came to the final Daryl opted to go with Rob, mainly
because he thought the little scrum-half's elusive footwork
could cause problems for Bradford's big men when they
began to tire. It was a bit like the Sinny situation at
Murrayfield three years earlier and was just as tough a
decision as leaving Rob out of the semi had been. We all
felt for Danny, but coaches have to make these decisions
and he's a good enough player to have plenty of finals in
the future. Ironically, Rob got a bang to the head shortly
after coming on as a substitute and only played for a few
minutes. He didn't get the chance to prove himself so we
will never know if the tactic would have worked. For what
it's worth, I think it was the right decision for that game; if
he had not been injured he might well have won it for us
in the final minutes, when we couldn't break their line.

Bradford had a try disallowed by the video referee in
the first couple of minutes, but they went ahead with a
Robbie Paul touchdown, though we felt the pass might
have been forward. We got back into it with a Gary
Connolly try, and then Dave Furner had a score disallowed
before Chris McKenna got a try to give us a lead we felt
we could build on. Unfortunately, Bradford got back level
at half-time with a Tevita Vaikona try, then Jamie Peacock

scored straight after half-time, so we had gone from 14–8 up to 20–14 down. They went further in front with a penalty goal, but we were still confident we could get back into the game and Dave Furner got us to within two points with a really good individual try. There was plenty of time left, but we just couldn't make the breakthrough. After being the hero in the semi-final Sinny got a lot of stick for not going for goal with a penalty late in the game which could have levelled the scores. Sinny and Bradford's Paul Deacon didn't miss a kick between them all game, so he would probably have landed it, but at that stage the Bulls were out on their feet and we thought we could score a try to win the final. The media made a big thing of it and savaged Kevin for not taking the two points, but no one in the team had any qualms with our captain's decision and we would all have done the same.

When time ran out a lot of our boys were in tears on the pitch, and it was a scene of utter desolation in the changing room. It's never nice to lose, but it's worse when you know you have given everything. The fact that we had suffered our first defeat of the year in the biggest game of the year just added to the pain.

That final was a case of what might have been, and so was our season. We were top of the league for most of the year, but faded a bit towards the end and finished second to Bradford, who were the only team we could not beat. As well as the cup final we played them three times in the league and once more in the play-offs, and lost the lot. They had a convincing win at Odsal a few weeks after Cardiff, which ended our unbeaten Super League run, but the rest of the games were all close. At Headingley there was only two points' difference, the same as the cup final, and they beat us by a point on their ground a few weeks after that. Bradford finished top of the table by three points, so if we had scored just one extra try in either of those games we would have finished as league leaders instead of the Bulls. It was that close.

Second place meant we had to win only one game in the play-offs to get through to the Grand Final, but we lost in the qualifying semi-final at Odsal after leading late in the game and then went down to Wigan at Headingley in the elimination play-off, when they kicked a last-gasp drop goal. That was another epic game, the lead changing hands all the way through, and we were absolutely shattered in the changing room afterwards. In the cold light of day we had no one to blame but ourselves. We should have won those games and we were so close to greatness, but we couldn't quite get there. A lack of composure and experience cost us.

Losing at Cardiff and failing to get through to the Grand Final was devastating, but something far worse happened that year when two of our team, Chev Walker and Ryan Bailey, got locked up for violent disorder after they had been involved in a fight outside a nightclub in Leeds. Chev got eighteen months in a young offenders' institution, and Ryan was sentenced to nine months. We knew about the court case, but none of us expected them to get sent down, especially as they pleaded guilty and showed their remorse. Another of our players, Dwayne Barker, got a community punishment order, and Paul Owen, who played for Rochdale, was also sent to prison. No one else was involved and everyone at the club and in Leeds thought the lads were harshly treated. They had been punished for who they were, not what they had done. If they had done other jobs and not been in the public eye, I don't think any of them would have been locked up. About a year earlier there had been a high-profile court case involving some Leeds United footballers, and I think our lads felt the backlash from that.

The effect the sentences had on the team was quite devastating. We were told the news at a training session and everyone was completely shocked. As a team you go through a lot together, you're just like an extended family, so when something like that happens to some of your own, everybody feels the pain. A lot of banter and joking goes on among the team and you can find something to laugh at in most situations, but no one ever tried to make a joke out of what happened to Ryan and Chev. Ryan served just under three months and Chev did about five. They were both allowed out as part of an early release scheme, but had to spend time wearing an electronic tag, which Chev wore during the trial games at the start of the following season.

Fortunately, Ryan and Chev are strong characters and good blokes and they both came through it unscathed. Everyone makes mistakes, it's how you deal with them that counts. They were very positive when they came out and I'm sure what happened won't stop either of them going on to have a great career.

We all took turns to visit them while they were away and they got plenty of support from fans and virtually everybody involved in rugby league. Some people were calling for them to be sacked by the club, but what would that have achieved? The club did not condone what they had done, but they said once they came out the slate would be wiped clean, and I think that was the right thing to do. Chev and Ryan made a mistake, but there was no need to keep punishing them for it.

The day after Chev and Ryan were locked up we had another bombshell dropped on us when we were told Daryl Powell was stepping down as coach at the end of the season, with the Huddersfield boss Tony Smith taking over. Unknown by any of us up to that point, Daryl had decided he wanted to take some time out to sharpen his skills by studying coaching methods at different clubs and in other sports, so he was moving up into a new role as director of rugby for two years before returning to the first-team hot seat in 2006. Tony Smith is an Australian, brother of one of their leading National Rugby League coaches and former Hull and Bradford boss Brian Smith. He came to England to join Huddersfield Giants and though he could not save them from relegation in 2001, he guided them back to the top flight the following year, when they lost only one game in all competitions. Huddersfield did well in 2003, including a home win over us, so we knew we would be in safe hands.

Tony carried on from where Daryl left off and we were again one of the top sides in 2004. Stability on the field was key to that. All the first-team squad stayed on and we made just two signings, both world class overseas players. Marcus Bai, a winger who plays more like a prop forward, became the first Papua New Guinean to play for Leeds and mid-way through the campaign the club pulled off a major coup by signing Kiwi Test forward Ali Lauitiiti after he was released by Auckland club New Zealand Warriors. Ali is rated as one of the best second-rowers in the world and he had offers from all Australian's top clubs as well as from Wigan, Bradford, Hull and Saints over here. The fact Leeds moved in to sign him showed the ambition which exists at Headingley and the desire to make Rhinos the top club in the game. A lot of that is down to Gary Hetherington. Gary has a lot of critics, but I have known him a long time and he is rugby league through and through, as are all his family – including his wife Kath, who is chairwoman at Hull. I owe Gary a lot and I will always be grateful for what he has done for Leeds and for my career in particular.

Time will tell, but I really think Rhinos could be on the verge of something special. The squad has a great blend of youth and experience and some of the top kids in the British game are either in the first team now or on the fringes of it. Lads like Rob Burrow, Danny Ward, Danny McGuire, Mark Calderwood, Wayne McDonald, Chev Walker, Chris Feather and Ryan Bailey had all become established Super League players by the start of 2004. I was pleased to be a part of their development. Another one to join that list was the young full back Richard Mathers, who must be one of the most enthusiastic players ever. Richard is a Leeds lad, he supported them as a kid and all he wants to do is play for Rhinos. He has got the talent to go all the way and his form was the main reason why Gary Connolly was released mid-way through Super League IX. Gary did a great job for Leeds and I was sorry to see him go. He didn't want to leave the club, but he was quickly snapped up by Wigan which, at the age of thirty-three, shows how highly he is thought of.

I get excited watching the young kids we've got coming through at Leeds and there's a similar situation right throughout the game, with youngsters like Hull's Shaun Briscoe and Richard Horne, Paul Wood at Warrington, Gareth Ellis, who joined Leeds in 2005, Sean O'Loughlin and Wayne Godwin at Wigan, Stuart Reardon and Karl and Leon Pryce at Bradford and Saints' Micky Higham all lighting up the competition at a tender age. They are all multi-talented and they can all play the game in several different positions. More and more in this sport, with full-time training and individual coaching, players are developing all-round skills, so props can kick, pass and read plays and half-backs make big hits and can drive the ball forward with power. When I started, there was an emphasis on bashing the opposition and making sure you dominate the game physically. That is still important, but under Tony Smith in 2004 we did a lot more work on technique, how to catch a ball; hands, feet and body position, playing the ball and other basics, as well as the traditional tough stuff.

It is a simple game made up of difficult components and Tony is a master of improving the way all his players do each of them.

I turned thirty-two in July 2004 and in a tough, physical sport like rugby league, that is getting towards the veteran stage. I am nowhere near ready for the knacker's yard yet and I am still enjoying my rugby as much as ever, but there comes a time when you have to start thinking about what you are going to do when you hang up your boots. As I said earlier in this book, I am confident I could carve out a career away from sport, but for the time being I am keen to remain in rugby league, preferably with Leeds, on the coaching side of things. The game has been good to me and I have picked up so much knowledge and experience, I would like to stay involved and to pass that know-how on to the next generation. Coaching is something I think I can make a success of. I would love to mould a group of individuals into a team that plays the way I want to play, with aggression, speed and skill and all the attributes I have tried to possess as a player. I already spend a lot of time trying to help young up and coming players and I would love it if in ten years' time players look back and say, 'The turning point of my career was when I met Barrie McDermott and he taught me about the game.'

17

DREAMS AND NIGHTMARES

*Dedicated to my team-mates, those who made it
and those who didn't, but who all enjoyed the
greatest game of all. And to my opponents.
I have won more than I have lost, but I have never
given in – and the bigger they are, the harder they fall.*

It is head-on-the-block time as I select Barrie McDermott's Dream Team – and my seventeen rugby league nightmares.

Picking the best seventeen players I have come across during my career wasn't easy, but the first name on the teamsheet was an obvious choice. Iestyn Harris is the best I ever played with and also the most impressive leader. He gave so much on and off the field and was an inspiration in both attack and defence. He tackled well above his weight, he could do whatever he wanted with the ball in hand, and he trained like a madman.

When Edgar Curtis was the conditioner at Leeds, fat counts – the percentage of your body weight made up by fat – were a big thing. We had a fat count one pre-season, and for the first and only time I actually beat Iestyn. He was so devastated that he trained his nuts off for the next six weeks and when he came back he was less than half what he had been. And that's a bloke who is as fit as a flea anyway. The standards he set himself were very high and he would never accept anything less.

Iestyn's best season at Leeds was 1998, when he destroyed the rest of Super League. He was the best player out there by a mile and everyone knew it. He won just about every individual accolade going that year, including the Man of Steel, which is definitely the most prestigious honour in the British game, and players' player. It was obvious right from the start of that season that Iestyn was going to do something special and he really began to get noticed in our second game, which was away to the reigning champions Bradford in a snowstorm at Odsal.

I was serving my five-game ban at the time following the red card in a pre-season run-out at York, and the club had told me to get away for a bit of a break, so I watched the match in a bar in Tenerife with a load of Bradford fans. For obvious reasons I was trying to keep a low profile, but the more the beer flowed and the further in front Leeds got, the louder I was getting. The Bulls fans got fed up by the end and they were telling me pretty forcefully to shut up. I don't think they had any idea who I was. Iestyn scored three tries that day in an absolutely brilliant individual display, and that just set the tone for the rest of the year.

He's a bit younger than me, but Iestyn's signing for Leeds was a turning point in my career. I learned so much off him and I became a much better player because of that. Iestyn is a very good communicator and he has the knack of getting the best out of people around him. He's probably an out-and-out rugby league stand-off, but I felt he played his best rugby for Leeds at full-back.

In 2001, when he decided to go to rugby union, he went through a really tough time and took plenty of stick from a lot of people, but he didn't deserve the abuse he got. Despite what people think, Iestyn did not go to rugby union for money. He was financially secure at the time and he could quite easily have seen out his career at Leeds. He went for the challenge, and I think that is a brave decision. The fact that Iestyn initially struggled to get to grips with rugby union just proves what a difference there still is between the two sports. Iestyn returned to rugby league with Bradford in 2004 and played against us in that season's Grand Final.

You have to be a freakish talent to be a success in both codes, and Jason Robinson was one of those. He certainly wasn't a better player in union than he was in league, but when he got into the England and then the British Lions sides in the fifteen-a-side game he became a huge national hero and a big celebrity, though it was a bit insulting to the rest of us in rugby league that he had to cross codes for the national media to recognize what a magnificent rugby player he is. Jason was a big loss to rugby league, but to be honest, most of us who didn't play for Wigan at the time were probably glad to see the back of him. If you read any big bloke's player profile from the late 1990s, under the heading 'most difficult opponent' every single one of them put Jason Robinson. He absolutely petrified us all. He had, and still has in union, amazing elusive skills, great footwork, agility and electric pace. You would try to tackle him and with a hop, skip and a jump he would be around you and away. His try that won Wigan the 1998 Grand Final. against Leeds was a perfect illustration of that.

Jason gets one of my Dream Team wing spots, and the other goes to Francis Cummins, who has been the cornerstone of the Leeds back division throughout my time at Headingley. Franny is not the flashiest of players. He's not the type of bloke to show off and he doesn't often grab the headlines, but he always does right for the team and he's the sort of bloke you need in any side. He made his first-team debut as a teenager and was the youngest player to appear in a Challenge Cup final, aged seventeen years and 200 days, when Leeds lost to Wigan in 1994. Franny has given great service to Leeds, and in 2003 he had a well-deserved testimonial season that netted him £150,000. He holds the Leeds record for most consecutive appearances, having played in 179 successive games between 1998 and 2004, and in the modern game that is phenomenal.

Keith Senior is an absolutely devastating centre, a really big, strong and powerful lad. I would not want him running at me, even though he is an outside back. He came to Leeds as a career move in 1999 after helping Sheffield beat Wigan in the previous year's Challenge Cup final, which was probably the greatest shock result of all time. He became quite notorious that season for knocking out Castleford's Barrie-Jon Mather, then the tallest player in rugby league, with one punch during a televised cup quarterfinal. Keith has since gone on to play for England and Great Britain, and he would be in anybody's Dream Team. He was named as one of the world's best centres at the end of the 2002 and 2003 seasons, and with a few years left in him I think he will be remembered as one of the all-time greats.

Gary Connolly is one of the few blokes I have played alongside at two different clubs and the only one from my Wigan days who later turned up at Leeds. He came to the Rhinos as a full-back, which is probably his best position, but he was known at Wigan as a centre, and that's where he features in my fantasy side. When I moved to Central Park Gary was at the top of his trade and was a key figure in a great Wigan team. He had just got back from a spell with Canterbury Bulldogs, where he played well and did what we all try to do, which is earn the respect of the Aussies.

He was just as impressive almost a decade later at Leeds. Joining the Rhinos gave him a new lease of life after it looked as though he was going to finish his playing days in union with Orrell.

Gary will always have my utmost respect because of what happened during and after the 2003 Challenge Cup final in Cardiff. He was named man of the match, even though we lost, and that was the first year the Lance Todd Trophy got presented on the pitch after the game. The Bradford Bulls lads were celebrating all around him and he was expected to go up and collect his trophy. He got a lot of criticism because people thought he was treating the award with contempt, but that wasn't the case at all: he was just absolutely gutted at losing the game. We had a bit of a get-together in the hotel four or five hours after the game. Gary stood up to talk and he was in tears again. That really got to everybody, and it showed just how much emotion he had invested in the day.

When I broke into the first team at Oldham one of the ball boys was Kevin Sinfield. Little did I know that a mere ten years later that fresh-faced youth would be my captain at Leeds. Kevin walks into my Dream Team at stand-off, though he is equally at home at loose forward and has played for Great Britain at scrum-half and hooker. I have known Kevin a long time and he has always been marked out for big things, but unlike countless kids who have been touted as great prospects he has gone on to fulfil his potential. He's still young, but in his early twenties he is already an established international and a very well-respected professional. He made his debut for Leeds at sixteen and was brought along quite slowly before becoming a first-team regular in 2000, going on to star for England and Great Britain and being named Rhinos captain at the age of twenty-two. Kev is a genuinely nice lad, and he's someone else I think could go on to be remembered as one of the greatest players of all time. He has it all: he's a great leader and he's very level headed, but he also oozes skill, class and determination.

The best scrum-half I have played with or against would have to be Shaun Edwards. I must admit I couldn't stand him when I first signed for Wigan, but that quickly turned into admiration. He was the first Wigan player to come up to me and wish me all the best, and when I was a young professional trying to make a name for myself he taught me a lot. Shaun was a natural winner, a great competitor and a fantastic leader. He won every honour in the game and his record speaks for itself. You don't collect eight consecutive Challenge Cup winners' medals without being an exceptional player, and Shaun was one of the very few stars who changed the way his position is played.

Terry O'Connor is my best mate in or out of rugby and he would never speak to me again if I didn't pick him in my Dream Team. But the fact is that he deserves a place on merit. As props go he is the opposite of me, which is why we have always been such a good combination when we have played together for Wigan, Great Britain or Ireland. Tez is an out-and-out grafter and one of the few front rowers in the modern game who can play the full eighty minutes if needed. He was regularly the top metre-gainer in Super League, carried the ball up as much if not more than any other prop, and could always get his team-mates going if they were starting to flag, which is why he was consistently voted into Dream Teams throughout his career. He is also a very nice bloke and someone I would always go into battle for.

Andy Platt was a Great Britain front-row/back-row stalwart when I first got into the professional game and was an icon for the heart and determination he showed whenever he took to the field. Andy must have been sixteen stone wet through at a time when front rowers were all big, immobile eighteen-stoners, but despite his lack of size he really held his own and played with 100 per cent enthusiasm. He was one of those players who would always run at a hundred miles an hour whenever he had the ball and who would tackle with every ounce of his weight. He had a great career with Wigan and Great Britain, and he proved how good he was by becoming a big success at

Auckland Warriors when they entered Australia's National Rugby League. They had a lot of respect for him in Australia and he was one of the British players they genuinely feared. A very honest worker, a really tough bloke and someone you would always like to have at your side. I missed him by a couple of months at Wigan so we were never in the same team, but we crossed swords plenty of times and he was a great player.

Probably the worst thing Leeds did during my time there was let Terry Newton go to Wigan. Terry is an exceptionally gifted player who has helped change the way hookers operate, from pass and tackle to a more creative role linking up with the half-backs and loose forward, though he is also very tough defensively. Terry's one of those players who is like ice on the field but warm and considerate off it, and he's a good friend of mine. He broke into the Leeds team as a teenager in 1996 after just a handful of games in the Academy, one of which saw him banned for his part in a huge brawl against Warrington. We have had a few battles since he joined Wigan, but I got a real taste of what he's capable of that night in Blackpool when we had a bit of a tiff and he knocked me on my backside with one punch. I think I've got a decent chin, so to knock me over takes some power. One Christmas while he was at Leeds he turned up with a big lump on his head, the worst black eye you have ever seen, and he was limping. When we asked him what he had done he reckoned he'd fallen off his bike. If that was true he must have been doing about 150 miles an hour at the time. I would hate to see what the road looked like.

I have played alongside Adrian Morley for club and country, and he is one of the players I most admire in the modern game. He's tough and skilful, the sort of individual who can totally dominate a game. He gets stuck into the big blokes and he's not content with taking just one of them on, he'll have a go at them all. Moz had a bit of a reputation for high shots early on in his career, but when he calmed down a bit he became absolutely devastating. He proved how tough he is by going over to play in Australia at a time when there were no other Brits playing at the top level over there. That, and the fact that he arrived with a big reputation, meant everyone wanted to have a go at him, but he stood up to them and earned their respect. When Sydney City Roosters won the Australian Grand Final in 2002 Moz was the only player skipper Brad Fittler mentioned by name in his post-match speech, which was a huge compliment and spoke volumes for him and how well he has done.

Moz has come a long way since our first days together at Leeds, when he was a bit of a teenage beanpole. I have to admit that at first I couldn't see what Bob Pickles, Leeds' chief scout, saw in him, but it didn't take long before it became obvious to me and everyone else that he had that X-factor all the great players possess.

Moz is also a tremendous bloke, a real character and a good friend. After one game in 1996 he and I stayed over for a few drinks together at a pub in Standish, in Wigan, and Jenny picked us up the next day. We dropped Moz off at his house, very close to Salford's ground at the Willows, and he introduced Jenny to his mum, dad and sister. The kettle was put on and Moz popped upstairs while we all had a cup of tea. We waited and waited for him to reappear, and after nearly an hour his dad, Leo, shouted up to find out what he was doing. All we heard back was snores. He'd only gone to bloody bed!

Alongside Moz in my Dream Team second row would be another star from the Oldham production line, Paul Sculthorpe. Scully came from my old amateur club Waterhead and was Man of Steel, British rugby league's highest individual honour, in both 2001 and 2002. What most impressed me about Scully was the way he completely reinvented himself. He began as a wide-running back rower, developed into a world-class loose forward and then became one of the sport's best stand-offs, and he played at international level in all three positions, which takes some doing. I place a lot of importance on being a good player and on being tough, but I also like to play alongside good blokes, and Scully qualifies on all three counts.

At loose forward I could have gone for all-time legend Ellery Hanley, but instead I have chosen Andy Farrell, who is already recognized as one of British rugby league's best ever products and is always an inspiration to play along-side at international level. Some people claim he is over-rated and he can't handle it when the going gets tough, but they are talking utter rubbish. In the latter part of my career, when I was Leeds' pack leader, vice-captain and club skipper, I modelled what I did on Faz and the way he carried himself on and off the pitch.

He is very much of the 'follow what I do' brigade and he likes to lead by example, though that doesn't mean he can't get his point across verbally when he needs to. I remember the Tri-Nations tour in 1999 when we played Australia at Lang Park in Brisbane. We had a look around the stadium the day before the game and Faz sat us down in the middle of the pitch and gave us a rousing team-talk about how much it meant to be playing for Great Britain against Australia at one of their most famous Test venues. I have never forgotten that speech, and it certainly inspired me. Mind you, we got absolutely hammered in the game the next day, so it obviously didn't work for everyone! As a kid I was a bit jealous of Faz because he seemed to get a lot of accolades at a very young age, but now I appreciate the fact that he was so focused and so single-minded.

Throughout my career I have played with a lot of Kiwis and a lot of Aussies, but Shane Tupaea, who is the first of my substitutes, was a bit of both. His family's from New

Zealand but he was brought up in Australia, and with a background like that I suppose it was inevitable he would turn out to have a talent for rugby. Shane wasn't the most gifted of players but he was an honest worker, and when he came to Oldham he had the job of tidying up everyone else's mess. Every team needs a player who's unselfish and doesn't grab the headlines, just gets on with his job and never makes mistakes. Shane was one of those, and he also passed on a few things that have stayed with me all through my playing days. He's a player I have a lot of respect for, and he's a great bloke as well. When our flight was delayed on our 1993 Tenerife trip he got his guitar out in the airport departure lounge and had everyone singing along to 'My Girl'.

Tommy Martyn had a fantastic career with St Helens, and if it hadn't been for injuries I think he would have become one of the truly great players. I played alongside Tommy at Oldham and, along with Chris Joynt, Tony Barrow junior, Richard Pachniuk and Ian Bates, he was one of the reasons why I joined them at the start of my professional career. I could see he was part of a new generation of youngsters coming through and he was one of the most skilful players I have ever come across. He could pass both sides, had a fantastic kicking game and an excellent rugby brain. Character is one of the most important parts of any rugby player's make-up, and Tommy showed plenty of that in the way he kept coming back from serious injury. He's a funny character and great for the dressing room, always having a joke to lighten the atmosphere. Another Lance Todd Trophy winner and someone who put his all into his game. As well as scoring tries, he was an excellent defender too, and there aren't that many players who are good at both.

Gary Mercer is one of very few players who have had two careers at Leeds. Once you leave Headingley you don't usually get a second chance, but Gary did, which is testament to what a good player he was. He had a spell with Leeds in the 1990s before moving on to become a player and then player/coach at Halifax. He did a good job there, but when that turned sour he returned to one of his previous clubs, Warrington, and then Leeds stepped in to re-sign him to help us through an injury crisis at the end of the 2001 season. When I came to Leeds he was in dispute with the club and had a spell frozen out, but Dean Bell later made him captain and he won all the player of the year awards. He was someone who always gave 100 per cent and really led from the front. When he came back, the then coach Daryl Powell just asked him to lift the young players, and he certainly did that. Another very strong character, Ming – after Ming the Merciless in *Flash Gordon* – was one of the most workaholic players in the game: he would always want to make two drives in every set of six and he never stopped toiling in defence. After leaving Leeds he joined the backroom staff at Castleford, and was appointed head coach in 2004. Ming later went on to coach my hometown club Oldham.

Ian Sherratt was a Waterhead lad who had spells with Oldham and Salford. When I was starting out as an amateur he was the first player I trained with who went on to join a professional club, so he was someone I really looked up to. When I got to Oldham Ian looked after me for a couple of years while I found my feet in the first team, and he was a good bloke to have at your side. He was another under-rated player who, like Darren Fleary at Leeds, did a lot of my donkey work, which paved the way for me to grab more of the headlines. When I was at Oldham he was also my drinking partner, so when he sees I have picked him in my Dream Team he might break the habit of a lifetime and buy me a beer.

My Dream Team coach would have to be Ellery Hanley. Though I only played under him for three matches in the

1994 Test series, he was an inspiration and he gave me the self-belief to go on and achieve what I have done in my career.

Without him I would not have had the confidence to get as far as I have in the game. Ellery is a legend in world rugby league and could have qualified for my team as a player as well. As Ellery's assistant I have drafted in Daryl Powell. I played alongside Daryl for Leeds and Great Britain and he had the job of Rhinos coach dropped on him midway through the 2001 season, when Dean Lance left the club. He could have got the boot a couple of times early on, but Leeds stuck with him and as he settled in to the job he repaid their faith and really improved as a coach, both tactially and as a motivator. We had some great times under Daryl and in 2002, when he had a lot of difficult personalities in the squad, he managed to balance everybody and keep the team happy and successful. It was a big surprise when he announced he would be stepping down as coach at the end of 2003, just when everyone else thought he was really beginning to get to grips with the job. His contract was up and he decided to take a break from the coaching role to become director of rugby for a spell, with Tony Smith taking over. The idea was that Daryl would be in charge of the development of the young players for few years and would also have time studying coaching methods at other clubs and in other sports before retaking the helm. The fact he is willing to admit he still has a lot to learn speaks volumes for his character and I am sure when he comes back to the job he will be even better.

All these super athletes will need someone to keep their bodies running, so my Dream Team has to have a physio and that must be rugby league legend Tommy Smales, who would merit a place for entertainment value alone. I could fill a whole book just talking about Tommy, who is one of the greatest characters in the game. Tommy lives in

Featherstone and had a fantastic career with clubs like Huddersfield, Castleford and Bradford, as well as Great Britain. After he packed in playing he ran a pub, the Traveller's Rest, but also kept involved with the game as a coach and then a physio, which is how I met him. He has treated me for all manner of injuries over the years and he has definitely kept me, and plenty of other top players, going.

Visiting a normal physio is a bit like being on a conveyor belt, but Tommy will treat you for as long as it takes. He uses a pressure point system that involves digging his fingers into your injuries to make them bleed and rid themselves of the badness. A trip to Tommy's is always a painful experience, but he keeps me laughing through the agony. Tommy always says the same things: it's always 'sorry about the pain, it's on its way out'; when he does something that makes you jerk in agony he'll say 'there's the joker'; and if he wants you to turn on your side it will be 'roll over Beethoven'. When I first started seeing Tommy he would finish by telling me to 'rise up and run'; later in my career that became 'rise up and limp'. More than anything, Tommy is a really nice bloke and a true rugby league man. He has done wonders for me and I owe him a lot.

Barrie McDermott's Dream Team

Full-back Iestyn Harris (captain)
Right-wing Jason Robinson
Right-centre Keith Senior
Left-centre Gary Connolly
Left-wing Francis Cummins
Stand-off Kevin Sinfield
Scrum-half Shaun Edwards
Prop Terry O'Connor

Hooker Terry Newton
Prop Andy Platt
Second row Adrian Morley
Second row Paul Sculthorpe
Loose forward Andy Farrell
Subs Shane Tupaea, Tommy Martyn,
    Gary Mercer, Ian Sherratt
Coach Ellery Hanley
Assistant coach Daryl Powell
Physio Tommy Smales

So much for the best players I have come across, but what about the toughest, the ones who are a real nightmare to play against?

As far as I'm concerned, there's more to being tough than just the ability to fight and dish out a few head shots, though that does come into it. I have known one or two really tough men who aren't much use in a punch-up but can produce the goods when the odds are against them, which is something I admire. For a bit of fun, I thought I would select my Nightmare Team, one you would never want to play against because everyone in it is either a hard nut, a cheap-shot merchant, a braveheart or just an out-and-out bastard.

If I had to pick the toughest full-back I have ever come across, it would be David Bishop, a Welsh rugby union convert who came north to play for Hull Kingston Rovers. The first time I saw him in action he was playing for Hull KR against Oldham, just before I turned professional. Our eighteen-stone Kiwi wing or second row Charlie McAllister, who was a big favourite at Oldham, made a burst on the right-hand side and Bishop came across to make the tackle, caught him with an elbow and left Charlie looking like the Elephant Man. That definitely grabbed my attention, and I always knew that whenever I played against David Bishop I would be in for a battle. He wasn't the biggest of blokes, but he was a proper tough guy.

You don't often think of wingers as tough men, but Des Drummond was someone who could really take care of himself. He had a great career at the top level with Leigh and Warrington and played on until his late thirties with quite a few lower division clubs. When I first moved into the Stones Bitter Championship I was used to the biggest guys being the toughest, but I remember Peter Tunks telling me that the hardest bloke in the game at that time was Des Drummond, who was a martial arts black belt. He was one of the quietest, nicest people you could meet off the pitch, but he was absolutely devastating with the ball in his hands.

Jamie Bloem is another winger who can give front rowers a tough time when he's in the mood. Jamie, who is South African, was probably more of a pantomime villain than a tough guy. He came over here and played for Castleford before transferring over to Oldham while I was there. He was the sort of bloke who could get into a fight with his own shadow. After leaving Oldham he had a spell with Doncaster when they got into the old First Division and I remember him barging the Leeds full-back Alan Tait off the pitch and into a stone post during a game at Tattersfield. Doug Laughton, who was Leeds coach at the time, was all set to sign him, but just before the deal was done Bloem failed a drugs test and got a long ban. He has been involved in plenty of scrapes since then, but you always know where you are with Jamie. He will always get stuck in whether he's playing within the rules or not.

Dean Bell's autobiography was called *Ultimate Warrior*, and that was a very apt title. He might not have been the most talented rugby league player ever, but he gave 100 per cent every week and it never seemed to matter whether he was fully fit or not. I have played with and against Dean and been coached by him, and I have seen him turn out with painkilling injections when he could hardly walk – and he wasn't above dishing out the odd high shot when he felt like it.

Dean would definitely be one centre in my Nightmare side, and Adrian Vowles would be the other. I played alongside Vowlesy when he had a brief spell at Leeds before going on to coach Wakefield, but he really made his name at Castleford. Like Dean Bell, he won the biggest individual honour in the game when he was named rugby league Man of Steel, and that was very appropriate. Vowlesy wasn't a dirty player, but he was one of the toughest tacklers I have ever come across, a real 100 per center. I remember him showing me his hands one day and they were in a terrible mess: his fingers were all in figures of eight because he had dislocated and broken them so many times. He was just pure aggression every time he went into a tackle. He always had big games against Leeds and I would definitely rather have him alongside me than against me. There are plenty of blokes who will have a duel with guys of the same size, but Vowlesy would always go straight for the biggest bloke in the opposition team.

Half-backs aren't usually the biggest of players, but I have come across some stand-offs and scrum-halves who have really known how to take care of themselves. Probably the hardest stand-off I have played against was Brendon Tuuta, who was known as the Baby Faced Assassin. A Kiwi, he was probably about thirteen and a half stone wet through, but he tackled with every ounce of his body. He always tackled you around the head and put everything into every hit. He had a bit of skill as well, but what really marked him out was the fact that he played so far above his weight. He was always a player you had to watch out for, but it never took him long to find you.

I didn't have to think too hard about the toughest scrum-half I have ever come across. Number sevens are usually the smallest guys on the pitch, and Bobbie Goulding was no exception, but he was as hard as nails. Pound for pound, Bobbie was one of the toughest blokes I ever played with or against. He had a spell at Leeds before my time in the 1990s, but left after a bust-up with one of the back rowers on a pre-season training weekend in Anglesey. It wasn't much of a scuffle, there were only a couple of punches thrown, but Bobbie was the only one left standing. Bobbie gets special bonus points for the high shots he put on Jamie Mathiou and Neil Cowie – they were both beauties. A top player, he should have been one of the all-time greats but for his habit of falling out with his team-mates or the management at just about every club he played for. Even so, he had an outstanding career and deserves respect as someone who always played with heart.

I like to think I know a little bit about tough prop forwards, and Kurt Sorensen would be at the top of anybody's list. Kurt was a Kiwi international who played for Widnes for a number of years. He was only a short bloke, but he started some almighty fights, which was probably his game plan. New Zealand at the time weren't too successful, but they were competitive and tough. When Kurt came to Widnes he had an aura about him and everybody was captivated by him. He has quite an unusual voice and he didn't say much, but that just added to his presence. One of Oldham's pre-season games in 1992 was against Widnes. As a young kid trying to make my name I thought I would get a good shot on Kurt and even instigate a fight, but he just swatted me off like a fly. I remember thinking at the time, 'I want to have presence like him.'

My other prop would have to be Stuart Fielden. I've already made it clear just how much I admire Stuart as a player, and how much I enjoy our many run-ins, but he's a nightmare to play against because he just keeps coming at you.

James Lowes is one of those players fans love to have in their team, and loathe if he's playing for someone else. He began his career as a half-back with Hunslet and signed for Leeds after a big game against them in a Yorkshire Cup tie at Headingley. When Dean Bell was appointed coach they didn't see eye to eye and Lowesy was shipped off to Bradford. He made Leeds regret it plenty of times before hanging up his boots at the end of Super League VIII. I played with him at the start of my Leeds career and a few times for Ireland and Great Britain, and he's probably one of the enigmas of rugby league. People who watch the game can't understand why everybody doesn't hammer him when they get hold of him because he's so niggly and annoying in a game, but off the field he's a very nice bloke and someone I have roomed with on many occasions. Although I have had more than the odd scuffle with him on the pitch, he's a top fellow and someone I would like to have at my side, because he does antagonize people and get opposition teams frustrated. He was a master at that, and he used it to his advantage. He's a tough lad and a fierce competitor. He wouldn't think twice about making up to forty tackles in a game and he was a very potent weapon with the ball in his hands as well.

As I have said, there are a few ways to measure toughness, and being willing and able to play through the pain barrier is one of them. Matt Adamson played one of the bravest games I have ever seen when we reached the Challenge Cup final in 2003. Matt joined us from Penrith Panthers after earning Test honours with Australia, and the only thing left in his career he really wanted to achieve was playing in a major cup final. We played St Helens in the semi-final and Matt fractured his cheekbone in a clash of heads with Darren Britt in the second tackle of the game.

He must have been in agony, especially when Paul Sculthorpe punched him right on the spot a few minutes later, but he played on until half-time. We won the game, and Matt was as delighted as anyone, but he was also absolutely devastated because he had set his heart on playing in a final and it looked like he would miss out.

He had three metal plates inserted in his face the day after the semi-final and nobody thought he had any chance of playing in the final fourteen days later – except Matt. I asked him straight after the semi if he would be all right for the big game and he told me there wasn't a herd of wild horses that could stop him. All through the build-up the medical staff were umming and aahing about whether to let him play, but in the end the doctor and our physio Patrick Moran reluctantly gave him the OK and Daryl Powell said he would pick Matt if he was prepared to play. He got targeted by Bradford fairly early on but managed to get through all but about ten minutes of one of the most intense and physical finals ever. What a lot of people didn't know was that Matt's three-year-old daughter Charlotte had broken one of her arms in an accident at the families' hotel the day before the game and he had spent the morning of the match at a hospital in Cardiff comforting her before she went into surgery.

My hero when I first started watching rugby at Oldham was Andy Goodway, who went on to play for and coach both Wigan and Great Britain, which is a fair achievement in anybody's book. Goodway was one of the first of the new breed of modern professionals. Although he went into the back row in his later days, he started off as a prop, and he was someone I tried to model myself on. He was very aggressive, and when he got up a head of steam he could skittle big guys out of the way. I played a season with him at Oldham, and to be honest, I was totally in awe at the prospect of playing alongside one of my idols. It took me a long time to tell him how much I admired him, but he later became a bit of a mentor and he was someone I went to for advice when things were going wrong for me at Wigan and I couldn't get many people to take me seriously. I got shunned by quite a few of the big names at Central Park, but Goodway would always meet me for a chat or to do a bit of training, and that helped me a lot.

I'm not sure what held Marc Glanville together – Pritt Stick and tape, I think. When he came to Leeds for the final two years of his career he was a complete wreck. His knees had so many scars they looked like a motorway map of Great Britain, he couldn't straighten his legs, and he hardly trained with us because it took him nearly a week to recover after every game. As we had to play thirty-odd matches a season, I never thought he would get through one year, never mind two. But he did, and he proved to be a great signing. He gave about an hour of pure quality every week, even if he did have to have about a gallon of fluid drained out of his knees the morning after every game. It's all right being a good fighter and a big hitter, but true toughness comes from inside and from what you've got under your shirt. MG typified that. He stuck his hand up every week and said, 'I'll take us forward and I'll tidy up the mess,' even when he knew he was really going to suffer for it later.

My Nightmare bench would, of course, be made up of four forwards. Paul Harragon has to make way in the starting line-up for Stuart Fielden, but he would be a useful man to bring off the bench. Harragon, who was known as the Chief, was one tough guy, someone who played at a hundred miles an hour. I was just starting out as he was coming to the end of his international career, but I liked the way he played the game. I came up against him at Wembley when we beat Australia in 1994. At the final whistle Mick Cassidy offered his hand to Harragon to say

'Good game, mate', as we do, but Harragon wouldn't shake. I said to Harragon, 'The game's finished, leave it.' He said, 'Well, do you want some?' I remember thinking, 'He's a big lad this one and I'm too tired to fight, but I'm not walking away.' So I did what I normally do, which is bluff it. 'You're picking on the wrong lad here,' I told him. 'I'll knock your teeth out.' One of his mates held him back and that was the end of that, but I breathed a huge sigh of relief.

The second sub would be Dave Furner, who joined Leeds from Wigan in 2003. Dave is a top bloke and one of the toughest competitors around. He never knows when to quit and he's a tremendous player to have at your side, and a real pain when he's among the opposition. He was very much in the MG mould and was an awesome boxer, so if there was a fight on the pitch you would be in safe hands with him behind you.

My other two subs would be Darren Fleary and Anthony Farrell, or Daz and Faz as everyone called them – and very often the wrong way round as well. When we played Bradford at Odsal at the start of the 1998 season they absolutely battered the Bulls forwards, and their performance that day, along with Iestyn Harris scoring a hat-trick, set the platform for the success we had over the next couple of seasons. Daz and Faz were big mates off the field and on it, and whenever I had them alongside me I knew no one would be going into my back garden. They were good tacklers, solid defenders and great wrestlers. Whenever an opposition player tried for a quick play-the-ball he would find himself flat on his back with his legs in the air, with one of them holding him down and the other trying to find something to pull, twist, snap or break off. They were both tough, competitive and aggressive, and they were great to play alongside.

I will need a coach for my Nightmare Team, and

Malcolm Reilly is the natural choice. He was famous as one of the hardest blokes ever to play the game and he got the same reputation when he moved into coaching. When I played under him I was baffled how one man could be so Jekyll and Hyde. He was an out-and-out gent most of the time, but whenever he spoke about the game there was so much passion it was frightening. Malcolm had a great career as a coach with Castleford, and he guided Newcastle Knights to the Australian Premiership, which was a great achievement. He played a big part in Great Britain's revival as an international force in the 1980s and had spells at Halifax, Leeds and Huddersfield before returning to Headingley as assistant coach and then taking over as director of rugby at Hull KR in 2004. He's the sort of bloke who, when he talks, you listen.

Malcolm is one of the fittest and most competitive blokes I have ever met, despite being another one with seriously dodgy knees. It's easy to get a rise out of Malcolm at training: challenge him to do anything and he'll do it. He can't help it, it's ingrained in him. When I trained with the Great Britain under-21s at Lilleshall, Malcolm was the national coach. I was more than twenty years younger than him and in peak physical condition, but when we were put through a series of really tough fitness tests Malcolm came top in all of them. He even managed to complete the sit-up bleep test, which is eight and a half minutes of non-stop sit-ups, getting progressively faster.

Malcolm was a notoriously tough guy off the field as well. Once, when he was coaching at Halifax, he got into an argument with a driver who had blocked the team bus in the car park. Malcolm asked him nicely to move it, then a bit less nicely, and each time the driver refused. Eventually Malcolm's patience ran out. He decked the driver with one punch and got in and moved the car himself. A legend.

Barrie McDermott's Nightmare Team

Full-back David Bishop
Right-wing Des Drummond
Right-centre Dean Bell
Left-centre Adrian Vowles
Left-wing Jamie Bloem
Stand-off Brendon Tuuta
Scrum-half Bobbie Goulding
Prop Kurt Sorensen (captain)
Hooker James Lowes
Prop Stuart Fielden
Second row Matt Adamson
Second row Andy Goodway
Loose forward Marc Glanville
Subs Paul Harragon, Dave Furner,
    Darren Fleary, Anthony Farrell
Coach Malcolm Reilly

18

THE REAL ME

To my family. No one can build a successful career in any sport without being selfish, dedicated and focused, but you were always the glue that held me together.

The biggest buzz I ever get on a rugby field is hearing the crowd singing 'There's only one Barrie McDermott'. That is probably the highest compliment the fans can pay you, but actually it's not true. I like to think there are two Barrie McDermotts, the one everybody sees out on the pitch and a separate, off-duty, non-rugby Barrie. And the two of them are very different people.

As a professional sportsman I get a fair bit of attention from people in the street, in supermarkets or at official rugby club functions, and I always try to send them away with a bit of a different impression to the one they had before they met me. I know I've got a notorious reputation and perhaps that's fully justified because of what has happened during my playing career, but it's not the full story. I would like to think I am every bit as much the dedicated, church-going family man as I am the fella who has been sent off more times than he can remember and has a season ticket to appear before the disciplinary committee.

One of the defining moments of my career, and my life, was when I met my wife Jenny. Our relationship has gone a long way towards separating the on- and off-field sides of my character. I will be the first to admit I had a fairly turbulent lifestyle in my teens and early twenties, and by the time I signed for Wigan it had already got me in quite a lot of trouble, but Jenny helped calm me down. I have known Jenny for a number of years because her mother lived just around the corner from my old amateur club Waterhead, so we were friends in the days when she had just left school and I was working on the building sites and playing rugby part-time. In those days I was really committed to my rugby, but I also enjoyed my social life a little bit too much, which was one of the reasons I got into trouble. Jenny has always been a steadying influence, and as my rugby career has progressed over the years she and the kids have really helped me keep my feet on the ground.

Our first son Billy was born in 1996, about a year and a half after we first started seeing each other. That was another big step, because it was the beginning of my settling-down period. I am no different to anybody else: once you become a parent your values, your outlook and your whole life changes. I came from a loving family that brought me up the right way, and I really wanted to do the same for my son. I wanted my children and all my family to be able to walk around with heads held high and to be proud of their dad, as I am of my mum and dad.

My parents have definitely been the biggest influence on my life. My sister Alison and I had a rock-solid upbringing, and if ever we wanted something my mum and dad would not think twice about sacrificing a few nights out just to give us a treat. I couldn't have asked for a better mother and father, or family in general. If I can be half as good to my kids as my parents were to me and Alison, I will have done a good job. I have been present at the birth of all three of my kids and I think that must be about the greatest experience a man can have. I saw Sophie being born in 1999, and I cut the cord when Jessica was born in 2002, which is worth more than anything that has happened to me on the rugby pitch. My children are my best medals and my sweetest victories.

All I want for my kids is for them to be happy. Although Mum and Dad weren't really poor, I had a relatively harsh upbringing in terms of material things, but we never wanted for love or affection and that made a big impression on me. I want to make sure my kids get a similarly good start in life. I don't want them to go without, but I aim to ensure they grow up to respect their dad for what he has given them in terms of love, not for what he has done on the rugby field.

A lot of what I have achieved in my rugby career I want to dedicate to my parents and especially my father. He wasn't able to play sport professionally, but he lives it through me. I'm thrilled to bits for him, but that's not necessarily what I want for Billy, Sophie or Jessica. I want them to be happy and successful in whatever field they choose; I don't want them to feel they have to better whatever I have done. The secret of success is to set yourself high goals, work hard, listen to all pieces of advice, use what you need and discard what you don't. I wouldn't want Billy to go on and play for Great Britain if that didn't make him happy. If he wants to try and make it as a professional rugby player I will support him all the way, but my attitude won't be any different whatever he decides to do. Billy has a bubbly personality and is a really open kid. He does what he wants, he plays all sorts of sports and he really enjoys himself. I would of course be thrilled if he became a professional sportsman, but no more so than if he did really well in any other job. And the same applies to Sophie and Jessica.

One of the nice things about the job I do is that I am able to ensure my kids have things we couldn't afford when I was growing up. Still, you can raise somebody in a bedsit or a mansion, but it's the way you bring them up, the upbringing you provide, that really counts. Money isn't really a motivation for me. It's nice to have a comfortable lifestyle, but that's not what makes me get out of bed in the morning. The fact that I enjoy my job is what makes me get up when the alarm goes off at six a.m. I want to achieve things in the game and to win honours – that is my greatest motivation. When I hang my boots up I want to be able to look back and say I did everything I could have done and I had a good time doing it.

The kids are still a bit too young to bother too much about what happens on the field, but obviously Jenny worries, mainly about me getting sent off or being hurt. She knows how much it affects me when either of those things happens. Whenever I am sent off, as soon as the red mist clears I always find myself thinking, 'What have I done here?' It usually means I'm going to be prevented from doing the job I love for the next four or five weeks and I'm going to be hit in the pocket, which affects the whole family. I know Jenny's parents Bob and Lyn Unsworth's and my mum and dad's hearts sink when I get sent off, and that's when I really need their patience and under-standing. I like them to be there in the good times, but they know to stay away when things go wrong. It can't be easy for them having to put up with the mood swings and the fact that not only am I pissed off with myself but also with life in general and everything that has contributed to the moment of madness that got me the red card. People are only trying to help when they come up and say, 'Never mind, keep your chin up,' but all I want them to do is leave me alone.

It's corny, but whenever that happens I think of the film *Rocky IV*, when the boxer played by Sylvester Stallone is all on his own training in the mountains. That's the sort of mindset I get into. I isolate myself and go into a really strict training mode, with the motivation that I'm going to be better when I get back from my ban than I was before. Things like that happen because of the way I play the game. I wouldn't alter anything – except, of course, the red card.

The same applies to being injured. You always want to come back better than you were before, but it's very difficult. Whenever you're not playing you start to lose some of the physical powers you have when you are fully match fit. At least if you are suspended you can train, but if you have a bad injury you might find yourself confined to sitting around doing nothing physical, and for a professional sportsman that is as low as it can get.

Being sent off has an effect mentally as well. When I was red-carded in 2002 after the punch-up with Stuart Fielden in a game against Bradford at Valley Parade, I picked up a four-match ban, and the first game after that was against Bradford again, at Headingley. The media made a big thing of that and I said in the papers and in TV and radio interviews that I was really looking forward to righting the wrongs against the same opposition. But deep down I knew I was in a corner, because I couldn't play with my normal ferocity. People were expecting me to mess up and to square up to anyone wearing a Bradford shirt, particularly Stuart. Everyone, including the referee, was waiting for it to happen, so I had to make sure it didn't. And with that very much in my mind it was impossible for me to play my normal game.

As I have said, what happens on the field does rebound on my personal life because it affects the way I am feeling, but I really do try not to take it out on my friends, family or anyone else. What I try to do is leave rugby behind on the Yorkshire border, so that when I'm back home in Oldham I am off-duty. If we have lost or I have had a particularly poor game I don't want to go home and kick the dog. For me, being tough and hard is a rugby thing. Being normal and non-aggressive is what comes naturally, so more often than not I can leave rugby behind without too much of a problem.

Sometimes after a game, once we have got changed, we have to do interviews, give autographs or speak to sponsors when all I really want to do is grab my kids and my wife and give them a kiss and a cuddle. After being tough and aggressive for a couple of hours I don't want to be like that any more; I want to sit down, stroke my daughters' hair and relax. That is not an act. Being tough and hard and ferocious is one thing I have to do as part of my job to get where I want to be, which is at the top of the tree. But it requires effort, and it can't be a twenty-four-hours-a-day, seven-days-a-week thing. That would take up far too much energy.

I am very conscious of the fact that I am a role model for a lot of youngsters, whether I like it or not. A lot of kids who come from tough backgrounds or who find it hard at school identify with me and get influenced by the things I do on the field, which is quite a responsibility. It's not something I would choose, it just happens. People put you on a bit of a pedestal because of the good things you do, but the bad things that sometimes happen are just as influential. So off the pitch I spend a lot of time trying to use my influence in exactly the opposite way, teaching kids to look after themselves and keep out of bother. I tell them to beat people with your mind, not your fists.

I want to give my friends and family something to be proud of even though I make mistakes all the time on the pitch and I do get stuck in. That's why I am admired by some people, but it's also the reason why I get so much attention off the field. I often get people writing and asking me to have a word with their lad because he has been getting himself into trouble. I spend a lot of my spare time visiting schools and youth or rugby clubs, and I inevitably end up talking to the kids who find it hard in lessons, or who are a bit different to all the rest. My dad's great with kids, and that's something he has passed down to me. I can usually get my message across. If I can help one kid get his life in order, even in a small way, then all the community work I do is worthwhile. I am not a teacher or a social worker and I would never want to be, but because of what I do for a living kids are usually prepared to sit down and listen to what I have got to say. I would like to think I can talk to them on their level, that I know where they are coming from, because I have been through exactly the same thing. Just because people put them in a certain category doesn't mean they have to accept that. Just because you have made some mistakes or you have had trouble at school doesn't mean that that is the way the rest of your life is going to be.

I made a definite change in my life. I made a conscious decision to stop being a bad example and to try to live my life in a positive way. That's not to say that I haven't messed up since, and I'm sure I will do so again in the future, but I do my best to ensure there's a positive aspect to everything I do. I try to tell kids that their destiny is in their own hands; just because they have a bad reputation at school doesn't mean they can't make something of their lives later on and change the way people think about them. People will not put up with you if you keep making the same mistakes, but if you learn from your errors you will generally get respected for that.

Many people will find it strange, but a lot of rugby players are church-goers, and most of them are the ones you would least expect, the assassins and enforcers. Vila Matautia, Apollo Perelini, Andy Farrell and Adrian Morley all spring to mind. I am not a bible basher by any means, but I want to give the right impression to my friends and family. The fact that I can get myself and my kids up on a Sunday morning, take them to church and sit with them through the service is a good thing for people to see. I am close to my priest, Father Eugene Dolan, and I hope he can use the fact that I attend his church to encourage others to come along. I know being a member of the Catholic Church is not seen as a cool thing to do, but by having me as part of the congregation Father Dolan can tell kids, 'If Barrie McDermott can do it, so can you.'

I am not embarrassed to say that I pray before matches. I don't pray that we win, I pray that I don't get sent off, that I don't lose my cool, that I don't let my family down, that I don't get hurt and that my family have a safe journey to and from the match across the M62. That is as much as I want to ask for. I wouldn't want to pray for a win because I want to earn my victories and to feel I deserve them. That is my job, rather than something I can ask for. A lot of rugby players wear their faith on their sleeve and enjoy talking about it and making it an issue, but my faith is very personal and it's something I rarely talk about, though I'm not embarrassed about it and I don't make an active effort to keep it secret. I would like my kids to grow up as church-goers, but if they get to an age when they decide it's not for them, then fair enough, I will respect their wishes. All my family are Catholic and my mum took me to church up to my middle teens, when she gave me the option to carry on or leave. I decided not to go for quite a few years, then I went back again.

My philosophies on religion and life in general have no real influence on how I play the game of rugby league. I play to win, and I will do whatever I can to ensure I do win. I have often gone to disciplinary hearings and been asked, 'Did you mean to hurt that player?' I might not tell them this, but the real answer is that I mean to hurt every player I tackle, though I don't go out deliberately to cause injury. I want any player I come up against to know he has been tackled, but I don't want to hit him so hard he can't get up or he's not able to play the following week. I aim to hurt rather than to wound, and there's a big difference. Rugby league is my job, but it's also a game. I often compare us to gladiators: it's as if we are battling for our very existence. I have had some tremendous wars with some very tough blokes, but once the final whistle has gone I would like to think I'm not too big to say, 'Yes, you got me there.' If someone does get the better of me I am always the first to shake his hand after the game and say, 'You played a great game.'

Rugby league is still a small world and most of the players know one another. A lot of the opponents I come up against when I'm playing for Leeds have been team-mates alongside me for Lancashire, Ireland or Great Britain, and after a game I will often ask them how their families are, because whatever goes on during the match is finished by then. It's never personal. I don't really care too much about whether players in the other team like me, but I do want them to respect me. The same goes for the fans. I am used to being jeered, abused and cheered in equal measure, and either way it's a compliment.

Still, you would have to be really thick-skinned not to notice thousands of people booing every time you get the ball, and the abuse I take is the reason I don't want my family to watch me playing in away games. If fans are singing 'He's only got one eye' it does bother me. It's personal, it has nothing to do with rugby and I don't see why my kids should be exposed to something like that. But if I'm getting a hard time from rival fans, I know the same supporters would be cheering me if I played for their team. I don't mind if they think Barrie McDermott is a dirty git. If they think that, then I'm doing my job right. Supporters have often told me after Lancashire or Great

Britain games, 'I don't normally like you when you play for Leeds, but I was glad you were on our side today.' Upsetting the opposition, whether that is fans or players, is part of the job for a front rower. As the old saying goes, it's a dirty job but somebody has to do it.

Prop forwards don't win too many man of the match awards. That usually gets left to the half-backs, the creative types and the try-scorers, and it's not something that bothers me much. It's nice to get recognition, but as long as my team-mates and coaches appreciate the work I and the rest of the grafters do, I am happy. I don't get jealous of the Kevin Sinfields or the Paul Sculthorpes or the Iestyn Harrises because I know they are just as grateful to me for the hard toil as I am to them for their flair play. Most games of rugby are won through forward domination, and Iestyn has said he would have me alongside him in any rugby league team because he respects the work I do. If I am on the pitch and my team scores a try, I can generally feel I played a part in it, whether it was jarring the ball loose from the opposition, a quick play-the-ball a few tackles back to get a roll on, or a dummy run to give someone a bit of space and fool the other side.

Rugby league is very much a team game, but if you haven't got the individuals to conduct the orchestra, you aren't going to get a tune out. It's all about piano players and piano carriers. If I didn't carry the piano for Kev or Iestyn or Scully, they wouldn't be able to play it. I would like to have scored more tries, to get a mention in some record book somewhere, but I'm still proud of what I do and what I have contributed to the teams I have played in. Certainly later on in my career there haven't been too many times when I've been left out when fit and available, so that's good enough for me.

I have done a bit of promotional work for various sponsors, but I don't suppose I am ever going to be seen as a glamour player. Because of the background I come from, I think the working man can associate with me. Every team has got someone who looks like he has just come off a building site, which when I was playing for Oldham was true more often than not. I have been a joiner, a plasterer and a hod carrier, and that has earned me a certain amount of respect, because there aren't too many of us left in the modern game of professional athletes.

I have to smile wryly when I'm driving to a game and I see the fans turning up. The young girls and the attractive women tend to be wearing a shirt with the number 13 and the name Sinfield on the back, and the big, burly blokes with tattoos and shaved heads are wearing 10 McDermott. It shows I am making an impression on somebody, even if he has just got out of prison!

I have been lucky to play with two of the biggest clubs in British rugby as well as my home town side, which is always something special. It's a privilege to play for a club like Leeds, which has so much standing in the game, and to follow in the footsteps of greats such as Eric Harris, Arthur Clues, Lewis Jones, John Holmes, Ellery Hanley and Garry Schofield. I wouldn't consider myself to be particularly famous, but being recognized and having people wanting to talk to you and feeling that you owe them something is all part of the business. As I have said, sometimes signing autographs is the last thing you want to do after a tough game, but it has to be done. I like to have a chat with my dad after I have got changed, but more often than not there's a queue of kids hanging around waiting for an autograph. Sometimes I wish they would just give me five minutes, but on the other hand I can see myself through their eyes and I wouldn't want them thinking I was an arsehole. If you refuse to sign your name you could ruin some kid's night, and there will always be someone there to accuse you of being a big-time Charlie.

As for getting nodded at in the street, that is quite flattering, and once I stop playing I'm sure it'll take some time
adjusting to not having people recognize me. As they say,
the only thing worse than being talked about is not being
talked about.

It certainly took some getting used to when I first started
playing. I would be enjoying a night out with some mates
and there'd be a bloke staring and smiling at me. I used to
think either he was gay or he wanted a fight. But being a bit
of a name does have its perks. I have never had to queue for
a nightclub, for example, and it's very rare for me to have
to pay to get in one. There are special privileges with res-
taurants and free sports gear, too, but at the same time you
always have to be aware that people are watching you and
if you're not careful you could end up in the newspapers.

Just after the trouble I had with the police in 1996
Franny Cummins came up to me in the changing room
after a game and asked if I had been out in Leeds the
previous Saturday night. I told him I had been at home
with my mum and dad and Jenny watching TV. One of
Franny's mates had told him I was in a huge brawl in a
nightclub and had spent the night in police cells. That
wasn't true, but it just shows how once you've got a bit of
a reputation people will invent stories if you don't give
them something to talk about.

I would like to think that over recent years I have
shed a bit of that image, that people now see me for how
I really am. I think I do surprise people when I talk to
them. I feel a lot of people expect me to be a bit thick and
a bit aggressive. I am not an expert on rocket science or
Middle Eastern politics, but I would like to think I can hold
a conversation with most people. And I do make an effort
to astonish people who don't know me with how nice I can
be. Of course I'm never going to change everybody's opinion of me, but sometimes when they are walking away I

will overhear them saying, 'He's all right, he's a nice lad.'
That always makes me smile.

So that's it. At the beginning of this book I said I wanted
to take you behind the name and the reputation, to reveal
the real Barrie McDermott. You've been with me through
all the ups and downs, the successes and the disappointments, and I hope now you will understand what makes
me tick off the rugby field, as well as on it.

To the media and the fans, I think I will always be
'the notorious Barrie McDermott'. You know me a little bit
better than that. Whether you agree with that description
or not is up to you, but I would like to think of myself
as a professional, who loves his sport, has always given
everything on the pitch and has managed to remain a fairly
decent sort of bloke off it.

And whatever happens in the future, I will always be
Made for Rugby.

Postscript

ON TOP OF THE WORLD

Victories aren't just a place you arrive at, they are about what you learn on the way. Dedicated to the Rhinos players of 2004–5, who made Leeds fans smile again.

If I had been told on 6 December 1987 that I would go on to have any sort of rugby league career – never mind such an enjoyable one which would influence so many people in a positive way – I doubt I would have believed it.

It is ironic that as soon as I finished writing my life story, I had probably the greatest moments of my entire playing career. The first edition of this book was published on Friday, 15 October 2004, and the very next day I finally got to collect a Super League Grand Final winner's ring.

The 2004 season was definitely the best I have ever had and was probably the finest in the Leeds club's history. We finished nine points clear at the top of the Super League, losing only two league games all season, and then won Leeds' first championship in thirty-two years by beating Bradford Bulls in the Grand Final at Old Trafford. And to cap it all, we defeated the Australian champions Canterbury Bulldogs in the World Club Challenge.

It was the sort of season I had long dreamt of but which, I must admit, I was beginning to think would never happen. I have always wanted to give the fans something to remember me by and being part of the first Leeds team in twenty-one years to win the Challenge Cup did that. After the Grand Final victory, our media manager Phil Daly told me I was only the twenty-second player to win a Challenge Cup and Championship final with Leeds, which is something I am extremely proud of. To go on and become the first player to win the Challenge Cup, Super League Grand Final and World Club Challenge for Leeds is something I will treasure for the rest of my life. I would like to think that when Leeds are inviting the old timers along to be introduced to the crowd in twenty, thirty or forty years' time, they will drop me a line.

What made our success in 2004 even more special was the fact we did it with such a great bunch of lads. I'm sure somewhere down the line we'll all get together for a beer and a chat and will remember that season very fondly.

We led Super League from start to finish and I played in thirty of our thirty-three games, so I like to think I did my bit. A big part of our success was due to the fact that we had very few serious injuries through the year, so our coach Tony Smith could select from more or less the same squad of players all season. That was a tribute to our physio Patrick Moran and the conditioner Steve Walsh, who both did fantastic jobs.

Tony Smith's philosophy is to look after the little things; we had probably skated over these in previous years. It was a great credit to him that in early 2005 the England rugby union squad, who had won their World Cup a year or so earlier, came to spend three days in Leeds to look at Tony's methods and the way Leeds Rhinos played. To be honest, we did not have anything too technical to show them. We didn't have a magic formula, it was just a case of practising the little things over and over again. When I start coaching, the first thing I plan to do is make sure all my players have a really good knowledge of the basics and a desire to improve. This is something I have learned from Tony.

Another thing Tony did which really paid off, was to give youngsters like Richard Mathers a chance. At the start of the 2004 season Richard was second choice full-back behind Gary Connolly, who was in the Super League Dream Team the year before and had played for Great Britain. Richard trained hard, got his head down and really focused on making sure Gary Connolly had to play at the top of his game every week to keep his place. As soon as Gary got an injury, which happened after the first few games, Richard stepped into the side and stayed there. By the end of the year, I thought Richard was very unlucky not to be chosen to play for Great Britain. I've no doubt he will go on to have a great international career.

We also saw people like Danny McGuire, Ryan Bailey, Danny Ward and Matt Diskin really begin to fulfil their potential. Danny McGuire had shown glimpses of his capabilities in the previous couple of seasons, with, for example, his two tries in the 2003 Challenge Cup semi-final, but he really came of age in 2004, scoring thirty-nine tries in thirty appearances, including the winner in the Grand Final. He was really influential in the team, but one of the best things about our championship-winning side was the fact we could still tick without our key men.

The two front-rowers, Wardy and Bailey, stepped up to the mark and had big years, both getting selected for Great Britain at the end of it. I was disappointed to miss out, though not entirely surprised, but the fact that two of Rhinos' other props were picked softened the blow.

Having packed down next to Disko for a few years I always knew how good he was, but he really proved it in 2004. He started the year in good form and just got better and better, unfortunately, he got to experience the down side of the game after he was named in the Super League Dream Team and got our player of the year honour. He thoroughly deserved to be called into the GB Tri-Nations squad, but suffered an anterior cruciate ligament injury on his debut against New Zealand. As any sportsman will tell you, that's about the worst injury you can get without actually breaking anything and it kept him out for much of 2005, though I am sure it won't affect his career in the long term.

Then there's other players like Nick Scruton, Lee Smith, Ashely Gibson, Jason Golden, Scott Murrell and Carl Ablett who have also really developed and I believe will go on to have big careers in Super League if they keep working.

We had the right mix of youth and experience and the team spirit was probably the best I have been involved with. My concept of team spirit changed a bit in our championship year. I used to think you had to interact with your teammates socially, perhaps over a beer or two, if you wanted to create an environment where you were all friends, but I learnt that isn't necessarily the case. What we did do was create a winning environment, a hard-working environment, one where it wasn't acceptable for you to come in at the start of the week tired or hungover and then expect everybody else to carry you.

If we played on a Friday we'd go swimming straight after the game and more often than not we were back in training the following morning with Sunday off. Then when you came in on Monday you were ready to start all over again at 100 miles an hour. If you hadn't looked after yourself over the weekend, you'd be found out.

So we had the right mix of players and the right attitude and it paid off for us. We had a couple of slip-ups against St Helens in the Challenge Cup and league and we lost narrowly in a Super League game at Wigan, but otherwise we were very consistent all season and had top spot on the table wrapped up with a month of the regular campaign to go.

We won twenty-four of our twenty-eight regular season games, with draws at London and Wigan, and finished on fifty points, nine clear at the top of the table. We had the best attack, scoring 1,037 points, and the tightest defence, conceding only 443, so it was a very pleasing campaign and the League Leaders' Shield was our first silverware since the Challenge Cup in 1999.

That meant a home play-off tie against our old enemy Bradford Bulls, who finished second in the league, with the winners going straight through to Old Trafford. We had won all our games at Headingley, including twice against Bradford, so we were confident, but they came and turned us over. They played really well and deserved the quick route into the Grand Final. That set a lot of nerves jangling – outside the team at least. We had to play Wigan at Headingley in the final eliminator and after what had happened twelve months earlier, when we lost to them at the same stage, a lot of people said we were going to blow it again and we would be the first team to finish top of the league and not reach the Grand Final.

As players we believed in what we were doing, we looked at what went wrong against Bradford and we were sure we could correct it. As it turned out, we were right to be confident. We won 40–12 to go through to our second Grand Final, which meant another anxious week for me and the rest of the lads. All that year Tony hadn't picked the same side two weeks running, so everyone who played against Wigan was looking over their shoulder wondering if they would miss out on the final.

I wasn't worried I'd be dropped, but I was a bit anxious that I had got to the final stage of something I had dreamed about for ten years and luck, as it had done sometimes in the past, might turn against me. I knew I had done every-thing Tony had asked of me and I'd had a good strong end to the season, so I was confident I would be in his plans. But you never know for certain, so it was a relief when I was named in the team, which, amazingly, was unchanged from the previous game.

Ever since, people have asked me what the build-up to the Grand Final was like. In fact it wasn't really different to any other game. All year we had tried to treat every game the same and prepare no differently whether we were playing Workington in the Challenge Cup fourth round or Bradford in the Grand Final.

There were a few different things we had to do, like go to a big press conference on Monday and visit Old Trafford to look round, but for the most part we just stuck to the tried and tested routine, with a short, sharp training session on the day before the game, pizza for lunch together at the Arc restaurant close to the ground in Headingley and then off home to relax. We didn't stay overnight in a hotel before the final, we just met up and travelled over on the day, as normal, and I think that helped. It is good to focus on the important games, but it doesn't necessarily mean you have to isolate yourself in a hotel and sleep in a strange bed and not eat the things you would eat on a normal day.

The game itself went more or less according to plan. We got off to a good start with an early penalty goal by Kevin Sinfield, but Bradford scored the first try when Lesley Vainikolo touched down at the corner after about five minutes. We weren't behind for long because Disko scored a great solo try to put us back in front. Sinny converted and kicked a penalty and we were 10–4 up at half time.

They scored another try right at the start of the second half through Shontayne Hape, but Paul Deacon couldn't kick the goal and there were just two points in it for a long, long time. We had most of the possession and territory, but couldn't find a way through until five minutes from time when the unfortunate Robbie Paul knocked-on near their line and Danny McGuire squeezed over after the scrum. Sinny kicked the goal to give us an eight-point lead and we knew then we'd got it won.

The reaction at the end was a mixture of relief and sheer

joy. Even though we'd won the league by such a massive margin, a lot of people were expecting us to choke when it really mattered, because that's what Leeds had always done in the past.

I was one of the substitutes and I came on midway through the first half. Just getting a taste of that big-match atmosphere, which is a mass of colour and noise, was fantastic, but to go up and get my hands on the trophy at the end was a very special moment. The Leeds fans had waited a long, long time for it and we were as pleased for them as we were for ourselves.

I was off the field in the closing stages and all the replacements and the people who hadn't been picked were lined up on the touchline counting down the last few seconds. I've watched the video and you can see us all jumping up and down with excitement. Francis Cummins is on the film, leaping about with the rest of us, even though he was waiting for a knee reconstruction! Franny had been hurt in the final league game and at that stage it looked as though he wasn't going to get a new contract, but he was as excited as everyone else, which shows the amazing team spirit and depth of feeling in the camp.

I have always been a big admirer of Franny, both as a player and a person, but the way he reacted before, during and after the Grand Final raised him even further in my estimation. I think a lot of the positive attitude he had to a selection disappointment came from the opening game of the season, when Franny was left out for the first time in five years, after 178 consecutive appearances. It must have been a big blow, but he knuckled down and showed true professionalism and that was a big inspiration to the rest of the lads. Franny is a real gentleman and an example to anyone, young or old. I was delighted when he was given a new contract and had the chance to work with the back-room staff after he had recovered from his injury.

People like Matt Adamson, Chris Feather, Wayne Mc-Donald and Andrew Dunemann all missed out on the Grand Final after playing a big part in the season, but they joined in the celebrations fully and that is a big test of character. I have been there myself and I know what it's like; 60 per cent of you wants the team to win, but 40 per cent of you wants to crawl off into a corner and be sorry for yourself. It is hard to feel a part of it, but the best policy is just to enjoy the moment and feel you've contributed to the team getting there.

After the final hooter we picked up the trophy, sprayed the Tetley's around and did the lap of honour. The thrill and excitement is something I've only felt a couple of times in my career and it's hard to describe. It's something you dream about and when it actually happens, it's quite surreal. I kept expecting to wake up.

I missed out on all the speeches in the changing room once the lads had got off the pitch because I was too busy invading the crowd. Straight after picking up my winner's ring all I wanted to do was find Jenny and Billy, because I had a promise to keep.

When I was fifteen and my grandfather died, I was left his black onyx ring as an heirloom, and I lost it on a building site in Oldham town centre. I suppose it's still there now, in the foundations. It's something that's bothered me ever since. It upset my family, and for years I kept asking myself 'How could you have done that?' I was deeply annoyed that my granddad had had the ring for most of his life but I had lost it in just a matter of months.

In Super League, the Grand Final winners don't get a medal, they get a ring. I always said when mine came along it was something I would give my son. I had often told him this, so once I collected the ring all I wanted to do was find my family and give it to Billy.

When we won the Challenge Cup at Wembley, all the

team's kids got passed over the fence onto the pitch, so they could be on the celebration pictures. At Old Trafford that was banned. We were told it would incur a £15,000 fine and there'd be action from the Rugby League if we even tried it. I was told later it was something to do with not having children on pictures which could be used to promote a brewer, who were the competition sponsor. We talked about it before the game. There was a strong feeling that if we won we should just wear the fine and do it because it was our day and we wanted to share it with our families, but in the end we decided to play by the rules.

After the victory lap I couldn't see my mum and dad, but I spotted Jenny, Billy and the girls and I set off on an expedition to reach them. As everyone else was heading for the changing rooms, I was climbing into the stand. Of course, my family seemed to be in Row Z and I had a real job getting to them. Normally, if you go anywhere near the crowd you're mobbed for pictures and autographs, but the fans realized what was happening and they all helped lift me up and over.

Eventually I got to Jenny and gave her a kiss and handed the ring to Billy, who was eight at the time. I am pleased I was able to do that. Since then I've got the ring engraved and it has gone in the trophy cabinet. When he's twenty-one, I'll present it to Billy at his party. Hopefully when he has a son, he can hand it on to him and it will go through the generations until somebody loses it in the foundations of a building site.

So I got to the changing rooms quite late, but apparently Dave Furner, who was retiring after the game, had made quite an emotional speech. He said he had planned to hang up his boots the year before, but decided to play on because he knew the group of people we had would win something in 2004 and he wanted to be part of it.

From Old Trafford we went straight back to Headingley

for a bit of a party with our families, people who worked at the club, sponsors and some fans who had managed to sneak in. The next day, there was a civic reception in Leeds, which is something I will never forget.

It was arranged at a day or two's notice, but more than 7,000 people turned up, which shows just how much Leeds Rhinos means to people in the city. It's fair to say there was the occasional drink consumed the night before, but we had to get up early on Sunday for a team picture with the trophy at Headingley, then we had another couple of beers before heading off to the civic hall.

I've been to 'homecomings' in the past, but this was the most enjoyable, seeing so many people there and the reaction the team and the trophy got. It was a wet day and to see all those people standing in the rain was really humbling. We get paid to play rugby and sometimes you can forget just how much what you do in your job means to thousands and thousands of people. The Leeds fans have had to put up with so many disappointments over the years, this was one time when they could go to work with a spring in their step and their heads held high, especially if they worked in Bradford!

After the reception we all decamped to the Skyrack, which is one of the most well-known pubs in Headingley, close to the ground. It's run by Carmel, who is the wife of Paul Fletcher, a former Leeds player who still works for the club, and is a hub of activity for the rugby community. We stayed there all Sunday night and not one of us had to dip his hand in his pocket, which is something I know Keith Senior was delighted about.

The day after that was the traditional end-of-season Mad Monday. We were a bit thin on numbers at first, though everyone turned up eventually. As a true professional athlete it was a long time since I had enjoyed a full English breakfast at 10 a.m. in a pub with a pint of beer, so I wasn't going to miss out. Later that evening we had a leaving do for Matt Adamson and Dave Furner and then the day after that we were back in training! Absolutely true.

Tony Smith called us in for a video session, which was basically a debrief of the Grand Final, very much in line with what we had done throughout the year. We looked at the bad points and laughed at the good bits, but just three days after the Grand Final Tony was already thinking about how we could improve for the next season, which is a tribute to his professionalism.

The Great Britain team for the Tri-Nations series against Australia and New Zealand was announced the Monday after the Grand Final, and I was in a pub when I heard the news. I was surprised and disappointed Kevin Sinfield wasn't selected after such an inspirational year for the Rhinos, though Ryan Bailey, Danny Ward, Chev Walker, Matt Diskin and Danny McGuire were all included.

Chev and Ryan made their Great Britain debuts in the series and I was delighted for both of them. After what had happened in 2003, they had both worked really hard to rebuild their reputations, on and off the field, and they deserved all the success they got. I think both of them will be regulars on the international scene for a lot of years to come.

I was keen to complete ten years as an international player, so I was delighted to accept an invitation to play for Ireland in the European Nations tournament. Daryl Powell was the coach and we had a group of young, up-and-coming players from the National Leagues.

I had the chance to do a bit of hands-on coaching and it was a couple of weeks I really enjoyed, though I must admit I was a bit off the pace at my first training session on the Thursday, having spent most of the previous week in the bottom of a pint pot.

We deservedly got through to the final against England

and I enjoyed the game, scoring a try and getting our man of the match award. England were 24–0 up at half time, but we dug deep. It finished 36–12, so we came out of the game with credit. Mark Calderwood and Rob Burrow scored tries for England, and Rob kicked six goals from as many attempts.

While all that was going on, I was also heavily involved in publicizing the hardback edition of this book. The publication date had been decided long before we knew we would be in the Grand Final, but it turned out to be a happy coincidence. The first review copies arrived on the day of the final eliminator, so Dave Howes, who was helping with the publicity, handed them out at the game and there were big features in most of that weekend's Sunday papers.

We had a cheese and wine party for 150 people at Headingley, which was Dave's idea, to launch the book and I must have done a dozen or so signing sessions all over Yorkshire and Lancashire. We held the first one at Philip Howard Books in Leeds, which is run by big Rhinos fans Phil and Ros Caplan. That was a week after the Grand Final and I took the trophy along to show off to people. I thought a few dozen fans might turn up, but hundreds came. There were queues down the street; we stopped the traffic and eventually the shop sold out of *Made for Rugby*, which didn't do my ego any harm.

I must admit I was a bit nervous about the reaction I'd get to this book. There is a lot of personal stuff in it and I thought if people didn't like it, that would be a reflection on me. Fortunately, the reaction has been really positive and I have been touched by people's nice comments. I was even more surprised to get letters from all over the rugby-league world, including New Zealand, Australia and Canada, and throughout the UK, not just Oldham and Leeds. I have since been told that I am very modest about my career, but for me the biggest compliment is for other people to talk about my achievements. I think it's important to tell people how I've done things, but it is up to others to decide what I've achieved.

In my first full season at Leeds, we almost got relegated. I could never have imagined then that as I started my testimonial year we would be crowned World Club Champions.

Since 2000, the British Super League champions have played an annual pre-season game against the Australian National Rugby League Grand Final winners. Saints and Bradford had both won it in the past and it was a game I had always dreamed of playing in. Straight after our win at Old Trafford, we were already thinking about taking on Canterbury Bulldogs, who had beaten Adrian Morley's side Sydney City Roosters in their championship final a couple of weeks earlier. It was probably the biggest game in Leeds' history and the whole city got behind us. We averaged crowds of 16,000 in 2004, but 37,000 people turned up at Elland Road for the World Club Challenge.

Great Britain had been thrashed by the Aussies at Elland Road in the Tri-Nations final two months earlier and I know a lot of people were looking to us to make amends. Personally, I still hadn't given up on another Great Britain cap at the end of 2005, so I was particularly keen to do well. I came back to training early and after a full off-season for the first time in years, I was raring to go. We only had a couple of warm-up games and were without Disko and Dave Furner from our Grand Final side, but Canterbury didn't play any trial matches and were missing some of their key players through injury, so we started as favourites.

We got off to a great start and we were 26–6 up at half time, which was better than anyone could have expected. It was one of those forty minutes when just about everything goes right. Chev got over for an early try to settle the nerves and then Mark Calderwood scored after he chased a kick which Canterbury's full-back Luke Patten made a mess of collecting. They pulled a try back, but I got an offload away for Danny McGuire, who showed what he could do with a great run from inside his own half, and Willie Poching and Rob Burrow also scored before the break.

We got another couple of tries just after half time through Richard Mathers and Jamie Jones-Buchanan to make it 38–12, but then Canterbury came back at us and once a team gets on a roll, it's very hard to stop. Canterbury scored five second-half tries to get the score back to 38–32 with nine minutes to go, but then Sinny managed to pop over a drop goal and we had the game won.

As well as the offload for Danny's try, my contribution was to lift the team when I came off the bench midway through the first half. When I talk about the game, people always mention one run into three or four Canterbury players which knocked their captain Tony Grimaldi unconscious and two others on their backsides.

It was a brilliant game and a wonderful occasion, though the aftermath was a bit low-key because we had our first Super League game of the season just a week later. We celebrated on the pitch and did a lap of honour to thank the fans, but an hour or so after the game we were at a local gym doing a swimming session to get over the bumps and bruises.

But any win for a British team against an Australian one is worth celebrating and what made this one extra sweet was the reaction of the Bulldogs' players. They were sledging all the way through the game and we weren't very impressed with some of their tactics. The game was full of scuffles and incidents and off-the-ball fouls and jibes.

The winding up didn't end with the final hooter. There was a bit of a set-to right on the last play of the game and, as we were all shaking hands, the Aussies were still at it, trying to belittle our victory.

One of their players said to Andrew Dunemann 'You've only beaten our reserve team,' but Andrew shut him up by replying, 'Don't be so hard on yourself mate, I didn't think you were that bad.'

We felt Canterbury's reaction was a bit disrespectful and we made sure the door was wide open so the Bulldogs' players could hear us when we did our victory song in the changing room after the game.

I went to church the day after the match and sat in my usual place at the back, out of the way. My priest Father Dolan knows I like to keep a low profile, but he pointed me out and told everyone, 'It's not often we get a world champion in the congregation.'

That was deeply embarrassing, but I suppose he was right. World champions; it doesn't get much better than that.

This would have been a nice way to finish, but unfortunately this story doesn't have the happy ending I wanted it to. After all the highs of 2004 and early 2005, there was one big low still to come.

We continued our World Club Challenge form into the 2005 season, getting through to the Challenge Cup final against Hull in Cardiff. The week before the final we were well beaten by Bradford at Headingly in Super League. I had a poor game and when Tony Smith named his side for Cardiff, I wasn't in it. That wasn't exatly a huge shock after the previous week, but it was a massive blow, particularly as I knew I wouldn't get another chance. A few weeks ealier I had announced that I would be retiring as a player at the end of the 2005 season, to join the backroom staff at Leeds. I had offers from various other clubs to stay on, but I didn't want to leave Headingley and I was keen to bow out with people saying I'd packed in a year too early, rather than telling me I'd gone on a season too long. Tony had a decision to make and unfortunately I was the one who missed out.

Keith Senior suffered an ankle injury against Bradford and he was in doubt all week. I was told if he didn't make it I'd be in, but Keith was passed fit and I had to watch from the stands. I was bitterly disappointed, upset and a bit angry, but I'd like to think I can hold my head up high. In these situations you can either throw your toys out of the pram, or you can be professional. If I had let my feelings show, it wouldn't have been fair on the other players. Inside I was hurting, but outwardly I was still Bubbly Barrie and I did everything I could do help the team with their preparation.

I didn't hold anything against the coaching staff and I desperately wanted Leeds to win, but sadly it didn't turn out that way. We scored first when Mark Calderwood was awarded a penalty try. Hull went 12–6 up, but Danny Ward grabbed a try to equalise. Another try and a drop goal put Hull seven points clear, but Calders and Marcus Bai both touched down and we were five points ahead. I thought that was going to be enough, but with three minutes left Paul Cook scored for Hull, Danny Brough kicked the goal and we lost 25–24. That meant the chance to create history, as the first Leeds side to hold all available trophies at the same time, had gone.

It would have been nice to close this final chapter on a better note, but in sport things don't always turn out how you want them to. As for the future, I'm preparing to begin a sports science degree – which wouldn't have seemed possible a few years ago – and looking forward to joining Rhinos' coaching staff. My playing story is almost over, but I am sure there are a few more chapters still to be written in my rugby league career, and if they are anything like the last fourteen years it will be a rollercoaster ride.

Barrie's Record

Born   22.7.1972

Amateur club   Waterhead

MATCH STATISTICS

		Appearances (plus as sub)	Tries	Points
Oldham	1991–92	4 (10)	3	12
	1992–93	10 (5)	2	8
	1993–94	10 (1)	1	4
	Total	*24 (16)*	*6*	*24*
Wigan	1994–95	8 (5)	4	16
Leeds	1995–96	9 (6)	0	0
	1996	16 (7)	3	12
	1997	14 (4)	9	36
	1998	5 (8)	3	12
	1999	29 (4)	4	16
	2000	29 (0)	1	4
	2001	26 (3)	6	24
	2002	27 (1)	3	12
	2003	27 (6)	2	8
	2004	11 (19)	3	12
to end of August	2005	6 (21)	6	24
	Total	*199 (79)*	*40*	*160*
Bramley (on loan)	1998	4 (0)	1	4

MATCH STATISTICS (*continued*)

	Appearances (plus as sub)	Tries	Points
Lancashire	3 (0)	0	0
Great Britain (Tests)	11 (4)	0	0
Great Britain (others)	1 (1)	0	0
England	0 (1)	0	0
Ireland	10 (0)	2	8

DISCIPLINARY RECORD

In rugby league, law breakers rarely get away with it. If you are a bad boy, the referee can, of course, send you off, but even if you escape a red card, that doesn't mean you will get away scot-free. When a referee thinks something untoward has gone on but he's not sure exactly what, he can place the incident on report to be studied by the Rugby Football League's disciplinary chiefs when they watch the match video later. Minor or technical offences, like the odd punch-up, can lead to a yellow card and ten minutes to cool off in the sin-bin. If clubs think one of their players has been fouled, they can cite the allegedly guilty party on video evidence. And even if you've done something that has escaped the notice of the referee and the opposing team, you can still get hauled up before the disciplinary committee following the after-match video review.

As you probably know by now, I am no stranger to Tuesday or Thursday afternoon sessions before the beak at RFL's Red Hall head-quarters in Leeds.

Full disciplinary offences (sendings-off)

12/4/1993   Oldham   Stiff arm to head. Suspended for two
                        matches.

11/7/1993	Wyong	Attacking head of an opponent. Suspended for four weeks.
7/11/1993	Oldham	High tackle. Suspended for four matches.
6/2/1994	Oldham	Careless high tackle. Suspended for two matches and official warning.
17/8/1995	Wigan	*(A team)* Head butt. Suspended for five matches.
29/11/1995	Leeds	Swinging forearm towards head. Sending-off sufficient.
20/3/1998	Leeds	*(Pre-season friendly)* Running in and punching. Suspended for four matches. Appeal dismissed.
14/2/1999	Leeds	Reckless high tackle. Suspended for two matches.
2/8/2002	Leeds	Punching in tackle. Suspended for four matches and fined £500. Appeal dismissed.

Referred disciplinary offences
(cited by other clubs or Rugby Football League)

8/10/1994	Wigan	Reckless high tackle – cited by Australia for deliberate attack to head with elbow on Paul Sironen. Suspended for two matches.
29/3/1997	Leeds	Reckless high tackle. Suspended for three matches. Appeal dismissed.
31/3/2001	Leeds	Punch to face causing injury. Suspended for four matches.
31/5/2002	Leeds	Late challenge and raising knee. Official warning.

On report

| 20/3/1998 | Leeds | *(Pre-season friendly)* Careless dangerous throw. Suspended one match. |
| 31/3/2000 | Leeds | Reckless high tackle. Suspended for two matches. |

11/11/2000   Ireland   Reckless high tackle. Suspended for one
                          match.

Temporary disciplinary offences (sin-binnings)

23/8/1992   Oldham   Punching.
31/3/1993   Oldham   Fighting.
30/10/1993   Oldham   *(A team)* Punching.
3/11/1993   Oldham   *(A team)* Fighting.
5/11/1994   Wigan   Fighting.
24/5/1996   Leeds   Fighting.
25/1/1998   Leeds   *(Pre-season friendly)* Trading punches.
16/7/1999   Leeds   Fighting.
7/9/2001   Leeds   Interference at play-the-ball.
16/6/2002   Lancashire   Fighting.
19/3/2003   Leeds   Fighting.
15/4/2005   Leeds   Fighting.

Others

4/12/1993   Oldham   *(A team)* Playing while suspended.
                          Received official warning. Oldham
                          fined £25.

Index

Ablett, Carl 280
Adams, Roy 233
Adamson, Matt 226, 258–9, 284, 287
Adamson, Phil 154
Adelaide Rams 121–2
air-rifle accident 1–7
Anderson, Chris 210
Anderson, Paul 36–7, 39
Annesley, Graham 90
Ashby, Bob 87
Aston, Mark 46
Auckland game 39–40
Australia
    1993 off-season 48–9, 58–72
    1994 Tests 11, 80, 83–95
    2001 tour 205–11
    2002 Great Britain tour 212–14
    2003 series 216–18
    Grand Final 68–71
    signing opportunity 177–8
    Tri-Nations tour 172, 193, 195, 197, 249
    Wigan game 84, 85–7
    World Cup 120–3, 204

Bai, Marcus 237, 292
Bailey, Ryan 236, 237, 279, 287
Barker, Dwayne 236

BARLA, New Zealand tour 22, 23, 36–41
Barnhill, David 67, 172, 203
Barrow game 131
basketball 17
Bateman, Allan 91
Bates, Ian 'Blaster' 53–4
Batley game 131
Bell, Dean 108, 109, 111, 113, 118
    Barrie's honeymoon 155
    Burrow trial 224
    Leeds sackings 114
    and James Lowes 258
    Nightmare Team 256
    steps down 127
    taxi incident 149–50
    World Cup Championships 123
Bell, Paul 172
Betts, Denis 77, 80, 89, 109, 161, 195
Bishop, David 254–5
Blackmore, Richie 135
Bloem, Jamie 255
Booth, Craig 129
Botica, Frano 97, 98, 111
boxing 7–8
Bradbury, David 37, 38, 43
Bradford 236
    1995 season 111–12
    1996 season 113, 114

Bradford (*cont.*)
  1997 Challenge Cup semifinal
    118–19
  1997 season 123
  1998 season 261
  1999 Challenge Cup semifinal
    162–3
  2000 Challenge Cup Final 174–5,
    195–6
  2000 season 176
  2002 season 226–7, 228, 268
  2003 Challenge Cup Final 231,
    233–5, 258
  Odsal ground 190
  signing 116–17
  video referee 191
Bradley, Graeme 119
Bramley, loan 130–2
Briers, Lee 212
Briscoe, Shaun 237
British Coal National Youth League
  30–1
Britt, Darren 258
Broadbent, Paul 85
Brough, Danny 292
building trade 20–1, 23–4, 25–7, 48,
  65, 188, 189, 274
Burleigh Bears 194–5
Burns, Gary 37, 43
Burrow, Rob 223, 224, 234, 237, 288,
  290

Caddick, Paul 117
Calderwood, Mark 191, 223, 224, 237,
  288, 290, 292
Campbell, David 86
Campion, Kevin 199
Cantillon, Phil 156
Carcassonne, Battle of 44–6
Carnekie, Alvin 18
Carney, Brian 200–1

Carroll, Tony 221, 229
Casey, Leo 51, 52
Cassidy, Mick 85–6, 159, 260–1
Castleford games 100, 127–8, 176
Chadderton 21, 30, 33
Chadwick, John 46, 54
Challenge Cup
  1995 final 100–1
  1996 season 113
  1997 season 118–19
  1998 season 127–8
  1999 final xi–xii, 164–70
  1999 season 157–63
  2000 final 174–5, 195–6
  2000 season 172–5
  2001 season 219, 220–1, 222–3
  2002 season 226–7
  2003 final 231, 233–5, 258
  2003 season 231–5, 244, 259
  2004 final 278
Chamberlain, Richard 41
Chambers, Brian 37–8, 39, 40–1
Charity Shield 106
Christie, Gary 37, 43
Civoniceva, Petero 211
Clarke, Phil 77, 89, 98, 101, 102
Clyde, Bradley 11, 90, 92, 224–5
Collins, Wayne 'Snoopy' 118
Connolly, Gary 93, 207, 211, 217, 230,
  237, 279
  Australia game 90
  Challenge Cup final 234
  Dream Team 244–5
  Regal Trophy 97
Connor, John 139
Cook, Mick 46–7
Cook, Paul 114, 292
Coulter, Gay 51
Cowie, Neil 97, 102, 103, 108, 145, 146
Craig, Andy 100
Craven, Steve 107

Crooks, Lee 100
Cross, Steve 191
Cumbria game 34
Cummins, Francis 'Franny' 123, 136,
    156, 165, 275, 283
  Challenge Cup Final 168
  Dream Team 243–4
  Tri-Nations series 194
Cunningham, Keiron 53, 196–7
Curtis, Edgar 154, 241

Daly, Phil 278
Davies, Jonathan 'Jiffy' 90, 91, 144,
    186
Daylight, Matt 173
De Vere, Michael 218
Deacon, Paul 235, 282, 287, 290
Deakin, Leigh 37, 41
Dewsbury game 44, 62, 172
Diskin, Matt 279
Divet, Daniel 45
Divorty, Robin 37
Dolan, Father Eugene 271, 291
Doncaster game 96–7
Donohue, Jason 30–1
Downing Street reception 231
drink driving 112, 140–2
driving licence 24, 82
Drummond, Des 255
Duffy, Stuart 111
Dunemann, Andrew 121, 230, 284,
    291
Dyson, Jeremy 37

Edwards, Doug 70
Edwards, Shaun 'Giz' 76, 79–80, 90,
    93–4, 245
Elliott, Matthew 116
Ellis, Gareth 237
England
  World Cup 111–12, 203, 204–5

    see also Great Britain
The Entrance game 62, 69–70
Erina game 66–7

Fabre, Michael 45
Fallon, Jim 112–13
fans 271, 274–5
  abuse 11–13
  Hull 173–4
Farrell, Andy 'Faz' 77, 119, 145,
    159–60, 161, 261
  Australia game 207
  Dream Team 249
  religion 270
  singing 144
  snoring 135
Feather, Chris 230, 237, 284
Featherstone Rovers game 51–2, 79,
    81
Field, Jamie 123
Fielden, Stuart 204–5, 207, 227–9,
    257–8, 260, 268
Fittler, Brad 210, 211
Fitzgibbon, Craig 218
Fitzsimmons, Eric 50
Fleary, Darren 'Daz' 34, 36, 132, 157,
    167, 261
Fleming, Greg 167
Fletcher, Paul 130–1, 210, 286
Ford, Mike 186
France
  game 207
  Leeds game 149–50
  Oldham tour 44–6, 54–5
  under-19 game 34–5
Fulton, Bob 92
Furner, Dave 230, 233, 234, 235, 261,
    285, 287, 289

Gartland, Brian 31–2
Gascoigne, Paul 144

Germany, pre-season training 230–1
Gibson, Ashley 280
Gibson, Damian 122–3
Gibson, Wally 74
Givons, Alex 54–5
Glanville, Marc 160, 172, 260
Godden, Brad 167, 168, 172
Godwin, Wayne 237
Golden, Jason 280
Goodway, Andy 49, 57, 74, 77, 135,
    161
  Nightmare Team 259–60
  Tri-Nations series 193–4, 197
Goulding, Bobbie 90, 257
grandfather Brian 5
grandmother 19
Great Britain
  1994 Australia Tests 11, 80, 83,
    87–95
  1996 New Zealand tour 115–16
  1998 New Zealand tourists 135
  2001 Australian tourists 205–11
  2002 Australia tour 212–14
  2002 New Zealand tourists 214–16
  2003 Australia series 216–18
  BARLA tour 22, 23, 36–41
  first Test 87–91
  Tri-Nations series 172, 193–5,
    196–7, 249
  under-19 squad 34–41
Griffiths, Clive 186
Grimaldi, Tony 290
Grimoldby, Nic 86

Halifax games 53–4, 123, 133, 134
Hall, Ernie 21
Hall, Martin 101, 145
Halstead, Roger 45
Hanley, Ellery 88, 91, 92, 154, 249
  Dream Team 251–2
Harmon, Neil 113, 115, 136, 137

Harragon, Paul 90, 260–1
Harrington, Paul 87
Harris, Iestyn 53, 114, 161, 272
  Bradford semifinal 163
  Cardiff 233–4
  Castleford game 176
  Challenge Cup final xi–xii, 166,
    167, 168
  chants 173
  Dream Team 241–3
  Leeds captaincy 119–20
  Leeds signing 119
  shaved head 156
  Tri-Nations series 194, 195
  union switch 186
  World Cup 204
Harrison, Karl 89, 93
Hassan, Phil 113, 123
hat-tricks 62–3
Haughton, Simon xi, 159–60, 161–2
Hay, Andy 175, 194, 229, 230
Hetherington, Gary 117, 118, 119,
    229–30, 232, 233, 237
Heugh, Cavill 48
Higham, Micky 237
Hill, Brendan 53–4
Hodgkinson, Colin 40–1
Hodgson, Nick 54
Holgate, Simon 41
Holgate, Stephen 37
Holloway, Bob 59, 67
Holroyd, Graham 123
Horne, Richard 237
Howard, Harvey 88, 113
Howes, Dave 288
Huddersfield game 51, 132, 174
Hudson, Ryan 237
Hull games 106–107, 132, 141, 172–4

injuries 82, 267
  broken leg 123–7

injuries (*cont.*)
elbow dislocation 47–8
groin 80, 82
hamstring 49, 68, 69
knee 111–12, 215
shoulder 100, 105, 132, 167
wrist 215
Innes, Craig 114
Ireland, World Cup 2000 183,
198–205

Jackson, Brett 66–7
Jackson, Lee 157, 168
Jepson, Harry 87
Jewitt, Roy 31–2
Johns, Andrew 211, 216
Johns, Matty 177
Johnson, Paul 211
joinery 20–1, 23–4, 48, 65, 188
Jones, Mark 51
Jone-Buchanan, Jamie 290
Joynt, Chris 53, 88, 203, 207

kangaroo cull 63–4
Kearns, Robbie 205, 216
Kelly, Andy 201
Kimmorley, Brett 218
Knowles, Matt 100
Knox, Simon 37
Kooga 47

Lancashire
under-17 squad 33
under-19 squad 33–4
Lance, Dean 171–2, 174, 175, 178–80,
221, 223, 252
Lanzarote 155–7, 158, 231
Larder, Phil 115, 186
Laughton, Doug 109, 114, 255
Laughton, Fred 9
Lauitiiti, Ali 237

Lawford, Dean 'Donk' 137
Lazarus, Glen 90
Leeds
1995 Challenge Cup final 100–1
1999 Challenge Cup final xi–xii,
164–70
2001 Player of the Year 206, 219
2003 Challenge Cup final 231,
233–5, 258
Charity Shield 106
contract 109
game against 80
Grand Final 133, 134–5
Headingley threat 116–17
interest 108–9
sackings 114, 229–30
signing 109–11
taxi incident 149
World Cup 120–3
Leigh game 30–1, 79
Lindner, Bob 49, 77
Lindsay, Maurice 79, 184
Locker Cup match 79
Lockyer, Darren 218
London Broncos game xi–xii, 164–70
Louther, Eric 21
Lowe, Graham 79
Lowes, Jimmy 114, 175, 258
Lucas, Ian 87
Lydon, Joe 180, 186

McAllister, Charlie 44, 56, 254–5
McCallion, Lesley 123–4
McCallion, Seamus 123, 126
McDermott, Alison (sister) 15, 16–17,
265
McDermott, Billy (son) 265, 266,
284–5
birth 115
Challenge Cup final 166
McDermott, Brian 115, 118

McDermott, Jacqueline (mum) 2,
    15–16, 265–6
  Barrie quits job 22–3
  Barrie's injury 48
  first Test 88
  letter to school 9
  Malcolm Reilly meeting 35
  Peter Tunks meeting 43
  religion 19
  rifle accident 4–5, 6
McDermott, Jenny (wife) 149, 151,
    163, 264–5, 266, 284–5
  Barrie's broken leg 126
  wedding 154–5
McDermott, Jessica (daughter) 266
McDermott, Robert (dad) 16–18, 29,
    265–6
  away games 12, 16
  Barrie quits job 22–3
  Barrie's injury 48
  first Test 88
  Malcolm Reilly meeting 35
  Peter Tunks meeting 43
  religion 19
  rifle accident 4–5
  size 15
McDermott, Sophie (daughter) 265–6
McDonald, Gerry 37
McDonald, Wayne 173, 232, 237, 284
McGahan, Hugh 108, 109
McGrath, Damian 132–3, 134, 137,
    153–4, 180
McGuire, Danny 232, 233, 234, 237,
    279, 282, 287, 290
McKenna, Chris 230, 234
McKnight, David 108
Mad Monday 71, 229
Maders, Dennis 19
Marshall, Richard 123
Martin, John 74, 84, 87, 141
Martyn, Tommy 53, 199, 226, 250

Masella, Martin 118, 122, 132, 134,
    157
Matautia, Vila 96–7, 270
Mather, Barrie-Jon 244
Mathers, Richard 237, 279, 290
Mathiou, Jamie 118, 119, 157, 175
  arguments 133, 134, 220–2
  Challenge Cup final 167
  Ireland team 203
  Leeds signing 118
Mears, Robbie 225–6
Mercer, Gary 137, 250
Moana, Martin 39
Molloy, Steve 51
Moran, Patrick 259, 278
Morley, Adrian 'Moz' 113, 136, 159,
    176–7, 178, 289
  Australia games 216–17
  Australia move 177, 209, 248
  Challenge Cup final 168, 174–5
  Dream Team 247–8
  Lanzarote 155, 156
  religion 270
  St Helens game 172
  Tri-Nations series 194, 195, 196–7
  World Cup 122, 203
Morrisey, Mike 36
Mullins, Brett 90, 224–5
Mumnorah game 62–3
Murdoch, Rupert 183
Murdock, Craig 100
Murray, Graham 119, 128–9, 130,
    132, 133, 137, 153–4
  Barrie's honeymoon 155
  Bradford semifinal 163
  Challenge Cup final 166
  Grand Final 134–5
  leaves Leeds 170–1
  Leeds appointment 127
  media 158
  Moz signing 177

Murray, Graham (*cont.*)
   team spirit 156–7
   Wigan sending off 162
Murrell, Scott 280

New Zealand
   1996 Great Britain tour 115–16
   1998 Great Britain tour 135
   2002 series 214–16
   BARLA tour 22, 23, 36–41
   Tri-Nations series 172, 193, 195–6,
     197
   World Cup 204
New Zealand Maori 197, 203
Newcastle Knights 177–8
Newton, Terry 113, 122, 133–4, 157
   Dream Team 246–7
   Lanzarote 155
Nickle, Sonny 226
Noble, Brian 206, 207
North Queensland Cowboys 121

O'Connor, Jane 146
O'Connor, Terry 'Tez' 103, 108, 136,
   144–5
   Australia games 207, 208, 211, 213
   BARLA tour 36
   Dream Team 246
   first meeting 33–4
   Ireland team 199, 201
   media 158–9
   Regal Trophy 97
   train incident 145–7
   under-19 squad 35
   Wigan debut 79
   Wigan signing 75, 77, 78
Offiah, Martin 80, 98, 101–3, 196
   argument 81
   Challenge Cup final 167
Oldham 73–4
   amateur signing 23

changing rooms 44
   doorman job 138–40
   final game 78
   French tour 44–6, 54–5
   fundraising 36
   groundwork 25
   pro signing 42–3
   quickest red card 51
   Second Division Premiership final
     55
   training 24, 99
   transfer fees 76–7
   under-19 district team 30–2
   wages 56, 74
   World Cup Championships 121
Oldham Evening Chronicle 9–10, 31, 45
O'Loughlin, Sean 237
O'Neill, Steve 201, 202
Owen, Geoff 37
Owen, Mark 18
Owen, Paul 236

Pachniuk, Richard 53
Paris game 114
Parker, Derek 73
Patten, Luke 290
Patterson, Tom 54
Paul, Henry 175, 195–6
Paul, Robbie 234, 282
Peacock, Danny 163
Peacock, Jamie 208, 234
Perelini, Apollo 192, 270
Perpignan 184
Phillip, Abraham 43
Phillips, Rowland 115
Pia game 44, 45
Pierre 65–6, 72
plastering 25–6
Platt, Andy 35, 75, 103, 246
Poching, Willie 39, 202, 227, 290
Poppie, Ralph 61

Poulter, David 77
Powell, Daryl 55, 89, 129, 159, 176, 230, 237, 287
  Challenge Cup final 234
  hair 156
  Leeds appointment 223
  and Matt Adamson 259
Powell, Roy 131, 252
Pratt, Karl 156, 221, 229, 230
Prescott, Steve 199
Presley, Steve 196
Price, Gary 51, 52
Prince, John 54
Pryce, Karl 237
Pryce, Leon 237

Quinn, Jim 24–5, 74, 76–7, 140, 190
Quinnell, Scott 96–7, 101, 108

Reardon, Stuart 237
Regal Trophy 80, 96–8
Reid, Jackie 37
Reilly, Malcolm 35, 262
religion 19, 104, 151, 270–1
Renouf, Steve 90
Retchless, Steele 164
Richards, Craig 51, 68
Ricketson, Luke 199, 218
Riverside Club 141
Rivett, Leroy 122, 156, 167, 168, 175
Roberts, Ian 93–4
Robinson, Jack 74, 87, 108, 141, 142, 147
Robinson, Jason 77, 135, 186, 187
  Dream Team 243
  Inga influence 104–5
  Widnes game 80
  rugby union 181–2, 183–4, 185–6, 187
Russell, Richard 45, 53
Russia 183

Ryan, Warren 177
Ryles, Jason 211

Saddleworth 7, 19, 21, 28
St Helens
  games 34, 172, 220–1, 222–3, 225–6, 227, 231–3, 259, 280
  signing interest 32, 108, 153, 154
St Hilaire, Marcus 163, 168, 175
Salem Hornets Cup Final 43–4
Salter, Matt 167
Samoa games 198, 202–3
Sampson, Dean 128
Schick, Andrew 128
Schofield, Garry 114
schooldays 7, 9–10, 19–20
Scruton, Nick 280
Sculthorpe, Paul 53, 208, 223, 232, 248, 259
Seddon, Joe 77
Senior, Keith 172, 194, 203, 207, 226, 244, 286, 292
Sheffield Eagles
  games 46–7, 55, 80
  signing interest 42
Sheridan, Ryan 122, 156, 163, 176, 229, 230
  Ireland team 202, 203
  Tri-Nations series 194
Sherratt, Ian 74, 251
Shiels, Peter 222
shirt numbers 113–14
Simpson, Robbie 167
Sinfield, Kevin 175–6, 226, 232, 235, 282, 283, 287, 290
  Australia Test 207
  car sharing 53
  Dream Team 245
  Widnes game 162
Sironen, Paul 85–7, 90

Skerrett, Kelvin 35, 74–5, 78, 81, 84, 108
Slicker, Mick 23, 31
Smales, Tommy 252–3
Smith, Ian 131
Smith, Lee 280
Smith, Russell 160, 234
Smith, Tony 237, 252, 278, 287, 291
Solomona, Tiny 49, 68
Sorensen, Kurt 257
South Africa, 2002 Leeds trip 226
South Sydney 177
Spain, La Manga 200–2
Sports Review of the Year 142–4
Spruce, Stuart 80
Standish, Derek 42
Steadman, Graham 206
Stephenson, David 58, 59–62, 63–6, 69, 71–2
Steptoe, Dave 69–70
Sterling, Paul 176, 178–9
Stevens, Jason 208
Street, Tim 54
Stuart, Ricky 11
Summerbee, Mike 36
Sun 158–9
Sunshine State Challenge tournament 220
Super League
  1996 114–15
  1998 season 132–3
  2000 season 174, 178–9
  beginnings 190
  Grand Finals 133, 134–5, 192
  mergers 184–5
Swinton game 113

Tait, Alan 186, 255
tattoo 34, 61
taxi incident 148–51

Taylor, Robert 'Rip' 59, 60, 66, 67, 70, 71
Tees, Gary 50–1
Temu, Jason 39
Tenerife holiday 56–7
train incident 145–7
Tri-Nations tour 172, 193–5, 196–7, 248, 287
Tuigamala, Va'aiga 'Inga' 76, 97, 104–5
Tunisia 137, 156
Tunks, Peter 42–3, 44, 45, 46, 49, 58–9, 68–9, 255
Tupaea, Shane 249–50
Tuuta, Brendon 256–7

Umina game 62
USA 182–3
  Leeds 2001 tour 220

Vaikona, Tevita 234
Vainikolo, Lesley 191, 282
video referees 191–2
Villeneuve game 46
Vowles, Adrian 128, 226, 256

Waddell, Hugh 46
Waikato game 37–9
Waite, David 206, 208, 210–11, 215, 216, 217
Wakefield
  game 174
  signing interest 42
Wales, World Cup 204
Walker, Ben 229
Walker, Chev 203, 236, 237, 287, 290
Walsh, Peter 'Spider' 58, 59
Walters, Steve 92
Ward, Danny 221, 237, 279, 287, 292
Warrington

Warrington (*cont.*)
  games 50–1, 79, 113, 114, 120, 174, 212
  Regal Trophy 96–8
Waterhead 7, 28–30, 33, 43–4, 147
  fundraising 36
  gym 21
  Mick Slicker's support 23
  social side 32
Watkins, John 54
Watts, Billy 233
Webcke, Shane 217
West, Graeme 79, 85, 97, 102, 105–6
Whitmore, Steve 88–9
Widnes games 80, 162, 226
Wigan
  1995 Challenge Cup final 100–1
  1999 Challenge Cup game xi
  atmosphere 81–2
  Australia game 84, 85–7
  Charity Shield 106
  debut game 79
  drink driving 140–1

driving licence 24, 82
  games against 47, 112, 119, 135, 159–62, 236
  Regal Trophy 80, 96–8
  signing 74–7
  signing interest 42
  Sports Review of the Year 142–4
  superiority 103–4
Williams, Danny 199
Williams, Darren 39
Wilson, Ken 21
Winterburn, Mike 54
Wood, Sir John 77
Wood, Paul 237
Workington game 131
World Cup
  2000 183, 197–205
  Championship 120–3
  England 111–12
Woy Woy game 68
Wyong 59–72

York game 31, 129, 131–2
Yorkshire Evening Post 136–7

extracts reading groups new
competitions books new
discounts extracts extracts
competitions reading groups
books new discounts
events books extracts events
new extracts reading groups
books new titles reading groups
interviews new
events extracts extracts books
discounts interviews new books extracts
new books events
events new
discounts extracts discounts books

www.panmacmillan.com

extracts events reading groups
competitions books extracts new